WITHDRAWN

HISTORICAL
ATLAS
—OF THE—

Viking
World

HISTORICAL
ATLAS
— OF THE —

Víking
World

Angus Konstam

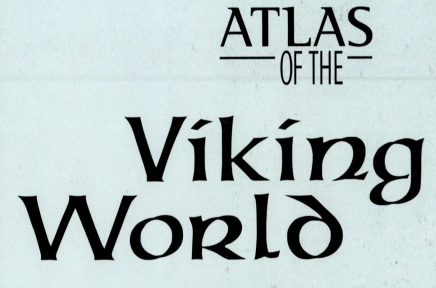

Checkmark Books™
An imprint of Facts On File, Inc.

HISTORICAL ATLAS OF THE VIKING WORLD

Checkmark Books
An imprint of Facts On File, Inc.
132 West 31st Street
New York, NY 10001

For Library of Congress Cataloging-in-Publication data, please contact
Checkmark Books. Control Number 12803030.
        ISBN 0-8160-5068-6

Checkmark Books are available at special discounts when purchased in bulk quantities for businesses, associations, institutions or sales promotions. Please call our Special Sales Department in New York at:
(212) 967-8800 or (800) 322-8755.

You can find Facts On File on the World Wide Web at:
http://www.factsonfile.com

For Thalamus Publishing
Project editor: Neil Williams
Maps and design: Roger Kean
Illustrations: Oliver Frey
Four-color separation: Proskanz, Ludlow, England

Printed and bound in Spain

10 9 8 7 6 5 4 3 2 1
This book is printed on acid-free paper

PICTURE CREDITS
Archivo Iconografico, S.A./CORBIS: 66, 84, 85, 113, 126, 157, 176; Elio Ciol/CORBIS: 41, 117; Dean Conger/CORBIS: 171 (top); Richard Cummins/CORBIS: 65; Ecoscene/CORBIS: 20; Oliver Frey/Thalamus Publishing: 13, 42–43, 47, 52, 67, 104, 109, 118, 128–9, 140–1, 152–3, 169, 171 (bottom), 177; David Hosking/CORBIS: 136; Peter Hulme/ CORBIS: 89; Wolfgang Kaehler/CORBIS: 16, 102, 184 (bottom); Bob Krist/CORBIS: 11, 26–7, 184 (top), 185, 189; Marc Lacey/Thalamus Publishing: 130; Lake County Museum/CORBIS: 186; Charles Lenars/CORBIS: 105; Chris Lisle/CORBIS: 34; Abilio Lope/CORBIS: 188; Gianni Dagli Orti/CORBIS: 72–3, 125, 156; Greg Probst/CORBIS: 18–9, 110; Carmen Redondo/CORBIS: 40; Kevin Schafer/CORBIS: 57, 83 (bottom), 135, 137 Paul A. Souders/CORBIS: 45; Ted Spiegel/CORBIS: 22, 23, 50–1, 52, 53, 54, 55, 70, 75, 77, 122, 124, 127, 131, 138, 147, 150, 153, 165, 167 (top), 167 (bottom), 180; Brian A.Vikander/CORBIS: 10, 21, 183 Patrick Ward/CORBIS: 63; Werner Forman Archive: 14, 30, 39, 44, 56, 60, 78, 79, 98, 106, 107, 144, 145; Werner Forman Archive–History Museum, Bergen University: 187; Werner FormanArchive–Liverpool City Museum: 32; Werner Forman Archive–Manx Museum: 143; Werner Forman Archive–Maritime Museum, Bergen: 154–5; Werner Forman Archive–National Museum, Copenhagen: 12, 24, 25 (right), 92 (bottom), 96, 99 (bottom), 112, 120, 148, 170; Werner Forman Archive–Statens Historika Museum, Stockholm: 1, 7, 13, 25 (left), 29, 35, 36, 38, 68, 69, 73, 76, 87, 92 (top), 97, 99 (top), 119, 121, 134, 160, 161, 162, 164, 168, 172, 175, 182; Werner Forman Archive–Stofun Arna Magnussonar a Islandi: 17; Werner Forman Archive–Thjodminjasafn, Reykjík: 173; Werner Forman Archive–Universitetets Oldsaksamling, Oslo: 2–3, 33, 37, 88, 93, 95; Werner Forman Archive–Viking Ship Museum, Bygdoy: 6, 46, 48, 49 (both), 80, 90, 91, 94, 116, 151; NikWheeler/CORBIS: 103, 108; Wild Country/CORBIS: 62; Adam Woolfitt/CORBIS: 61, 83 (top).

Page 1: Detail of a carved funerary stone showing a Viking longship and warriors, c.8th century AD, from the island of Gotland.

Pages 2–3: Detail of a 12th-century carving from a stave church at Stetesdal, Norway, depicting the saga of Sigurd the dragon slayer. The story illustrates the legendary Viking attributes of courage mixed with cunning. The dragon's treasure of gold, however, brought Sigurd only woe, and he ended his days in the snake pit, but still gamely playing his harp with his toes.

Contents

Introduction

The period that we call the Viking Age lasted almost 300 years, beginning just before AD 800. During these three centuries Viking raiders ravaged the coasts of Europe, then followed up their initial attacks with military conquest and settlement. At the same

Below: Carved dragon-head post from the ship-burial at Oseberg, Norway.

time other Vikings ventured west, east, and south on voyages of exploration, and embarked on trading expeditions which made Scandinavian commerce a major force in the development of medieval Europe.

At the heart of the Viking world was Scandinavia, now comprising the modern countries of Norway, Denmark, and Sweden. To a lesser extent Viking settlements existed in what is now Finland. From this cold and often inhospitable region, the Vikings engaged in commerce, settlement, and military conquest in distant lands, extending their influence as far as

the coastline of North America, the steppes of Russia, and the Mediterranean Sea. These people, therefore, exerted an influence out of all proportion to their numbers. They have also passed into history as the ultimate pirates—marauding barbarians of the early medieval period.

The word "Viking" is derived from the Old Norse (Norwegian) word *vikingr*, meaning a sea-raider. While a Viking was a kind of pirate, Viking expeditions could involve thousands of men, and were undertaken with the endorsement of the rulers of their Scandinavian homelands. However, since a pirate is someone who operates outside the law, and since most Viking raiders returned from their expeditions to resume the peaceable cultivation of their farms, it is misleading to call them pirates.

The term "Viking" is also applied to the peaceful inhabitants of all of early medieval Scandinavia, whether they went raiding or not. Scandinavian settlers, farmers, fishermen, merchants, and craftsmen quietly continued with their lives throughout the period and played a vital part in the story. They provided the stable society and economy that allowed their counterparts to engage in their raiding.

The trouble is that "Viking" has become so widely used that it is now virtually impossible to separate the true Viking raiders from the rest of contemporary Scandinavian society. Nowadays it is used to denote all of these hardy Scandinavian people, and the word has provided the label with which to identify a particular three centuries of history.

During these centuries the nature of Viking society changed. At the start of the period, Viking raiders struck fear into the coastal communities of the British Isles (including Ireland), northern Germany, western and southern France, and the Low Countries (now Holland and Belgium). Using rivers, Vikings struck deep inland to attack monasteries, towns,

emerging nations of Scandinavia became even more closely integrated into the political development of the rest of Europe.

A new era was ushered in during the late 11th century, as Viking settlers, merchants, and even armies became intermingled and indistinguishable from the general populations of northern Europe. For example, the Vikings who settled around the Seine estuary in France became Normans (from *Norsemen*) rather than

Above: 7th-century brooch in the form of the World Serpent from Oland, Sweden.

and even walled cities. The Christian Church was threatened with extinction in parts of Europe, but somehow it survived, and then spread its influence into the Viking heartlands.

Conquest and integration

Settlers and armies of occupation or conquest followed the first raiders. As the power of Scandinavian kings increased, so too did the scale of Viking involvement in Europe. While large parts of Britain and France came under Viking control, new Scandinavian states were also formed. The incidence of raiding and pillaging diminshed as the Vikings converted to Christianity. Gradually, those Vikings who occupied overseas domains or ruled in the

Vikings, and from their state of Normandy looked toward France, England, and Italy rather than Scandinavia for their political development. The failure of the last great Scandinavian invasion of Anglo-Saxon England and an increasing level of national identity helped to bring the Viking era to a close—although its historical and cultural legacy survives to this day.

Who were the Vikings? Why did they suddenly burst beyond the confines of their Scandinavian homeland? How and why did the Viking era come to an end? How did these people live? How did they acquire such a fearsome martial reputation? And what did they believe in? This book sets out to answer these questions, and more.

Scandinavia and the Baltic Sea during the Viking age.

▨	Viking Norway
▨	Viking Sweden
▨	Viking Denmark
○	non-Viking town
●	early Viking town
●	late Viking town
●	settlement
□	early trading center
●	royal site
⚓	ship-burial/ship find
Fosna	pre-Viking tribe

Varangerfj.

Porsangen

Einmark

Lofoten Islands

Troms

Vestfjord

L A P P L A N D

Hålogaland

Kosma

N O R W E G I A N   S E A

Nordland

Norrland

GULF OF BOTHNIA

Trondheim ● ● Lade

Trøndelag

Dalarna

Åland

GULF OF FINLAND

Urnes ● ● Ytra Moa

Sogn ● Borgund

Dalälven ⚓ Vendel
⚓ Valsgärde

● Bergen

Hordaland

Värmland

Uppland ■ Uppsala

● Siguna

Sveland

Rogaland

Borre ⚓ ● Oslo

Oseberg ⚓
Gokstad ⚓
Kaupang □

Birka ● □ Helgö

Hiiumaa

Fosna

Jæren

Agder

Oslofjord

Ranrike

Lake Vänen

Lake Väner

Skara ●

Lake Vätter

Östergötland

GOTLAND

Saarenaa

SKAGERRAK

Västergötland

Småland

Emån

Paviken □

B A L T I C   S E A

Cimbri

Lindholm ●
Høje

KATTEGAT

Skåne

ÖLAND

● Eketorp

NORTH

Viborg ●

Jutland

● Arhus

Vorbasse ● ■ Jelling

Skuldelev ⚓

Roskilde ● ● Lund

● Grobin

SEA

Schleswig ● ● Hedeby

Fyn

Sjæland

Lolland

Bornholm

□ Ribe

Egernsund ⚓

Frisian Islands

Elbe

● Wolin

Vistula

● Truso

CHAPTER I

The Scandinavian Homeland

The Vikings did not emerge fully formed from the North Sea mists. Their roots can be traced back to their earliest prehistoric forebears: the hunter gatherers, then the farmers and fishermen who inhabited Scandinavia long before the first European written records.

Through the centuries before the classic Viking age of the eighth to eleventh centuries AD, these northern European peoples developed their culture and formed the basis of the Viking society that followed. This development was molded by the nature of the land itself, and the sea lanes that linked the isolated pockets of habitation. The Vikings maintained a characteristic social and political structure that was similar throughout Scandinavia—although in time this changed, so that by the end of the Viking era the region was divided into separate and well-defined national political entities.

Above all the Vikings were an agrarian people, and their social and political structure reflected this. Centered around the yeoman farmer and his extended family, these freemen and the slaves they owned provided the wherewithal for the political and economic development of Scandinavia during the early medieval period. These social building blocks were linked together to form larger communities, and they in turn were grouped into *land* or provinces.

The growth of royal authority continued throughout the Viking era, and with it came a restriction on the political independence of the provinces, and of the *jarls* (earls) or oligarchies who ruled them. Set among these rural communities was a handful of non-agricultural communities, whose specialist craftsmen, builders, and shipbuilders supplied the needs of a commercial community. Like the slaves who assisted the yeoman farmers, these artisans provided Viking merchants with the tools needed to develop Scandinavian trade with the rest of Europe.

While much attention is paid to the first Viking raids on the rest of Europe, less dramatic events were ushering in a new era in Scandinavian political and economic history. The opening up of trade links through the rivers of Russia and Germany meant that commercial centers such as Hedeby in Denmark and Helgö in Sweden served as conduits through which Scandinavian slaves, furs, or sea-ivory could be exported, and precious metals, weapons, and domestic items could be imported. Far from being merely a land inhabited by sea-raiders, Scandinavia boasted a sturdy economy based on agriculture, timber, an increasingly powerful political administration, and a mercantile community that reached deep into Europe.

The Lands

In order to understand the Vikings it is important to understand the lands in which they originated. Topographically diverse but united by a network of fjords, rivers, and seaways, Scandinavia provided the resources of people and raw materials that allowed the sea-raids of the early ninth century to take place, and which led to the emergence of the Viking Age.

Below: Typical Scandinavian farmhouses with sod roofs have been used for centuries. Vikings began using the sod roof as insulation against the harsh winters and to keep the house cool during the summer months.

The geographical makeup of Scandinavia, the variations of climate, landscape, and the way in which the land was settled all played a part in shaping the course of events during the era. In the west, Norway's jagged coastline is dominated by mountains, and arable land is in short supply. The thousands of islands that lie off the coast provided a network of sheltered waterways linking the few pockets of workable land. Some of the country's narrow fjords extend deep inland, and the best farmland is located at their tips, where rivers cut their way through the mountain ranges.

Other cultivated pockets exist in the Jæren district of southwestern Norway, in the Trøndelag region around the modern city of Trondheim, and around the Oslofjord, where the modern Norwegian capital of Oslo now stands. These last two regions were linked by roads, and maintained close contact with the Swedes to the east. Still further north, beyond the Arctic Circle, the population was very sparse indeed, although small communities of hunters and fishermen clung to the inhospitable shorelines. Outside the three main cultivated areas the rest of Norway was sparsely populated, but these communities made use of the leads (inshore seaways) to maintain links between communities, and to trade.

To the east, Sweden displays a more varied landscape. In the Norrland region in the far north, dense forests and rocky soil meant that agriculture was limited to a narrow coastal strip on the Gulf of Bothnia, and the Viking-age population was consequently extremely sparse. Further to the south the central portion of Sweden is divided into two fertile and populous regions, and one less hospitable one. Svealand is the traditional home of the Suehan (or Sweden)

people, who gave their name to the entire country. This region encompasses the province of Uppland, the powerbase of the Swedish crown, which ruled from the capital of Old Uppsala. To the north of Uppland is the region known as Dalarna, a trackless waste of mountains, lakes, and rivers and largely uninhabited in Viking times.

Scandinavia meets Europe

To the south of Svealand lies the Götar region, named after a tribal grouping of the same name. The region is bordered to the west by Lake Väner, and incorporates the provinces of Östergötland and Västergötland (east and west Götar), separated by Lake Vätter. Both were lightly populated during the Viking age, although the town of Skara developed in Västergötland toward the close of the era. At the southern tip of Sweden, the poor soil of the Skåne region meant that the area was largely uninhabited until the Danes founded the township of Lund on its coast during the late Viking age. Similarly Småland to the north was sparsely populated. Off the Swedish coast the islands of Öland, Gotland, and to a lesser extent the Åland Islands were populous areas with arable land.

Denmark comprises the low-lying Jutland peninsula and more than 500 islands off its eastern shore. In addition, the Danish realm during the Viking age incorporated the southern province of Holstein, the Baltic island of Bornholm, and the southern portion of Sweden. During the Viking era much of Denmark was covered with forest, while the soil of the North Sea coast was sandy and poor. The best arable land lay in the archipelago of islands (particularly the two largest ones, Sjaeland and Fyn) and in the area around the Viking royal capital at Roskilde.

Unlike the rest of Scandinavia, Denmark was suited to the raising of horses and cattle, and its Dark Age population was well placed to trade with their neighbors to the south. The relatively narrow neck of land connecting Denmark to the German lands to the south meant that the border was easily defended, and trading links could be established without much danger of invasion. Consequently Viking commercial centers such as Hedeby thrived as conduits of Scandinavian trade. The region also exerted some degree of control over sea links between the Baltic and North Seas. During the Viking era the Danes endeavored to exploit this by expanding their political control into the lands across the narrow waterway to their north.

Below: Good arable land was at a premium in much of Scandinavia. Here animals graze on a Viking burial site.

Scandinavian Prehistory

The Vikings were a product of their environment, the direct descendants of the prehistoric Scandinavian peoples. These societies and their descendants established the pattern of kingship, community, and culture that governed the lives of the Scandinavians of the Viking age.

Below: A votive offering most likely made to celebrate the sun, this bronze horse and chariot date from about 1200 BC. They were cast into a peat bog at Trundholm in Denmark, probably during a religious ceremony.

As early as 12,000 years ago, people were living in Scandinavia. From the occasional archaeological find, we know that these early Scandinavians were hunter-gatherers. Among the signs of their passage, they left a trail of flints and worked antlers. These traces of human activity are rare, indicating that the region was sparsely populated. However, as the millennia passed, enough material survived to provide a clearer indication of what these people were like.

In southwestern Norway (south of the modern city of Bergen) a group of people known as the Fosna settled the region, probably after migrating there from the southeast. Further to the north, another group identified as the Kosma occupied the northern portion of Norway and Sweden in prehistoric times. By 4000 BC, both peoples showed evidence of using the bow and arrow, the harpoon, and the spear for hunting. There is also evidence that fishing and farming became more widespread. These were the ancestors of the Vikings, and their partially settled hunting culture has a modern parallel in the Lapp culture of northern Finland.

By 1500 BC, these people began to leave behind more substantial artifacts. The Bronze Age inhabitants of the settlements on Oslofjord in southern Norway and Varangerfjord in the far north lived in settled communities, with a relatively stable economy, and both groups

shared the same ethnic background with the even more prosperous inhabitants of Denmark. The Danes of the Bronze Age traded amber from the Jutland peninsula in exchange for gold, copper, and tin. Archaeological evidence suggests that these communities thrived. Grave finds include decorated weapons and personal ornaments; so clearly these societies supported specialized artisans and craftsmen. As for their beliefs, religious artifacts such as the bronze sun god chariot from Trundholm in Denmark and the plethora of rock carvings throughout Scandinavia indicate the nature of their beliefs.

The carvings and picture slabs provide us with a superb pictorial insight into these communities, from the nature of their small oared vessels that were the true precursors of the Viking ships, to the animals they hunted or harnessed. Male figures predominate, and almost all are shown naked, an artistic convention that obviously offers no indication of the clothing worn by these people. Fortunately the thousands of tumuli (burial mounds) provide well-preserved remains of dress: woolen cloaks and kilts, leather shoes, and fur hats.

Recognizably Viking culture

The Bronze Age in Scandinavia ended about 500 BC, and the development of ironworking came at a time when burial practices changed, with tumuli being replaced in some regions by boat-shaped graves outlined by stones. These *skibsætninger* were the cultural precursors of the boat-shaped Viking graves and ship-burials of the Viking period. The early Iron Age was a period where the cultural affluence of the late Bronze Age seems to have come to an end. It has been suggested that the spread of the Celtic culture in the rest of Europe meant that during this period Scandinavia was economically and politically isolated from the rest of Europe.

Climatic change was also a problem, and early iron was too brittle to survive the temperatures of northern Scandinavia, which lack led to regional stagnation and decline. This was the period when the Scandinavians received their first written mention. About 300 BC, the explorer Pytheas described the Iron Age Scandinavians as "barbarians who lived by agriculture." The Roman geographer Strabo, writing in the first century BC mentions the Cimbri of Denmark, the people linked with the part-Celtic Gundestrup cauldron (*see picture*).

During the Roman period these people traded skins, sea-ivory, slaves, and fur with the Roman Empire, and Roman finds have been recovered throughout Scandinavia. From that point on, the dearth of hard information about pre-Vikings was replaced by a body of written accounts of early Scandinavian society, provided by Roman observers. Although still fragmentary, these records provide us with solid information about the ancestors of the Vikings, and the way in which they structured their society.

Left: This stela, or incised rock carving, is typical of the many Viking images found in Scandinavia. This particular carving from central Sweden most probably depicts a weapon.

Above: The pre-Viking Gundestrup Cauldron was found in a Danish peatbog. Its side panels had been dismantled from the lower bowl and the whole buried probably as a votive offering. Experts still argue over the origins of the gilded silver bowl. Although the images are early Celtic, from the 1st century BC, they also have a distinctly Germanic slant, which reinforces the theory that this is Cimbric work, and therefore as much pre-Viking as it is Celtic.

Pre-Viking Scandinavia

During the half millennium or more between the arrival of the Romans in northern Europe and the start of the Viking age, Scandinavians developed a culture that would emerge as the true Viking society of the seventh century AD. This Scandinavian society was both dynamic and productive.

As far as the Romans were concerned, Scandinavia was the homeland of the Cimbri, a Germanic tribe who ventured south in search of land and plunder during the first century BC. Worse was to come, as throughout the Roman period further waves of barbarians clashed with and eventually toppled the Roman world: the Langobards, Burgundians, and the Goths. All were reputedly Scandinavians, the inhabitants of *Scandza*. The Romans provide us with a profile of these people. In the first century AD, Pliny the Elder wrote of the "bay" beyond the Jutland peninsula where the "island" of *Skandia* was situated, and Tacitus recorded that the Suiones (of Sweden) who inhabited the "island" were noted for their warriors and their ships, which had "a prow at each end."

These people were bordered by the Sitones

(of northern Sweden and Finland), who had a woman ruler. Consequently, northeastern Scandinavia became incorrectly associated with *terra feminarum*, the land of the amazons. The following century, Ptolemy charted the region, placing the Saxons and Cimbri in Denmark, and the Finns and Lapps to the north of *Scandia*. Over the next few centuries, few descriptions of the Scandinavians (accurate or otherwise) exist, although numerous grave and hoard finds indicate a thriving trade between Scandinavia and the Roman world. The arterial trade routes of the Vistula and Elbe rivers linked both Sweden and Denmark with the Gothic races to the south, and trade southward from Denmark brought Roman glassware, jewelry, coins, and weapons north into Scandinavia, in return for skins, furs, slaves, and amber, among other commodities.

Wild northern tribes

The collapse of the Western Roman Empire at the start of the fifth century AD led to a period during which there were no written descriptions of Scandinavians. However, Cassiodorus in writing his history of the Goths a century later described the destroyers of the Roman world as coming from Scandinavia. To the north of the "island" were the Adogit people and the Screrefennae, while to the south lay the realms of the Suehans (Swedes) who produced fine horses and furs, and the Hallin, Liothida, Bergio, Gautigoth, Rugi, Augandzi, Granni, and Raumarike tribes.

The Swedes emerged as a confederation of several of these smaller tribal groups. Similarly, to the south the Dani (Danes) were formed from lesser groups. The Byzantine historian Procopius described the land of the Danes, and the island of Thule (the north) that lay beyond, as being a barren and desolate place where the sun shone at midnight. Procopius went on to describe the Lapps, claiming their life was "like to that of beasts." Their clothing and sustenance came from the wild animals they hunted, while the other Scandinavian tribes were "not much different from the normality of men," apart from their religious beliefs.

Turning to later Scandinavian sources, the early political unity of both Denmark and Sweden is recorded in the sagas, although Norway remained disunited longer than the rest

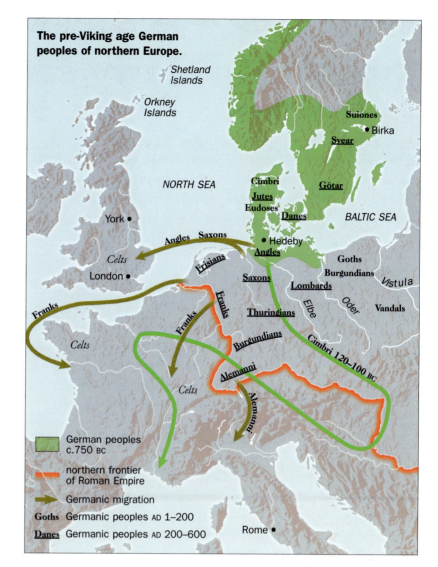

The pre-Viking age German peoples of northern Europe.

Shetland Islands
Orkney Islands
NORTH SEA
York
Celts
London
Franks
Celts
Frisians
Angles   Saxons
Angles
Saxons
Franks
Franks
Celts
Alemanni
Alemanni
Thuringians
Burgundians
Cimbri
Jutes
Eudoses
Danes
Hedeby
Goths
Burgundians
Lombards
Elbe
Oder
Vistula
Vandals
Cimbri 120–100 BC
BALTIC SEA
Suiones
Birka
Svear
Götar
Rome

German peoples c.750 BC

northern frontier of Roman Empire

Germanic migration

Goths Germanic peoples AD 1–200

Danes Germanic peoples AD 200–600

of the region. By the early sixth century AD the Swedes of Uppland were ruled by a powerful monarch, as described in the *Ynglinga Saga* and other works. In *Beowolf*, the Scandinavian "sea-kings" are mentioned, reflecting the emergence of the region's people as seafarers. Similar powerful kings are recorded in Denmark, so by the sixth century strong and unifying monarchs ruled both regions. Similarly the mechanisms of political administration were also in place, allowing these monarchs to better supply their armies, raise revenues, and administer justice.

This is supported by archaeological evidence that indicates that Scandinavia was developing an agrarian economy, where artisans such as smiths and potters found ready markets for their goods. Political unions came and went, but Scandinavian society continued to develop, and settlements turned into towns, which in turn provided ready markets for traders. Although backward compared to the rest of Europe, Scandinavia was a stable and buoyant region at the dawn of the Viking age, and its people had laid the political, mercantile, maritime, and martial foundations for the Viking achievements that followed.

Facing: This petroglyph (rock carving) near Litsleby, Sweden, of a man is drawn larger than life. Shown brandishing a spear and with an erect phallus, it was carved on top of older petroglyphs of boats. The carver was a member of the Boat-Ax culture, dating from the early Bronze Age.

Kingship in Early Scandinavia

During the centuries preceding the Viking raids of the early ninth century, most of Scandinavia became unified under powerful monarchs. In order to understand the Vikings themselves, we need to examine the political landscape of their Scandinavian homeland.

It is difficult to avoid labeling the Scandinavian countries according to the boundaries of the modern states of Sweden, Norway, Denmark, Iceland, and Finland. In the ninth century, political boundaries were far less defined, and borders changed in accordance with the success of military campaigns or changes in the fortunes of royal houses. Despite this, the Viking attacks on the rest of Europe were not the result of political unrest at home, and the largely agrarian economies of the various Scandinavian states continued to flourish throughout the raiding era. Instead the expansion was the result of an increasing population and the attractions of greater wealth in southern lands, so commerce and raiding overseas were seen as increasingly lucrative activities.

At the start of the Viking period, Scandinavia was divided into a number of *land* (provinces), each controlled by either an independent ruler, a regional *jarl* or a king, or a more powerful political governor. Many of these regional entities still exist today as recognizable political units. The *land* were also organized on a military basis. Each was divided into *hund*, which supplied a body of about 100 fighting men. While the *land* frequently changed hands, amalgamating, dividing, or otherwise changing their political boundaries, the *hund* remained as clearly defined local areas. As time progressed, the *land* tended to become increasingly absorbed into a greater political entity ruled by a king. In turn this fostered something akin to national identity, although the modern definition of the term is not directly compatible with national unity in the early medieval sense, when nations were in a continual state of flux.

As centralized monarchies became established, the political and military structure of Scandinavia altered, and independent *land* became increasingly rare. As an example, the island of Gotland in the Baltic Sea remained under the independent control of an island oligarchy, but during the Viking era it was amalgamated into the Kingdom of Sweden. By the 13th century, the hitherto independent landmasses of Greenland and Iceland were brought under the control of the Norwegian crown, and the process of political amalgamation was completed. As the Scandinavians converted to Christianity,

Right: A hearth, alcoves, and thick external walls form the interior of a building at the Jarlshof settlement in Shetland. The lack of local wood meant that the usual form of timber construction used in Scandinavia was impossible.

Left: Illumination from the Icelandic manuscript *Flateyjarbok,* which shows King Harald Harfagri (Fairhair) cutting the fetters from the giant Dofri, who according to folklore was to become his foster father. Harald's increasing amalgamation of power under his monarchy would be responsible for driving independent-minded Vikings to seek new lands over the sea (*see pages 104 and 136*).

the administrative structure of the Church was used to reinforce the power of the monarchy by adding stability and encouraging the codification of laws.

Emerging nation-states

Sweden derived its name from the principal region in the country, and throughout the Viking period it remained an agrarian entity, lacking the bustling population centers found in Denmark. Royal authority grew under the Uppsala dynasty, and all of the *land* were absorbed into the emergent Swedish kingdom by AD 1000. Internal colonization was further augmented by expansion into Finland and Russia, which had the effect of increasing national revenue. However, further extensions of royal influence were hindered by the late conversion of most of Sweden to Christianity.

In Denmark, the growth of royal power was both steady and comprehensive during the early Viking period, and the region (including territory as far south as the Elbe) was united under the control of a single powerful dynasty

by AD 900. As in Sweden, kingship was part hereditary and part elective, since royal candidates required the backing of the *land* in order to win the throne. State control was even more centralized than in Sweden, and the royal army was the power behind the throne. The political, economic, and military growth of the State was ensured by campaigns against the Franks in Germany and the Saxons in England. At the same time, the Church spread its influence outward from the kingdom's capital of Roskilde to guarantee that both monarch and State maintained close ties with itself.

As for Norway, the land of the North-men (Norsemen), the growth of royal power was hindered by the broken topography of the land. In southern Norway (Vestfold), the ruling dynasty was originally of Swedish descent, but elsewhere the *land* were largely self-governing. These northern *land* were finally tamed by King Harald Harfagri (Fairhair) in the late ninth century, and thereafter his dynasty retained control of the crown throughout the remainder of the Viking period.

The Viking Family

The basic social unit in early medieval Scandinavian society was the extended family. In what was almost exclusively a rural society, communities of families came together for mutual support, and formed the building blocks of both the Viking raiding fleets and of the emergent kingdoms of the region.

Although detailed accounts of domestic life only exist from the end of the Viking age, it is evident that the family was considered a political entity in its own right. Kinship through blood or marriage provided bonds that are a recurring theme in contemporary histories. Administrative records show that descent was recognized through the male line, but male offspring tended to remain in the paternal home after marriage, thus ensuring a continuing association between a family and the land on which it farmed.

In addition, families held a form of collective responsibility for their members, as reflected in Scandinavian law, which was codified during the late Viking era. For example, the laws concerning atonement for a man's murder involved the payment of a settlement from one family to another, with the whole family assuming financial responsibility for the

Below: Reconstruction of Norse longhouses at L'Anse aux Meadows National Historic Site, where Vikings first settled in Newfoundland.

payment. The more distant the relationship of the family member to the killer, the proportionately smaller the fine for that individual.

Family units were measured back over three or four generations, so an individual was considered to be part of the family if he shared a great-great-grandfather (i.e., third cousins). The lack of family mobility ensured that local communities were often closely linked by blood and marriage and, on a regional scale, the status of certain communities or areas within a *land* was measured by the standing of the family who lived there within the wider community. Families usually observed religious events together, feasted together, and farmed together.

When required, these same close family ties were used to create Viking warbands, and together they formed part of the *hund* system of regional military organization. As with the family reputation, the social standing of a family was influenced by its performance in battle, or in the marketplace.

Individuals broke away from this mesh of family ties either by sea-roving or because they were ostracized by their family or their state. Conversely, due to the increasing influence

of a centralized royal authority, bonds were also formed between individuals or families and regional leaders. This included the loyalty of a warrior to his chief (such as a local *jarl*), or the bond between a freed slave and his former master. In time, this evolved into something akin to the feudal system, but Scandinavians never adopted the rigid structure of Frankish feudalism during the Viking era.

Family bond

Similar social changes came about with the growth of towns toward the end of the period, while Christianity also served to undermine traditional bonds. By the 13th century, a significant portion of the Scandinavian population was removed from the solidarity and kinship of the traditional family with its emphasis on the family farm. Although isolated from traditional patterns of society, individuals were also freed from the heavy weight of collective responsibilities and obligations.

The yeoman was at the core of Scandinavian society, a free farmer who worked the land for his family, and who fulfilled occasional military or economic obligations to higher authorities as required. This meant he also formed the core of any Viking army or raiding party. The term *bondi* (meaning householder, landowner, or farmer) is traditionally associated with these yeomen, even though yeomen could work as

hired farmworkers, or they might share their household with other family members. Various levels of *bondi* were denoted by such terms as *edalbondi* or *hauldr*, representing lesser or greater social standing respectively, although these terms were not used universally throughout Scandinavia.

Naturally, *bondi* were family men, working family farms. The spread of royal control brought in its wake an increasing level of administrative and legal bureaucracy, making inroads into both family ties and the perceived freeman status of the *bondi*. This encroachment by monarchs on traditional values is often offered as a partial explanation for the migration to Iceland and Greenland, and also for the explosion of Viking raids during the early ninth century. Despite this, family loyalty and bonding within the rural Viking communities of yeoman farmers remained the cornerstone of Viking society during the period.

Above: A Viking home. At its center was the hearth. Raised platforms served as sitting and sleeping areas. The woman in the background is working a loom. Most utensils were made from wood. Clay pots only became common in the later Viking era.

The Structure of Viking Society

Beneath the emerging kingships of early medieval Scandinavia lay a stratum of society that administered justice, ruled the land in the name of the king, and protected the population. Although the nature and title of these chiefs varied from region to region, the role remained the same.

Above: A farmer on Mainland, Shetland Islands, makes hay by spreading cut grass across a field to dry, a technique performed for centuries by Scandinavian farmers and Viking settlers.

At the top of Viking society stood the king (*konugr* in Old Norse). Kings were usually selected by the community to rule. Because fealty and military service was given in exchange for protection and administrative leadership, this was a two-sided task. The monarch ruled only by the popular consent of his subjects, a government far removed from the feudal system that was emerging in northwest Europe at about the same time.

The king had access to a treasury (known as Uppsala-wealth in Sweden), and to the resources of royal lands and livestock, but otherwise his opportunities for revenue collection were limited. Although all Scandinavian economies were predominantly agrarian, the kings of the Viking era derived the bulk of their income from revenues gleaned through the control of trade, or from military conquest or raiding.

A social elite provided regional leadership and military force to help the king rule his country. The title earl (*jarl* in Old Norse) means a distinguished man; a regional figurehead, who in this case controlled the destiny of large parts of Scandinavia or of colonies overseas. For example the earls of Orkney ruled both Orkney and Shetland, and at times their lands extended into the mainland of Scotland and the Western Isles. Founded at the end of the ninth century, the Orkney earldom was seen as subservient to the Norwegian king, but its titleholders ruled with hardly any royal interference. The Hlaðajarlar (Earls of Lade), who ruled northern Norway on behalf of the Norwegian king, had less independence, but at times they managed to extend their influence south to encompass virtually the whole country. In the Viking territories of mainland Britain or Ireland, regional leaders often assumed the title of king, but in effect they were sub-kings, or earls in all but name.

Local administration

Further down the social ladder came the men who ruled small provinces, either in their own name as independent rulers, or more commonly on behalf of a king or an earl. Their level of independence and power varied greatly with time and geography, but the steady growth of monarchical influence began to erode regional power, and petty chiefs gradually evolved into a new social elite, whose power was closely linked with that of the king. In Denmark and Sweden landsmen (*landsmenn* in Old Norse) administered the *land*, assisted by a cluster of more lowly officials known as *styræsmen* in Denmark, or *hirdsmen* in Sweden. In Norway the *hersir* provided local or regional leadership, but from the onset these magnates ruled as servants of the king. In most cases these leaders became military commanders in charge of regional levies in time of war, or provided quotas of ships and men for royal use when required.

On a lower level of the social order, the *gæðingar* in the Orkneys or the *hauldr* of Norway comprised a social stratum above that of the yeoman. These superior yeomen were described as "men endowed with or possessed of goods." In effect, they were landed magnates whose holdings were more extensive than those found in the rest of the rural community. A term used elsewhere in Scandinavia to describe superior yeomen was *lendr maðr*. Another kind

of local magnate, the *sæslumaðr* (sheriff) was appointed directly by the monarch and administered royal holdings on the king's behalf.

Beneath these more exalted landowners, administrators, or magnates were the bulk of Viking society, the *bondi* or yeoman farmers. While there were several levels of *bondi*, for the most part they were farm owners. Their often extensive families existed throughout Scandinavia and formed the bulk of the Viking colonists who migrated overseas. These agrarian workers were free men, unlike their counterparts the peasant serfs found elsewhere in feudal Europe. As well as landowners and their tenants, the *bondi* also encompassed local craftsmen. Beneath the *bondi*, slaves formed a sizeable portion of the Viking population. These were captured during raids into Russia, Germany, or northwestern Europe. Although these unfortunates could be granted their freedom, most had no hope of betterment, and were treated as chattels.

Below: A Scandinavian farmhouse on the upper summer pastureland in Norway. Viking dwellings were built in a similar manner to this later structure.

The Viking Rural Economy

The Viking world was one based almost exclusively on agriculture, fishing, and hunting. Although merchant settlements became increasingly important during the Viking age, the mainstay of the Scandinavian economy was the farmer and his land.

Vikings were tied to the land and the adjacent coastal waters, and their life was dictated by seasonal patterns. While Viking raiders ventured far from home, they almost always returned in time to perform the main agricultural tasks of the year, such as planting and harvesting. Although merchants, some state administrators, and religious leaders lived in the handful of Viking towns, they probably only did so for part of the year, when the markets were open for business. The Viking population lived almost exclusively in isolated farms and settlements.

Although extended families or neighbors gathered for religious festivities, weddings, or social gatherings, most Vikings spent the winter in relative isolation, guarding their reserves of food and fuel. In such northern latitudes, this meant surviving in cold and darkness for almost half of the year, and smaller less well-stocked farms faced the prospect of hunger. Such hardships played a major part in the desire to find richer pickings overseas.

Certain general observations can be made about Viking rural economy. The further north the farm, the less likely that it relied on cereal crops, and consequently animal husbandry became increasingly important in the north of Norway and Sweden. Beyond the Arctic Circle a handful of scattered settlers made their living by hunting or fishing; however, Viking farming implements have been found in the far north of Norway. Fishing was an important element of

Below: Hand-hewn shingles shaped with an adze were used to build walls in a Viking house. Reconstruction from the town of Hedeby, Denmark.

life in the populous coastal regions or lakesides, while farmers who relied on animal husbandry tended to move their herds to mountain pastures in the summer to conserve local fodder.

There were marked regional variations to this overall pattern. Farmers in Denmark enjoyed lusher pasture and so relied on cereal production and animal husbandry. By contrast, in less hospitable Iceland, the larger and more profitable farms existed almost exclusively on animals for their sustenance and imported most of their cereal crops from the Scandinavian mainland.

Land and sea

In the forests of the far north (and to a lesser extent further south), Viking hunters stalked deer, bear, reindeer, seabirds, ducks, and seals among other quarry. A thriving fur trade also created a demand for animal skins, of which seal, bear, reindeer, and walrus were the most popular. By the middle of the Viking period the fur trade had become a major factor in the Scandinavian economy. Sea-ivory from walrus tusks, oil from whales, and eiderdown for bedding were all valuable exports, and traders made annual voyages up the Scandinavian coast to collect these commodities before returning south in the high summer to sell the goods in the Viking markets.

The agricultural system was basic, but well-suited to the land. Horses, cattle, pigs, and goats were raised, with the weakest being butchered in the short autumn. The flesh was

then cured and stored to provide nourishment for the long winter months ahead. Among the cereals, archaeological samples indicate that rye was the most popular crop, but oats and barley were also grown widely, particularly in southern Scandinavia. Farmers also grew vegetables such as cabbages, leeks, and peas, and the basic diet was augmented by wild berries, nuts, and even seaweed. Much of this was grown in order to ensure survival, but cattle and cereal crops were also taken to the few Viking towns or royal centers and sold or bartered, or else sold at regional fairs or markets.

Beyond the rural economy, the Vikings maintained extensive trading connections across Europe and through Russia to the Mediterranean Sea. Market towns served as conduits for this trade, but they also provided the means for local enterprise, which was even more important for the development of the Scandinavian economy. Archaeological finds suggest that this internal trade was widespread, as traveling merchants or tinkers passed through the countryside each year peddling their wares. From 975, the first Scandinavian coins were minted, but even before that silver had become the principal medium of exchange, used by merchants, royal administrators, and farmers alike. The basic early Viking economy altered as the importance of towns increased, turning from a predominantly agricultural one to a more mercantile system.

Above: A carpenter carves a post using an ax for a standing loom that will be used in the reconstructed Viking town of Hedeby, Denmark.

Merchants and Craftsmen

The Viking era is associated in the popular imagination purely with the excesses of the Viking raids, which for the most part occurred during the early part of the ninth century. Consequently it is an unfortunate fact that most people are unaware of the lasting achievements of Scandinavian merchants in forging new trade routes.

Below: Despite the increasing spread of Christianity throughout Scandinavia, the older Viking gods retained an influence. Craftsmen who ensured that they catered for all prospered. This Viking metalsmith's mold found in Denmark was used for casting both Christian crosses and Thor's hammers.

Merchant traders helped build the market towns of the Viking world into centers where local craftsmen could utilize their skills to full effect. The fact that Vikings were traders more than they were raiders is one that has only recently been acknowledged through the excavation of settlements such as Hedeby in Denmark, Kaupang in Norway, and Birka in Sweden. Viking traders established and maintained a sprawling network that stretched as far as France, the Mediterranean Sea, and the Middle East. Although small regional trading centers were established in Scandinavia before the start of the ninth century AD, the Viking age witnessed the development of larger towns. These—often founded by royal initiative, as was the case with Hedeby and Bergen—provided a vital source of revenue through taxation.

The basic trading commodities included: sea-ivory, furs, and hides from the north of Scandinavia, slaves from Britain and Russia, iron and timber from central Scandinavia, and amber from Denmark. In exchange, Viking merchants purchased silver (the most desirable of imports), wine, ceramics, personal adornments such as jewelry, and even silks and spices from the Middle East and beyond. Archaeology shows us that Viking Scandinavia was well provided with metalwork from all over Europe and Arabia as well as Mediterranean glassware, Rheinish pottery, and gold or silver personal ornaments.

Merchants were exceptions to the Viking rural norm, and their success is demonstrated by the widespread distribution of trading artifacts throughout Scandinavia. Clearly trade was important outside the main centers, and Viking merchants made coastal voyages and inland treks in order to reach the isolated and scattered rural markets of the region.

the basis of local market economies. Both iron ore miners and blacksmiths formed a skill base that existed alongside the farming community and produced the tools farmers needed.

While regional craftsmen such as carpenters, silversmiths, and shipwrights existed, most of these specialized artisans required the trade generated by a larger market in order to thrive. They made the leather goods, ivory combs, and jewelry which have been uncovered in Viking burial sites. Above all they made the armor, weapons, and ships which the Viking raiders used during their attacks on the rest of Europe.

Surviving artifacts make it evident that the standard of artistic craftsmanship was extremely high. Goldsmiths, silversmiths, ironsmiths, ivory or stone carvers, and woodworkers were all producing uniquely Scandinavian products by the start of the Viking age, although artistic production reached a peak during the tenth and eleventh centuries. Given the Scandinavians' warlike nature, it is hardly surprising that some of the most exquisite workmanship was applied in the production and decoration of arms and armor. The armorer and weaponsmith were deemed the principal specialist Viking artisans.

There is evidence that by the 11th century artists and craftsmen had established guilds, while written records suggest that sometimes quite complex financial alliances were being forged, as merchants and noblemen provided venture capital for Viking expeditions and trading ventures. Given the influx of imported finery and weapons, it is a testimony to the artistic skill of Viking craftsmen and the merchants who sold their goods that these stunningly beautiful products became so widespread.

Above: An amber head from the Viking age. Amber, much prized in the Russian principalities, was extensively mined and worked in Denmark.

Left: An early Viking silver-gilt pendant of the 6th century. The figure represents a Valkyrie offering a drinking horn.

The markets themselves were seasonal affairs, and while much of Scandinavia was virtually sealed off from the rest of the world during winter, spring brought the start of mercantile activity.

Early medieval industries

One commodity became vital in the Viking world. Iron extracted from veins of ore in central Scandinavia was wrought into bars before being taken to a blacksmith for fashioning into tools or weapons. The climate precluded the use of iron in northern Scandinavia in the early medieval era, but the iron goods produced in the south formed

CHAPTER 2

Viking Religious Belief

Below: Marker stones lie scattered across a Viking burial ground near Aarlberg, Denmark.

Religious beliefs of the pre-Christian Viking world were largely influenced by the land itself, and by the presence of the Vikings' forebears, buried in the hundreds of funeral mounds that covered Scandinavia. During the period before Scandinavia's adoption of Christianity, believers had to balance their traditional need for close proximity to their ancestral dead and inherited family land with the stimuli provided by the fresh sights and cultures they encountered on their raiding or trading expeditions. Pre-Christian belief therefore underwent something of a transformation during the eighth and ninth centuries, as religious ideas were adapted to encompass the changes in lifestyle brought about by these migrations.

The old pagan beliefs of the Vikings were tolerant, pantheistic, and culturally binding. They believed that many gods and lesser deities had special powers that could be summoned to assist people who found themselves in difficult circumstances, such as encountering a tempest, or harvesting the crops, or attacking an enemy.

The Vikings horrified contemporary Christian Europe with their sacking of monasteries and churches, but this is not evidence that they lacked spiritual beliefs themselves. To them, Christian religious communities were rich storehouses of plunder, nothing more.

At first glance, the pagan gods and beliefs of pre-Christian Scandinavia were far removed from Christianity. Deities such as Odin, Thor, and Freyja were interwoven into a complex tapestry of belief, but many of the themes of this pagan structure had rough parallels with the new religion. Aspects of pagan belief such as the afterlife, heaven, hell and resurrection were all part of pre-Christian Scandinavian belief.

When the time came, this synergy made it easier for Christian missionaries to persuade the Vikings that the new faith was similar (while being superior) to their old ways.

The change from one religion to the other is most noticeable in the way in which the deceased were interred. The old forms of burying the dead accompanied by the goods and chattels needed in the afterlife were replaced with a simpler form of burial in hallowed ground in the Christian tradition. By the end of the Viking era, the old religion had gone, and the new nations of Scandinavia were firmly part of European Christendom.

A family of Gods

The numerous Viking gods had particular characters and functions, but all shared a common family known as the Æsir, a sort of divine tribe that ruled mortals from on high. Like Zeus to the ancient Greeks, Odin was the supreme divinity, and the remainder of the Æsir assisted him in his supervision of the mortal world, while at other times they acted independently.

Facing: This tapestry of the 12th-century from Skog Church, Halsingland, Sweden, shows three Viking deities. On the left, one-eyed Odin carries an ax, with a representation of the tree Yggdrasil from which he hung. In the center, Thor carries his symbolic hammer in his right hand. On the right stands Frey, symbolizing fertility by holding an ear of corn.

We learn of the pre-Christian gods of the Vikings from contemporary poems and prose, from later Christian chroniclers such as Adam of Bremen, and from medieval Icelandic literature. Odin was the chief of the Æsir, a father figure similar to those of other pagan cultures. Odin was described in the Icelandic *Prose Edda* of Snorri Sturluson, written in the 13th century:

"Odin is the highest and oldest of the gods; he rules all things, and however powerful the other gods are they all serve him as children their father. Odin is called All-father, because he is the father of all the gods; he is also called Valfather because his chosen sons are all those who die in battle. Valholl [Valhalla] *is for them."*

Valholl, valfather, and valkyrie are all derived from the Old Norse word *valr*, meaning those slain in battle (and which gives rise to the modern word "valor"). Odin was also associated with birds and animals, particularly those such as ravens and wolves which feed on carrion. This rather gruesome link is tempered by Odin's association with wisdom and poetry, and Odin was accompanied by his two ravens, Huginn and Muninn (Thought and Memory), and by his gray eight-legged horse Sleipnir.

Although Odin was the father of the gods, his supremacy did not always go unchallenged. Some later chroniclers describe Thor, the god of thunder and war, as the most powerful of the gods, and certainly there is evidence that when the Vikings referred to "the god" in the singular, they were referring to Thor, not Odin. Certainly for many Viking warriors Thor was the most important of all the gods, and personal jewelry associated with Thor is commonly found during the excavation of warrior burials. The item that is most clearly associated with this martial deity is Thor's hammer, Mjöllnir, which returned to the god's hand whenever he threw it.

Foreign gods

In addition to the gods of the Æsir, a divine tribal group known as the Vanir was attached to the main grouping of gods, rather like a group of outsiders who were allowed to participate in heavenly affairs when permitted. It has been suggested that these Vanir gods (who included the popular deities Frey and Freyja) originated in Asia, and were brought to Scandinavia through migration and trading contacts.

Their tribal chief was Njörd, the god of the sea, whose children were the siblings Frey, the handsome god of fertility, and his sister Freyja, who was married to Odin, and who helped him to gather souls. Next to Odin and Thor, this family pair ranked among the most venerated of the Scandinavian pagan gods. Baldur was Odin's second son, and his blind elder brother Hödr was tricked into killing him with a spear by Loki, the "father of all lies." As a result, Loki was bound by his son's entrails, shackled to a rock, and tortured with snake venom for all eternity (*see picture, page 79*).

In a way, the Scandinavian pagan deities were an extended family, and as such they mirrored the central focus of Viking society. Most of the gods were related in some way, and Odin ruled them like a protective father supervising his often wayward offspring. The mythological tales of these gods are sprinkled with tales of mischief, jealousy, retribution, and love; harsh gods for a hard people.

In the mythology Odin is eventually killed, only to be avenged by his son Vidar, and the children of Baldur are resurrected to join a new generation of godlike offspring. These include the children of both Odin and Thor, who ruled until the end of the world, when a last battle was fought between gods and men on one side and giants and monsters on the other. This long-awaited twilight of the gods never came. Instead, the Scandinavians simply abandoned their old gods, and adopted Christianity.

Asgard, Valhalla, Yggdrasil

That any warrior who fell valiantly in battle would be rewarded by Odin with a place in Valhalla, the eternal heaven for heroes, was central to the Vikings' belief. Ascension to the meeting hall in Valhalla ensured that Viking warriors lived for eternity in a corner of Asgard, in the center of the mythological universe.

Left: A carving on the side of the wooden stave church at Urnes, Norway, depicts the deer eating Yggdrasil, the World Tree. Staves (derived from *staf*, "staff") are thin, shaped lengths of wood set edge-to-edge.

For Viking believers, the universe as they knew it was framed by the branches of Yggdrasil, the world tree. This mighty ash encompassed the Viking world, and was preyed on by four stags who nibbled at its leaves, and by the dragon Dreadbiter, who lay at its base. The tree's trunk was partly rotten, but further decay was prevented by a trio of guardians (Norns). It was a male tree, full of vibrancy, virility, and magic, and in its branches Odin hung in a sort of self-crucifixion, in an attempt to understand the meaning of the tree and the universe it supported.

In the center of the Viking universe itself lay Asgard, the heavenly dwelling-place of the gods. Asgard lay on a mountaintop above the clouds, while the mortal world lay beneath it, where the gods could watch over mankind and steer the humans through life. The worldly place of humans was known as Midgard, or middle earth. Beneath it lay Hel, the lair of giants and monsters, which the gods kept at bay until the day of final reckoning. The parallels with Christian belief in heaven and hell are striking, but the Vikings were far more specific about the nature of the afterlife and other worlds in their universe.

Warriors' fate

When a Viking died, he went to one of two places. The truly worthy Viking warriors who had died heroes' deaths in battle were summoned by Odin and ascended to Valhalla, the hall of heroes in Asgard. Their passage was assisted by the Valkyrie, the mythical armored handmaidens of war whose appearance in the skies presaged a bloody battle. If any mortals managed to climb the mountain that housed Asgard, entrance to the realm was barred by a fast-flowing river and Valgrind, a gate that only opened for the chosen few. The Valkyries simply flew their heroes over such obstacles, and deposited them on the steps of Valhalla itself. The banqueting hall had 540 giant doors, and each door accommodated 800 warriors marching abreast. The hall's rafters were fashioned from huge spears, and shields were used as roofing tiles. Here the Viking heroes sat in the banqueting hall for eternity, feasting, drinking, and celebrating with their fellow warriors and with servants to care for their every need.

For those who failed to make the selection, eternity was spent in Hel. This belief in Valhalla and Hel was strongly espoused by the Vikings, and constituted a powerful incentive for bravery in battle. When the Viking universe was threatened with collapse during the twilight of the gods (Ragnarök), these warriors fought shoulder-to-shoulder with their gods to defend Asgard and Midgard from the forces of Hel.

Unlike other religions, Scandinavian paganism was based on specific descriptions of the worlds of gods and giants, monsters and mortals. In part this reflected the close link between the agrarian Vikings and the land itself, a link that further manifested itself in the choice of places to worship. Specific sites were chosen, often at a particular natural feature such as a hill, lake, or rock outcrop. Religious decoration of stones litter these sacred places, where the pagan Vikings felt closer to their gods than elsewhere in the Scandinavian landscape. Certain sites even had particular links with particular deities, as the evidence of carved religious markers testifies.

At other times, religious observance was carried out at home or in communal gatherings, where the unity of the family and local community was strengthened by common religious worship or feasting. While the gods themselves indulged in occasional human sacrifice, so too did the Vikings, and this aspect more than any other appalled the Christian missionaries who eventually made their way into Scandinavia toward the end of the Viking age. However, although the Viking religion had its bizarre aspects, there were sufficient parallels with Christianity to allow the missionaries some opportunity in persuading the Vikings that the new religion was a superior one.

Ragnarök: End of the World

That the world would end in chaos and the fall of the gods is unusual in a religious faith, but it has similarities to the Christian Day of Judgment. For the Vikings, Ragnarök took the form of a cataclysmic battle between good and evil, in which the gods sacrificed themselves in an attempt to save mankind.

Sigurd's legend (Siegfried in the German form), as it was recorded in medieval Icelandic literature, gives us some idea of how the Vikings believed their world might come to an end. The young warrior fell in love with Brynhilde (Brunhilde), one of Odin's valkyries. Brynhilde was part human and part deity, but as punishment for using her powers to protect her lover, she was placed in a trance-like sleep by Odin, and protected by a curtain of fire. Sigurd was already seen as a Norse hero; a mighty warrior and a dragon slayer. According to the tale, his father Sigmund had already ascended to Valhalla when the love affair took place.

In the banqueting hall he learns that the death of Odin will be brought about by Fenrir, a gray wolf, during a final cataclysmic battle between the gods and the monsters from Hel. As Snorri Sturluson the medieval Icelandic chronicler put it:

"The wolf will swallow the sun… then a second wolf will seize the moon and he too will do great damage. The stars will disappear from the heavens…. The wolf Fenrir will then be free. The sea will invade the land because Midgardsom turns in a giant rage intending to come ashore."

This reveals that Ragnarök and Fenrir's approach will be marked by natural calamities: the onset of a fearsome winter lasting for three years and the collapse of human values and morals. War, pestilence, and flooding will bring mankind to its knees.

In Asgard, Baldur's death (*see page 28*) presages the coming catastrophe, while Loki allies himself with the giants. Once the sun and the moon have been eaten, the wolf Fenrir seeks out Odin. The wolf—the result of a union between Loki and the ogres of Hel—is joined by Jörmungand, the world serpent, who slithers up into Asgard to wreak havoc. As the Fire Giants, led by their chieftain Surt, cross the rainbow bridge of Bifröst into Asgard, Loki breaks free from his bonds and joins in the destruction. The gods defend Asgard with the help of the Einhergar, the heroes of Valhalla, summoned by Heimdral, the watchman of Asgard.

The legions of Hel then struggle with the gods and heroes for domination in one final and cataclysmic battle. Odin wields his magic spear Gungnir in the fight, but Fenrir avoids Odin's lunge and devours the father of the gods. Odin is instantly avenged by his son Vidar, who kills Fenrir, but himself dies at the hands of Surt. However, Thor kills Jörmungand before he succumbs to his wounds. Flames engulf heaven and earth, and the gods are given a fiery cremation amid the ruins of Asgard.

The cycle continues

Following the destruction of the old order of gods and mankind comes a resurrection of life and decency. Baldur's offspring rise up to greet the dawn of a new sun, daughter of the first sun, which had been eaten by the wolf. They are joined in the ruins of Asgard by the children of Odin and Thor, and between them they rebuild a new age of gods and men.

Lying in the scorched grass

Below: Fulfilling in Viking tradition a similar function to the Cross in Christian belief, representations of Thor's hammer were popular throughout Scandinavia.

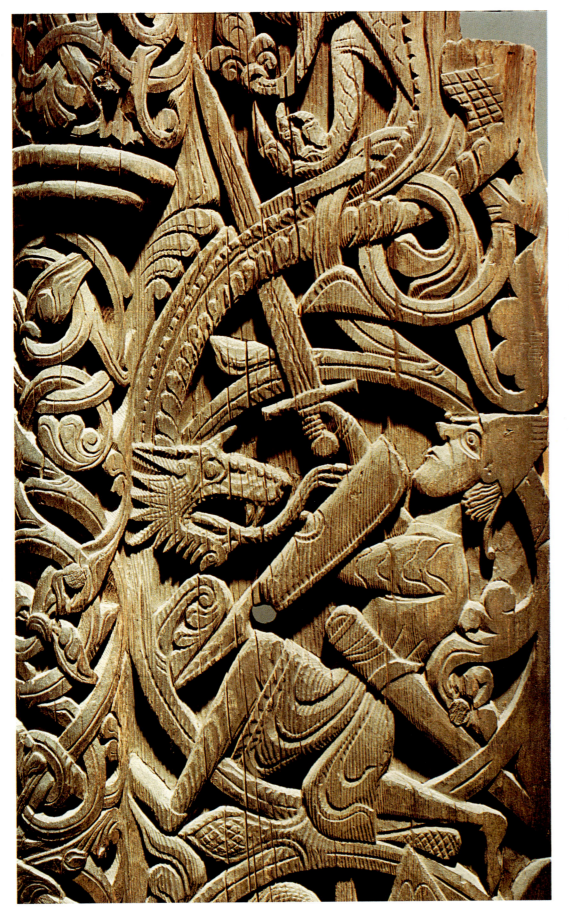

of Asgard, the children find the golden playing pieces used by the gods, and use them to restore order from chaos. Two mortals also survive the final conflagration and, like Adam and Eve in Christian belief, they repopulate the earth. It is even hinted that a new supreme deity, possibly even Tyr, the almost forgotten forerunner of Odin, will emerge to govern this new Viking universe, rising phoenix-like from the ashes of the old. The Viking belief in the inevitability of apocalypse and resurrection has obvious parallels in the Christian Book of Revelations.

Burial and the Afterlife

Of the archaeological evidence we have from the Viking age, the most prolific source of information comes from burial sites. As with most religions, the way a society dealt with death tells us a great deal about the belief system and customs its people followed.

Above: A Viking grave of stones in the shape of a longship rests in the middle of a pasture on the island of Gotland.

In the pre-Christian Viking period it was important to maintain the reputation of both the individual (for example as a great warrior), and of the family. The worst event that could befall a Viking was to undergo a shameful death, and leave behind him an odious reputation. Finds made in burial sites make it clear that the Vikings believed in an afterlife. The dead were often laid out accompanied with the items they might need on their eternal journey. These included animals, agricultural tools, household utensils, weapons, or even whole ships.

In the Oseberg burial mound (*see pages 48–49*) in southern Norway the richly decorated Viking ship that formed the centerpiece of the burial was filled with all manner of household goods, domestic animals, and even beds. This rich find is a spectacular example of what was regularly carried out on a less grand scale by the majority of the population. Equipping the dead for their future included providing warriors with the weapons and armor they would need to fight alongside the gods during Ragnarök, and others with the trappings of their station in society or their trade, so that they could perform a useful function for eternity.

Ships seem to have been a recurring theme in burials, although the interment of bodies in complete vessels is rare. More common was the burial of a body in a boat-shaped plot, where stones lining the grave are arranged in the shape of a vessel with a clearly denoted stem and stern. Large graveyards of these stone ship-burials indicate that this method of interment was common in central Sweden and southern Norway, and most probably denote the last resting place of the upper echelons of Viking society. In AD 960 King Harald Bluetooth built two monument mounds at Jelling in Denmark over the top of earlier stone ship-burials (*see picture, page 39*), marking a break with this ship-burial tradition, immediately before he and his people adopted Christianity.

Many possible fates

While some Norse legends speak of the afterlife in Hel, others mention living "under the hill" with dead family ancestors, a reference to the burial mounds that littered the Scandinavian landscape. Local burial mounds would have been a constant shadow on life, because the Vikings viewed the mounds as gateways to some kind of dark underworld. Viking mythology tells us that the Scandinavians dreaded the "dead walkers" (*see below*) and part of the tradition of inhumation with such a wealth of objects was to appease the gods, and for them to accept the soul of the deceased into a better afterlife. What became of the spirits was in the hands of the gods.

In addition to the extremes of Valhalla and Hel, it was believed that the gods provided eternal homes for the dead in some form of afterworld. This was perhaps the equivalent of purgatory, amid the ogres, monsters, serpents, and giants. For the unlucky ones who had to enter Hel, they crossed the underground River Gjöl by a bridge, guarded by Garm, the hound of Hel. Beyond lay the Hills of Darkness, the lair of the wolf Fenrir, where the air rang with the wails of the eternally damned. An even worse possibility for a Viking was that of being refused entry to an afterworld, and being left behind

to be a "dead walker." Conversely, an improvement over Hel was Niffheim, the land of eternal ice and mist, while the more fortunate entered Folkvang, the hall of Freyja.

Vikings believed that, on their death, they would be held to account for their reputation, the manner of their death, their performance in battle, and their character. On the balance of these values the gods decided the deceased's eternal fate.

Part of this reputation was determined by the manner in which they were interred, hence the elaborate burials that dominate the archaeological evidence for the Viking age. A good send-off, an elaborate and costly burial, and a legacy of respect were the ideals to which every Viking aspired.

Below: This carved Viking funerary stone from the 8th century was found on Gotland. In the top panel it depicts Odin riding on the eight-legged horse Sleipnir being welcomed to Valhalla by a Valkyrie holding a horn. Valhalla is shown at the left as a round-topped building. In the lower panel heroes are shown sailing in a longship. Compare this fragment with the stone pictured on page 87.

Mythology and Poetry

Much of our understanding of Scandinavian mythology comes from the Icelandic chronicler Snorri Sturluson. His 13th-century written reworking of the old myths safeguarded the rich legacy of Scandinavian mythology for subsequent generations, and his works reveal the complexity of pre-Christian Scandinavian belief.

Facing: In a segment from Sigurd's story, Sigurd roasts the dragon Fafnir's heart and burns his finger, while Regin the blacksmith sleeps. Tasting the dragon's blood on his injured finger, Sigurd gains the power to understand the birds. He learns from them that Regin is planning treachery. Carving from the Hylestad stave church in Norway.

Sturluson's *Prose Edda* (1220) retold the older myths in the form of Skaldic poetry, a bardic tradition that emerged about the beginning of the Viking age (*see pages 86–87*). He bound these together with a collection of more modern Eddic poems.

Traveling bards and storytellers played for their supper during the long Scandinavian winters by entertaining the kings and nobles with religious tales, sometimes interwoven with references to everyday life. These were the Skaldic verses. In this manner the complex and interwoven belief system of pagan Scandinavia was explained and passed on from one generation to the next. Toward the close of the Viking age in the 12th century, a new series of Eddic poems began to emerge, concentrating on the deeds of specific gods and heroes. Like the earlier poetic versions of Scandinavian mythology, these intertwined to form a rich mythological tapestry, filled with gods, heroes, and the battles of good versus evil. Around 1230, Sturluson followed his masterly rendition of these old poems with the *Heimskringla*, a history of Norway whose opening chapters provided a summary of the mythological roots of Scandinavian society (*see pages 90–91*).

While many historians have questioned the accuracy of Sturluson's writing, and have pointed to the numerous obvious parallels between these mythological tales and Christian beliefs, others argue that the myths are genuine. Sturluson explained the nature of the old pagan beliefs to a Christian audience by claiming that the pagans had lacked spirituality, which was a divine gift. Regardless of their critics, these works present Scandinavian mythology as a coherent entity, and while earlier versions of some of the tales existed (such as in the *Voluspá* or Prophesy of Sybil), these were incomplete. Sturlusun presented an entire world of gods and monsters which was far from simple pagan superstition. While with the hindsight of a millennium it is difficult to understand how people could have accepted this interwoven fabric of mythological belief, the inhabitants of pre-Christian Scandinavia most certainly believed in Odin, Thor, and Freyja. Their conviction was as fervent as was that of the Ancient Greeks who worshiped Zeus and the deities of Olympus. For these people this was not mythology. It was the way of the world.

Tree of Life

To Vikings, their position on the earth was as part of a greater entity, and their Midgard, or middle earth, was just part of the interwoven assemblage of heaven, earth, and hell encompassed within Yggdrasil, the World Tree. The three roots of the tree support the three levels of this universe, and these supportive roots are fed by a spring. The three women (the Norn) who guard the tree from predators also decide the fate of men. In many Scandinavian settlements, a tree was planted to symbolize this universe, and to emphasize the continuity of the succeeding generations of a family with the soil. The poems do not say what lies beyond the tree,

but Sturluson mentions Útgarðr (the world outside), while other poems link this with the world of the giants, the allies of the legions of the underworld.

The Christian concept of heaven, earth, and hell is similar, but lacks the totality of the Viking concept of the universe. Even the notion of an apocalyptic end when the dead will rise again is similar in both religions. It is little wonder, then, that when the time was right, Christian doctrines were able to easily replace the tapestry of the old beliefs. For the poets who retold these tales during the Viking age the old ways were already under threat, as the more shamanistic elements of Viking belief, such as human sacrifice and druidic worship, seem to have been abandoned. From that point on all the Christian missionaries had to do was to convince the Scandinavians that the old belief system was partly valid but much of it needed updating. The similarities between the two belief systems made that task simpler than it might otherwise have been.

Facing: A pair of harness mounts from Gotland in the form of Odin's birds. The exaggerated beaks and talons emphasize the ferocity of eagles, which—together with ravens—were widely associated with the cult of Odin.

The Coming of Christianity

During the migrations of the Viking age, Scandinavian raiders and traders came into contact with Christian Europe, and gradually elements of this new religion made their way back to Scandinavia. Resisting the pressure of missionaries, most Vikings retained their old faith until well into the 11th century, and seemed to be weighing up the merits of both systems of belief.

An enterprising mid-tenth-century artisan from Trendgården in Denmark's Jutland peninsula left behind a soapstone mold that had allowed him to produce two religious emblems

Throughout Scandinavian territories in Britain, and to a lesser extent France, this duality of belief continued. It has been suggested that the very polytheism of Viking belief encouraged the adoption of Christianity, since to many, the Christian God was just another useful deity, who could be invoked in time of spiritual need.

The late introduction of Christianity to Scandinavia was in large part a by-product of the barbaric nature of the region. The Vikings had never been conquered by the Romans or Franks, and they remained outside the bounds of the safe, known world of western Europe.

Above: Tapestry detail illustrating the struggle between Christianity and paganism. The three figures to the right are ringing bells to frighten away evil Viking spirits and pagan Gods. From the Skog church at Halsingland, Sweden.

at the same time: a small Christian crucifix and a model of Thor's hammer (*see picture, page 24*). This superb piece of archaeological testimony shows that the two religions existed side by side for some considerable time before Denmark officially became a Christian kingdom late in the tenth century.

In the 13th century, Icelandic chroniclers tell of a group of Viking settlers who adopted Christianity, and even named their farm Kristnes (Christ's Point), but still retained some of their old beliefs, such as the worship of Thor, reserved for invocation in times of crisis.

In the eighth century, the first Frankish missionaries ventured into Denmark. In return for political alliances with the Carolingian Empire, the Danish monarchs permitted them to preach within their kingdoms. In 826, King Harald of Denmark was baptized in Mainz, but a revolt at home prevented the convert from enforcing his new beliefs on his subjects. Four years later the missionary Anskar entered Sweden, but had little success converting the inhabitants. By the mid-ninth century Denmark's trading centers of Hedeby and Ribe boasted small churches, but another century passed before the Danish king Harald Bluetooth finally adopted Christianity on behalf of his people, as a result of observing a miracle. Missionaries had to be adept at such "methods," but the effect was clearly dramatic, because the new religion was firmly established by the start of the 11th century.

Steady conversion

In Norway, Anglo-Saxon missionaries ventured across the North Sea, and established links with King Harald Harfagri during the early tenth century. The king's son Håkon was schooled in Christian England, but his early death in 960 prevented any enforced conversion of the Norwegian people. Instead, conversion in Norway and Sweden was less dramatic than in Denmark, and took place over a period of several decades up to the mid-11th century.

It is evident that a duality of religious beliefs continued until the very end of the Viking period. Enforced adoption of Christianity was certainly attempted, often with seemingly spectacular results. In 997, King Olaf Tryggvasson of Norway marched west into the Vizen region to enforce the baptism of the entire population. However, tactics such as this caused resentment, and ultimately led to the defeat and death of the monarch in a sea battle (*see page 91*).

These methods gave Scandinavia a Christian veneer, but although the old religion had lost the backing of all of Scandinavia's monarchs and leading nobles by the start of the 11th century, many of the common people adhered to the old beliefs, or combined them with Christianity. Viking grave slabs in Middleton, Yorkshire, England are shaped as crosses, but depict Viking warriors surrounded by their weapons,

a visual legacy of old pagan burials, in which the warrior still needed such accoutrements in Valhalla. Nevertheless, Scandinavia gradually became Christian.

In Norway, King Olaf Haraldsson (St. Ola or Olaf) reaffirmed the adoption of Christian beliefs throughout his realm, which included Orkney and Shetland, and Sweden slowly and reluctantly followed suit. The Scandinavians had moved from Odin to Christ, encouraged by monarchs who saw in the new faith the opportunities it presented to them for increasing their grip on society—as it had in the rest of Europe.

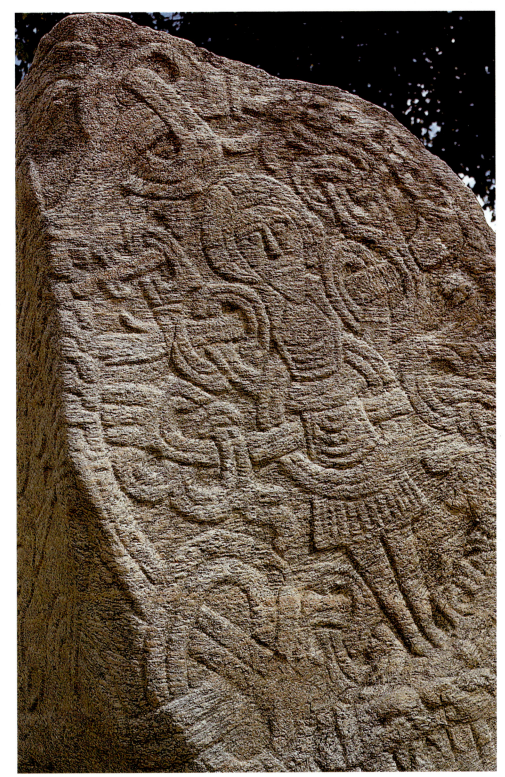

Above: The three-sided pyramid called the Jelling Stone was erected over an earlier ship-burial by Denmark's first Christian king, Harald Bluetooth, in memory of his parents. This face depicts the crucifixion; the others contain a picture and an inscription.

The Scandinavian Church

As Scandinavia became Christian, changes in culture, administration, and the law soon followed. Encouraged by monarchs who saw the Church as a stabilizing influence within their kingdoms, Christian centers of worship became the new focal point of the Viking community during the last years of the Viking age.

By the start of the 11th century, Christianity was firmly established in all but the remotest parts of Scandinavia. Old codes of conduct such as revenge killings to maintain family honor were discouraged, as were Viking raids themselves. The process of changing from a religion that emphasized prowess in battle to one that embraced strong central control must have been difficult for some, but these religious changes also came at a time when the emerging nation states of Scandinavia were placing an increasing demand on military endeavors.

Early Christian monarchs such as Norway's St. Olaf (r.1015–30) combined martial prowess, and a policy of religious and political consolidation, with fervent Christian beliefs.

Below: The wooden stave church at Urnes, Norway.

Following his death at the Battle of Stiklestad in Trøndlag (1030), several marvels were attributed to him. The warrior king subsequently became a cult hero in Scandinavia, and was later canonized. At this time the Church needed heroes, and a rash of churches in Britain, Scandinavia, and even in Russia celebrated Olaf's achievements. This embracing of Christianity allowed Scandinavian rulers access to the diplomatic and political powerplay within the rest of Europe.

St. Olaf's half-brother Harald Hardrada married the daughter of a Novgorod king, and was linked by kin to the royal houses of Sweden, France, and Hungary. By the time King Olaf Sköttkonung died in 1022, Christianity had been firmly established in Sweden, and a bishopric was founded at Skara. For the rest of the century Church and State maintained close links throughout Scandinavia, and royal grants of land and money encouraged the rapid expansion of Church authority.

A new moral tone

As for the churches themselves, the earliest examples in Scandinavia were simple timber structures built near the main trading centers. By the 11th century, these had evolved into a host of more complex edifices, all of which shared certain architectural features, and maintained a distinctive architectural style. Stave churches had been built at Hedeby and Trelleborg in Denmark, but few signs remain of these early churches, except the ones built from stone in Greenland (Brattahlid), or those where modifications were laid on top of earlier foundations (Urnes in Norway).

These traces that can be seen indicate that 11th-century Scandinavian churches were simple rectangular structures, with a square chancel built at the end of the nave. By the following century these had developed into the distinctive stave-built churches found as far afield as Borgund on the Sognefjord in Norway, and Novgorod in Russia (although the latter followed distinct regional variations of the standard pattern, *see picture, page 171*). Although only of wood, these structures soared far above the other buildings in the communities they

served. By the late 11th century the first stone churches had been built. A prime surviving example is the simple but beautiful St. Magnus Cathedral in Kirkwall, Orkney built in the last decades of the century (*see picture, page 137*).

On a less visible level, Christianity affected the moral tone of Scandinavian society. A new form of writing was introduced, and with it came access to the collective learning of the rest of Christendom, interpreted through the Church and its representatives. In effect Christianity led to the Europeanization of Scandinavia, and legal, moral, and spiritual influences brought Scandinavia in line with the rest of medieval Europe. For example, the notion of sin was alien to pagan Scandinavia,

but as a central doctrine of the Church, sin was linked to the older concept of eternal damnation.

Christianity did not end the Viking age, but it altered the consciousness of the Viking raiders. It removed some of the old martial rules that had encouraged the Vikings to seek distinction in battle while at the same time encouraging the development of peaceable settlement. Through the introduction of Christianity Scandinavian society became more hierarchical and organized, while an increasing emphasis was placed on the rule of the law rather than that of the sword. Christianity altered the nature of Viking society. As the old ways ended, so too did the aggressive raiding that had characterized the previous centuries.

Viking Ships

The longship has become a symbol of the Viking achievement, and is easily the most readily-identifiable vessel type of the early medieval world. These were the ships used by the raiders to wreak havoc on the coastal communities of Britain, Ireland, and the Frankish Empire, and which struck fear into the hearts of those who saw them emerging from the North Sea mists.

Multi-oared, and renowned for their speed, elegant lines, and stability, these ships represented the high point of a particular development of northern European boatbuilding. Of course, longships were not the only type of vessel the Vikings used. Behind the first waves of raiding longships came a stubbier, more robust trading vessel known as the *knorr*, which carried Scandinavian merchants and their goods into Russia, western Europe, and beyond. The *knorr* also carried Viking explorers and settlers to Iceland, Greenland, and even Newfoundland in their quest for land.

In addition to these two well-known types, the remains of Viking ships recovered from the Roskilde Fjord near Skuldelev show that they were part of a whole range of Viking vessels.

These varied from tiny fishing boats and *faerings* (tenders) to over-sized and richly-decorated longships known as dragon ships, the flagships of the men who ruled the Viking world. What these vessels all had in common was a shared style of construction, and perfect balance between style and function. Given the age and the raw materials available, they were the ideal vessels for the purpose.

The archaeological legacy of the Viking world is substantial, but it is hardly surprising that the most spectacular and evocative finds from this age are the remains of Viking ships. Archaeological discoveries such as the ships from Skuldelev, and the spectacular ship-burial finds from Gokstad, Oseberg, and other locations have provided us with the opportunity to examine the Viking ships themselves, and to marvel at their graceful lines and perfection of purpose. The finds have allowed archaeologists to reconstruct the vessels of the Viking world in a way that we can experience first-hand how these vessels were built, how they sailed, and above all, how they appeared to the terrified populations of coastal Europe over a thousand years ago.

Viking raiders return to their longships with their plunder of valuables, livestock, and children destined for the booming slave trade in Hedeby and other major Viking trading centers.

A Perfect Raider

In the seventh century, the vessel known as the longship first appeared. A derivative of earlier Scandinavian ship types, it became the symbol of the Viking age, and carried Norse raiders and warriors as far as the Mediterranean and North America.

Facing:
A reconstruction of the 9th-century Gokstad ship, displayed in the Vikingskiphuset Museum, Oslo.

Below: A crude but effective Viking anchor made from wood and stone.

Archaeological evidence and surviving examples allow us to build up a vivid picture of this vessel, which played a pivotal role in the history of European seafaring. At Nydam in Denmark, longship-like vessel remains were discovered dating from approximately AD 350. These longship prototypes were oar-powered, and had no mast. They were clinker-built, meaning that the outer planks were fastened to a series of frames rising from a keel. The edges of the outer planks overlapped each other to create a sturdy structure for the hull.

In 1920, the remains of two Norse ships were found at Kvalsund in Norway. Dating from about AD 700, these were broader than the earlier vessels, and may have carried a mast. The adoption of the sail in northern European vessels took place about the mid-seventh century, allowing raiding craft to sail across the North Sea, or make the journey from Norway to the Frankish coast.

These first longships were fighting vessels, although they could also be used for coastal trading. We can determine from archaeological and pictorial evidence that they were generally about 100 feet long, with a 20-foot beam. The smallest had 16–20 oars a side, each pulled by two oarsmen. Larger versions had 25, 30, or even 40 oars. The latter type of longship was known as a *draka* (dragon ship) and usually served as the flagship for a Norse king or warlord. These dragon ships were the pride of the Scandinavian world. In 998, King Olaf Tryggvasson of Norway ordered the construction of the *Long*

Serpent, a dragon ship 160 feet in length, with 34 oars a side. The bow and stern were decorated with gilded carvings of a serpent's head and tail. Not all longships carried such prized adornments, which were usually removed to storage when the ship was not in use.

Whatever their size, all longships shared certain characteristics. They were long, slim, elegant vessels, with double-skinned clinker-built hulls. Although powered by oars, they also carried a single mast with a large square sail. Made from local cloth, the sail was reinforced by a pattern of diagonal stitching. The development of the longship coincided with an expansion by the Norsemen into Russia and western Europe and, from 800, longships carried Viking raiders as far south as the Mediterranean. They were built from timbers, cut radially for maximum strength, from oak (in preference) or fir trees.

Surviving treasures

The well-preserved remains of ship-burials from southern Norway provide us with examples of these craft. The Oseberg Ship (*see pages 48–49*) dates from the ninth century, and is highly decorated, with a low freeboard; probably a royal pleasurecraft rather than a warship. Historians have linked this vessel with a type known as a *karv*, a form of coastal craft. Although not a true longship, its hull is built along the same lines as contemporary warships. The Gokstad Ship is larger, and its clinker-built hull is pierced for 16 oars a side. It has a more powerful mast and a higher freeboard than the Oseberg Ship, and was evidently capable of making long voyages. A replica of the craft made a successful Atlantic crossing in 28 days. The Gokstad vessel has been dated to the tenth century, and was probably a cross between a warship and a trading vessel.

Norse sagas contain numerous accounts of longships being used in action. Longships were sometimes lashed together to create large rafts that served as fighting platforms. Although the Vikings used archers, combat at sea involved hand-to-hand fighting, and the side with the best fighting platform had an advantage over

their adversaries. Evidence from the sagas suggests that some longships had decked platforms at the bow and stern called *lyfting*, which were used as fighting platforms.

While Norse longships were among the most distinctive vessels of their day, they also represented a dead-end in warship development. Improvements in sailing rigs and the inherent vulnerability of oared vessels in battle led to the gradual abandonment of the longship during the tenth to twelfth centuries. Just as the invention of the longship had ushered in the Viking era, so its replacement by more advanced vessels marked the end of the Viking way of life.

The Scandinavian Trader

Icelandic sagas describe the foremost trading vessel of the Viking age. However, apart from these sources, a handful of contemporary illustrations, and the cargo vessels found at Skuldelev, we know little about this type of ship. These were the vessels that carried Viking explorers and settlers of the era, and were the backbone of the trading network of Viking merchants.

Of the five Viking ships excavated at Skuldelev in Denmark (*see pages 50–51*), Skuldelev #1 is the only one that has the lines and cargo capacity of an ocean-going trading vessel of the type the Sagas referred to as a *knorr*. Measuring over 53 feet in length, with a beam of 15 feet, it has a sharply rising stern and stern post, and was probably built during the early 11th century. Reconstruction of its hull shows that it was built for both its cargo capacity and its seaworthiness. A *knorr* could carry up to 20 tons of cargo, or a similar load of animals, or passengers such as settlers. This made them ideal vessels for the exploration and settling of Iceland, Greenland, and Newfoundland, and they formed the basis for the Viking trade routes that spanned the North Sea, the Baltic Sea, and the river networks of Russia.

This cargo capacity was made possible by the rounded shape of the hull. Its low freeboard and rounded bilge also made it ideal for use where no harbor was available. The ships depicted in the late 11th-century Bayeux Tapestry show Norman vessels of this type being used to transport men, supplies, and horses across the English Channel during the Norman Conquest of England in 1066. The Tapestry also shows these *knorr*-type vessels being loaded while the ship rode at anchor off a beach, or lay grounded on the shingle.

In 1963 a group of Danish boy scouts built a reconstruction of the Ladby ship (known as the *Imme Gram*), which was a longship. Although not even a *knorr*, this reconstructed vessel was tested as a horse transport, and it was found that horses could be loaded on board while the vessel lay beached in the surf. The hull capacity of the Ladby ship is far less than that of a *knorr*, but it demonstrated the effectiveness of the low freeboard of Viking ships.

Viking workhorse

In 1991 staff at the Viking Ship Museum at Roskilde in Denmark built the *Roar Ege*, an exact replica of the Skuldelev 1 vessel. Again, the cargo capacity of the vessel was tested, along with its practicality and seaworthiness. The vessel lacked the speed and maneuverability of the large longships (the museum also built the *Helge Ask*, a replica of the smaller Skuldelev #5 longship), but it carried a prodigious amount of cargo, was easy to sail, and performed well. The internal layout of the typical *knorr* was designed to make the best possible use of its shape and capacity. A single mast mounted amidships—which was rarely stepped (taken down)—carried a square sail, rigged from a single yard. A central hold area occupied up to half of the ship, while raised platforms toward the stem and stern were fitted with rowing benches (if required), a helmsman's position, and rowing ports. Although any exact reconstruction of the layout is conjectural, this fits in with contemporary depictions of the vessel, and with the archaeological evidence.

The two biggest drawbacks of this design is its slowness and its lack of protection for either cargo or crew. It is quite possible that on long ocean voyages screens would be rigged to provide some cover over the hold and the forecastle area, but the helmsman's position was by necessity exposed to the elements. He provided the sole means of steerage, apart from using the sail, Like all other large Viking vessels, a large steering oar was fitted over the starboard quarter.

As for speed, an account of the Viking pirate Gauti Tófason described how he overtook four Danish *knorr*s in his longship, and was only prevented from capturing a fifth because of a rising storm. The *knorr* may have been slow and vulnerable, but it was the means by which Vikings carved out overseas colonies, and built a thriving trading network. Without the *knorr*, none of this would have been possible.

Facing: Carvings on the stem/stern of the Oseberg ship of c.850 have "gripping beast" motifs that echo the mischief wrought by Loki. For a more detailed explanation of the "gripping beasts" motif in Viking art, see page 93.

Below: A Viking *knorr* trading vessel sets sail.

Gokstad, Oseberg, and Thune

The three Norwegian burial mounds at Oseberg, Gokstad, and Thune in the Oslofjord region produced probably the best-preserved and best-known archaeological remains of Viking-age ships. All these ship-burials produced vessels that contained a wealth of objects, some of them the finest examples of Viking art and craftsmanship yet discovered.

Below: This stern view of the reconstruction of the Gokstad ship reveals the beautiful curvature of its clinker-built hull, and the shallow draft that made these vessels ideal river raiders and transports.

In early 1880, a team of Norwegian archaeologists excavated a burial mound near the farm of Gokstad, to the southwest of Oslo. The feature was known locally as The King's Mound, and the expedition came about as a result of local attempts to break into the mound and plunder the contents. On the second day of the dig, a highly decorative ship's figurehead was uncovered from the blue-clay soil, and by the end of the season a virtually intact vessel had been uncovered, together with its contents, and the remains of the nobleman who was interred there.

He was a tall, well-dressed man, of about 50 years, and had been laid out on a bed in the center of the vessel.

His weapons lay beside him, and the ship was filled with the goods he needed in the next world: beds, tableware, small boats, a sled, games, and all the fittings a ship of that type would require. In addition, a dozen domestic animals had been slaughtered and interred next to the mound, and a peacock was sacrificed and laid on top of the vessel before the mound was sealed. From the finds, archaeologists dated the burial to about 900, but it seems that the ship itself was constructed up to a half-century earlier.

The ship is 76 feet in length, 17 feet in the beam, and is built from oak. More sturdily constructed than the Oseberg ship, it could accommodate 16 oarsmen a side. Its keel and mast step were also sturdier and the sides were two strakes (planks) higher. The oar holes could be closed while the ship was under sail, and the single mast and square sail allowed it to attain speeds of up to 12 knots. Sixty-four painted wooden shields were found during the excavation, and it appears they had been fastened to the outside of the ship's gunwale. A replica was built during the late 19th century, and this vessel sailed across the Atlantic in 1893, demonstrating the design's seagoing qualities.

Sacrificial victims

The Oseberg ship was found in a burial mound in Vestfold, some 20 miles north of Gokstad, and was excavated in 1904. Built in the early ninth century, the ship had been in use for almost a decade before it was interred. The body laid to rest in this ship was that of a richly-dressed woman, together with its servant (sacrificed so that it could serve its mistress in the afterlife). They died about 834, and the sacrifice included the bodies of 13 horses, three dogs, and an ox. The blue-clay of the site protected the ship (and bodies) from extensive decay, providing a useful nucleus of knowledge about the ship itself.

Also built from oak, it measures 71 feet in length, with a beam of 16 feet 5 inches. This makes it slightly shorter than its Gokstad counterpart. It was clinker-built, with 12 strakes,

and carried a mast as well as 15 oarports per side. A steering oar was fitted to the starboard quarter. In all probability this vessel was a royal pleasure vessel for use in Oslofjord, and as a result, it was extensively decorated with animal carvings. Its contents were even more sumptuous than those at Gokstad: carved sleds, a four-wheeled cart, beds, a loom, tents, a chair, domestic utensils, and a rich array of ship's fittings. Foodstuffs were also provided to nourish the travelers on their journey through the afterlife.

A third ship-burial discovered at Thune, Østfold was excavated in 1867. This vessel is a contemporary of the Gokstad ship, and was used as a burial-ship some decades after its construction. Although the hull is not nearly as well preserved as those at Gokstad and Oseberg, enough information was recovered to further the understanding of how these ships were built.

Above: Detail of the decorative carving on the Oseberg cart, which depicts the torment of Gunnar in the snake-pit. The imagery is full of "gripping beasts" (*see an explanation of this term on page 93*).

Below: The reconstruction of the Oseberg longship.

The Skuldelev Ships

At the end of the tenth century, five ships were scuttled to form a barrier across Roskilde Fjord. This was clearly meant to protect the harbor of the nearby Danish capital from seaborne attack. The ships, discovered in the 1950s, have been excavated and now form the largest single maritime legacy of the Viking world.

At the time of the scuttling, Roskilde was the capital of Denmark, and a ring of land and marine defenses incorporating ditches, watchtowers, and blockships surrounded the town. During the 1950s, Danish archaeologists decided to investigate reports of sunken wooden vessels in the narrow waterway, near the town of Skuldelev. An initial investigation of 1957 determined that the vessels were of the Viking period, and were well worth further study. At that time underwater archaeological techniques had still to be developed, so the archaeologists had to resort to building a coffer dam around the shipwrecks before draining the site.

By 1962 the cofferdam was completed, the site drained, and the wrecks exposed. The seabed of the fjord consisted of thick mud, and this had helped to preserve the hulls from decay over the centuries. In addition, the craft had been pinned beneath the very boulders that had been used to sink them. Five ships were examined and excavated by the Danish National Museum, which then conserved and examined the timbers. It was discovered that the ships were all similarly constructed using clinker-building methods, like the Oseberg and Gokstad ships. It was clear that these ships were Scandinavian, and probably Viking. Floor timbers were laid over the frames, supported by a series of cross-beams and all five vessels were fitted with a single central mast. This all demonstrated a common Scandinavian shipbuilding tradition; but what really excited the archaeologists were the variations between the five Skuldelev ships.

Wealth of knowledge gained

Despite sharing common shipbuilding methods, the Skuldelev wrecks were also subtly different from each other, betraying the adaptation of a basic design to suit a specific function. The first ship to be examined, Skuldelev #1 was a *knorr*, the basic seagoing ship used for trading and exploration during the Viking period. This was the type of ship used by Leif Eriksson when he discovered America (*see pages 108–9*); roomy, strong, and capable of carrying a reasonable load of supplies or cargo. Skuldelev #1 was 50 feet in length, 15 feet in the beam, with a rounded hull, finishing at a sharp point at bow and stern. Its cargo capacity was determined at about 25 tons. The combination of pine and oak used in Skuldelev #1's construction indicate that it was originally built in Norway.

Skuldelev #2 was poorly preserved, but what remained showed that it was once the most impressive of all the Skuldelev blockships. It was a large longship, almost 100 feet long, with a 12-foot beam. Propelled by 30 oars a side, it would have been one of the largest longships of

its day, indicating that it was probably once a *draka*, the flagship of an important Scandinavian warlord or leader. It was built from Irish oak, but was repaired with timber from Denmark. In its prime, the longship may have played a role in the Norse occupation of Ireland before the Battle of Clontarf (1014), but that can only remain supposition.

Skuldelev #3 was the best preserved of all the wrecks, and one of the smallest. Measuring 45 feet by 12 feet, this oak-built vessel was fitted with six rowing ports a side as well as a sail, making it a small but versatile raider or trader. There was no ship designated Skuldelev #4, but Skuldelev #5 has been identified as a *leidangr*, or local guardship, 56 feet long, with an 8-foot beam. It bears remarkably similar construction features to Skuldelev #3, so it is likely that both vessels were built in the same Danish shipyard. Skuldelev #6 was poorly preserved, but was probably a small fishing vessel from southern Sweden. It was 38 feet long and 8 feet wide.

The remains of the Skuldelev shipwrecks may now be viewed in a purpose-built display near the site of their sinking. Together, they form a unique collection of ships, from which vital knowledge of Viking shipbuilding techniques has been gained.

Left: Model of Skuldelev #3, a coastal trader.

Below: Interior view of Skuldelev #1, an ocean-going merchant vessel.

Building a Longship

It has been established that while Viking ships ranged in shape and function, they shared certain design characteristics. From the evidence of archaeological remains, we can reconstruct how the shipwrights of the Viking world built their vessels.

When it was available, oak was the Viking ship-builder's timber of choice, although other woods were also used extensively, particularly in Norway where pine was abundant. The logs were split radially by employing wedges, and the freshly cut timber used straight away since green wood is easier to work. The open nature of the vessels themselves meant that this newly-cut timber was unlikely to get the chance to rot. Straight logs were used for the hull strakes (planking), while timbers with a slight curve were preferred for the stem and sternposts.

Ship-building took place adjacent to the timber-felling operation, and Viking shipwrights used a small but efficient selection of tools.

A depiction of ship-building in the Bayeux Tapestry and a selection of tools recovered from archaeological sites tell us what Viking carpenters used, and what each implement did. Axes and adzes were the most commonly employed tools, used for cutting or shaping timber. Knives, augers, molding irons, and chisels were also employed for more refined shaping or drilling, while hammers and tongs were used to drive home iron fasteners or fittings. There is no evidence of saws being used.

Tried and tested techniques

Construction was relatively simple. No real shipyards were required since the ships were simply built on flat ground next to the sea, either in the open or protected from the elements by a temporary shelter. First the keel was laid out in one or more sections on wooden chocks. The stem and stern posts were then bolted into place and supported by external wooden supports. The basic profile of the ship was now in place. Because there were no drawn plans master shipwrights of the Viking age had to rely on their experience and their keen eye to ensure the best possible hull shape and ratio of length to breadth. Typically, while a *knorr* or other merchant vessel had a length to breadth ratio of about 4:1, a longship lived up to its name by having a 7:1 ratio.

After the stem and stern were fitted, the garboards (first strakes) were fitted to the keel with iron nails. The next pair of strakes were added by overlapping the garboards, with caulking to seal the overlap, before the strakes were fastened together using iron spikes. This method of overlapping hull-planking was the clinker style of construction (*see pages 44–45*), and was a typical feature of northern European ship construction during this period. Indeed, the same principles are still used in Scandinavian small-boat construction to this day. The remainder of the side strakes were continued until the desired height of freeboard was achieved. As the hull sides rose, the width of the strakes varied, and the hull sides grew out, then up, forming the shape of the finished vessel. The Skuldelev ships have from three to seven strakes a side, while the Gokstad ship has 11.

In the next step, internal supports were added to the hull. First, a layer of floor plank was fastened to the strakes by means of wooden pegs, then a keelson to support the mast was fitted to the top of the keel, and a series of angled frames, or knees, were fastened to the inside of the strakes, binding them together. Crossbeams (known as stringers) were then used to span these frames, creating a series of

D-shaped braces, usually supported by a central vertical support. The stringers were left out if a central hold featured as part of the design, while on longboats they served as the thwarts or benches for the oarsmen. On a *knorr* the same crossbraces on either side of the hold area could support deck planking.

The result was a pliable yet resilient hull, capable of remaining seaworthy in all but the worst of conditions. After being built the ship would be launched, fitted out with its mast and fittings, and then provisioned for its voyage. Although there were variations to the basic design, the techniques and designs used to produce these Viking ships remained the same throughout the period, whether the finished vessel was to be a dragon ship, a small fishing boat or a *faering*.

Above: An ax is used to shape the stempost for a *faering* (tender). Traditional methods of ship-building still survive in Norway, while others have been re-introduced.

Sailing the Longships

The building of replica Viking ships has meant that historians and mariners have been able to test out the performance of these amazing vessels. The lessons they learned provide us with a wealth of information about how the Vikings sailed their ships.

Facing: Sailing a replica Viking ship.

Below: With the sail furled, Scandinavian scouts row a replica longship. This view emphasizes the low freeboard of the longship. The oar ports could be covered in rough weather to gain a few further inches of freeboard.

During the Viking age, ships sailed on regular journeys between Scandinavia and Orkney, Iceland, and Greenland, or the Faroes and Norway. Long ocean voyages were not considered too hazardous for these seafarers, which suggests that they had a supreme faith in themselves and their ships. We also know from written accounts that voyages were not usually attempted during the winter months, and that the Vikings were well aware of the tides, winds, weather conditions, and anchorages they visited and the areas of ocean in which they sailed.

Navigation was rudimentary after the ships left the sight of land. They had no form of compass or way of determining the latitude or longitude. Instead they navigated by the stars during their long North Sea voyages, such as on passages from Iceland to Scandinavia. The prime navigational aid was the Pole Star, which gave the position of North. They were also well aware of the attitude of the prevailing winds at a particular time of the year, and these could be used to determine an approximate course.

Similarly, when it was visible the sun's progress through the sky provided a crude but reliable navigational aid. The sun determined the east and west cardinal points, and the time of sunset indicated if the vessel was sailing on a northerly or southerly heading. Much of this navigational skill came from experience; the knowledge of the positions of stars or planets, and when or how they moved in the sky, was passed on from one generation to the next.

True ocean-going vessels

As for performance, the ships' seaworthiness has been demonstrated by the passage of the replica Gokstad ship *Viking* from Bergen to Newfoundland in less than a month in 1893. The captain on that voyage (and those who commanded other later replica ships) noticed how the hull's structure moved with the motion of the seas, reducing the effect of the waves on the hull, but increasing the need to bail out water as it seeped through the seams. These ships were superb seaboats, and although they appeared fragile, their method of construction made the vessels supple and seaworthy.

Operating a longship under oars was backbreaking work, but the light hull and narrow entry into the water made for speed. A reconstruction *faering* (tender) proved that speeds of seven knots was possible even in small boats, and larger replica longships such as the reconstruction of Skuldelev #5 demonstrate that 12 knots was attainable. With a full crew, a shift system meant that such speeds were sustainable. Exact speeds with the square sail rigged are difficult to quantify, but eight knots or more is probable. The simple square sail rig meant that the sailing arcs were restricted to beyond about 60° from the wind direction. This meant the use of sailpower was highly dependent on the wind remaining in the right quadrant, and any unexpected changes could result in lengthy voyages or else hard pulls on the oars.

Both the oars and the sails could be used to adjust the course of the vessel, but the side rudder shipped over the

starboard quarter of the boat was more useful. It extended well below the keel, giving it a substantial bite into the water, and it pivoted around an externally-fitted pintle. The rudder could be raised in shallow water to avoid the risk of damage.

The light construction of the longship's hull meant its displacement was small and consequently they were capable of sailing in very shallow water without the need for deep-water harbors. This factor, combined with the hull's shape, made the landing of cargoes, men, provisions, or animals on a beach easy. It also allowed longships to sail far inland up rivers, and for Viking raiders to land almost wherever they chose. As raiders they were perfect, as cargo ships they were versatile. That these vessels still impress the seamen who sail modern replicas demonstrates how advanced and suited to their environment they were.

Medieval Developments

For three centuries, the ships used by the Vikings remained largely unchanged. After the 11th century, the longship gradually faded from view, and the Viking trading vessel was replaced by larger European ships. Despite this, it can be demonstrated that this was an evolutionary process, linking the ships of the Viking age to the medieval ships that succeeded them.

The longboat and the *knorr* were not the only vessels of the Viking age. In the Sagas, longships were defined by how many "rooms" they had, which was another term for a rowing position. The Gokstad ship had 16 ports (or rooms) a side, but others were even bigger. These were the draka, or dragon ships, which served as the flagships of their age. Ledung ships were permanent royal ships, crewed as part of a standing fleet. These were led by the *skeid* or *draka*, having up to 32 rooms, while monster dragon ships also existed.

Below: A late Viking age ship's anchor. Although still using stone encased in wood, this anchor is more sophisticated than the one pictured on page 44.

Olaf Tryggvasson's Ormen Lange was 34-roomed, and even bigger vessels are mentioned in the sagas.

However, these larger vessels were stretching contemporary ship-building technology too far. Wooden vessels over 150 feet long were fragile, and lacked the robust qualities of smaller longships. In design terms, the longship represented a dead-end in warship development. Improvements in sailing rigs and the inherent vulnerability of oared vessels in battle led to the gradual abandonment of the longship during the tenth to twelfth centuries. They also lacked the capacity of post-Viking merchant ships for carrying fighting men. As depicted on the Bayeux Tapestry, William the Conqueror's invasion fleet consisted of longships and *knorr*s. The cargo vessels transporting soldiers, horses, and military equipment are shown carrying no oarsmen and powered by sail (*see picture, page 156*). Like the *lyfting* (covered deck) on some Scandinavian longships, some are depicted with raised stern platforms, a feature that would eventually develop into the sterncastle.

Evolutionary design

Northern European cargo ships of the 12th century were descended from the *knorr*, but they boasted improvements to the traditional design that would render the older Scandinavian vessel type obsolete. The best evidence for this development comes from surviving coins and seals. The *knorr* design developed very gradually. As ships became larger, hulls became more rounded, and decks were fully planked over to create enclosed cargo holds. Vessels like this served as troop transports and warships as well as cargo carriers.

Two seals from the English town of Hastings show small clinker-built wooden vessels with temporary castle structures at the stern, and sometimes both bow and stern. A platform or top was fitted to the masthead, to serve as a lookout post or as a fighting platform. At some time during the late 12th century, the rudder was moved from the starboard side to the stern. This development coincided with the introduction of the bowsprit, and the combination made ships

Left: A Viking longship prow, with decoration based on that of the Oseberg ship, stands on the harborside at Stockholm, Sweden.

far more maneuverable under sail.

In 1962, the remains of a vessel dating from c.1329 were discovered off Bremen, Germany. This vessel type was known as a cog, and formed the standard form of craft found in northern European waters during the rest of the medieval period. Cogs are associated with the bustling ports of northern Germany, and are depicted on seals of the ports run by the Hanseatic League. Similar vessels were used throughout Europe, as evidenced by port seals and manuscript illustrations. Their characteristics were a barrel-like hull, with a permanent stern structure, a decked-over cargo hold, and a single mast and square sail. They had a very high freeboard, a stern rudder, and sharply inclined stem and stern posts.

Although primarily a cargo vessel, the cog could be fitted with fighting platforms at the bow and stern and turned into a warship. Cog design continued to develop over the next two centuries as sterns became larger (and permanent) and forecastles smaller, but the linear transition from Scandinavian *knorr* to medieval cog can still be traced—a clear line of development linking the vessels of the eighth century with those of 500 years later. No longer sleek longships, warships were now simply fortified trading vessels. While the Viking longship faded from view, the *knorr* just kept on adapting to suit almost every northern European maritime need during the medieval period.

CHAPTER 4

The Sea Raiders

During the last decade of the eighth century, Viking invaders crossed the North Sea and landed on the Holy Island of Lindisfarne, off the northeastern coast of England. In the ensuing raid the monastery on the island was destroyed through "plunder and slaughter," marking a turning point in European history. That day over 12 centuries ago, a 30-year reign of terror began that left the coastal communities of Europe devastated and the fragile economies of their kingdoms in ruins. At one point these violent invasions threatened to wipe out the Christian Church in northwest Europe, and the inhabitants who fearfully stared out to sea must have thought the end of the world had come. For many, it had.

Raids on isolated villages, then on towns, followed the first attacks on coastal and riverine monastic settlements. These Vikings were merely a vanguard. Increasingly large fleets of raiders came to plunder, and then to colonize. What had begun as a series of raids from Scandinavia south and west into the rest of Europe had turned into a cultural migration and a military campaign of conquest by the start of the tenth century.

Vikings established thriving forward bases in the Shetland and Orkney Islands, the Western Isles, and the Isle of Man. While the monastic communities of the Celtic fringe of the British Isles were damaged and sometimes destroyed, the raids moved on into the heart of the Frankish Empire. Once all-powerful under the leadership of Charlemagne the Great, the Franks were unable to prevent Viking raids and even the conquest of substantial chunks of their territory. Frankish resistance only stiffened when local warlords took steps to organize their own defenses, and in the process laid the foundation for the establishment of the feudal system.

Wide-ranging in scope and effect, the Viking raids changed the map of Europe, and marked the end of an era of relative peace and prosperity. Faced with these depredations, the Celts, Saxons, and Franks were hard-pressed to survive, let alone organize any concerted counter-attack. For more than a century, the Vikings had a free-reign in what was virtually an undefended continent. They took full advantage of that golden opportunity.

Viking raids on western Europe between the late eighth and eleventh centuries.

NORWAY
Kaupang •

SWEDEN
Birka •

GULF OF BOTHNIA

Lake Ladoga

GULF OF FINLAND

Carolingian kingdoms
Muslim states
first raids
main raids
late raids

DENMARK
Hedeby •
Hamburg •
Wolin •
Elbe
Oder

EAST FRANCIA
East Frankish Kingdom
Main

EMPIRE
Danube

KINGDOM OF ITALY
Venice •
ADRIATIC SEA
Pisa •
Livorno •
CORSICA
Rome •
SICILY

STRÆCLED WALAS
(Strathclyde)

NORTH HYMBRE (Northumbria)

Lindisfarena
(Holy Island/Lindisfarne) **793**

In Gyrwum
(Jarrow) • **794**
Uiræmutha
(Wearmouth)

NORTH SEA

796

MÆNIG
(Isle of Man)

IRISH SEA

Eoforwic ceaster
(York) •

c.860

854
834
851
842

LINDESSE
(Lindsey)

841

841

MON
(Anglesey)

Chester •

853–4
850

Merscware
(Marschman) **841**

EAST ENGLE

Contwaraburh
(Canterbury)

NORTH WALAS

MIERCE
(Mercia)

Sceapig
(Isle of Sheppey)
854–5

841

MIDDLE SEAXE

EAST SEAXE

Pedridanmutha
(Mouth of the R. Parret)

BEARRUCSCIR
Basingstoke •

WILSÆTE

Lundenburh
(London)

SUTHRIGE

Hrofesceaster
(Rochester) **850**

CANTWARE

850–1

c.850

845

843

851
Carrum
(Carhampton)

SUMORSÆTE

Wiggadon
(Weare Giffard?)

DEFENASCIR

WEST WALAS

Hengestesdun
(Hinxton Down)

838

SUTH SEAXE

Wintanceaster
(Winchester)

DORNSÆTE

Dorchester •

Port
(Portland)

c.795

Hamtun
(Southampton)

840

840

Tenet
(Isle of Thanet)

850

Sondwic
(Sandwich)

ENGLISH CHANNEL

BYZANTINE EMPIRE

Viking raids on England, 793–860.

Kingdom of Northumbria
Kingdom of Wessex

The Coming of the Vikings

Much of the eighth century was a relatively peaceful period for Europe, but toward its end, the threat of the longships loomed. For a while, Vikings limited themselves to the fringes of the British Isles. Then on June 8, 793, the monastery on Lindisfarne was attacked. The next 30 years of increasing raids changed the political landscape of Britain forever.

The Anglo-Saxon cleric Alcuin described the effects of the Lindisfarne raid to his patron, the King of Northumbria: "Never before had such terror appeared in Britain as we have now suffered from a pagan race, nor was it thought such an inroad from the sea could be made." But it was only the start. The raids on

Northumberland continued until the following year, when a Norwegian raiding party, caught by a storm, was shipwrecked and killed.

In fact, it now seems likely the Vikings first made an appearance in 789, since the *Anglo-Saxon Chronicle* reports the sighting of three ships in the English Channel, near Portland (*see page 62*). In 792, the year before the Northumberland raid, the Anglo-Saxon King Offa was reportedly involved in improving the defenses of Kent because his kingdom was threatened by "pagan seamen." This must be a reference to the Vikings, but whether they were Danes or Norse (Norwegian) is unknown. The attack on Lindisfarne was therefore not the first appearance of the Vikings in English waters, but it was the first all-out attack.

In 794, an Irish monk recorded the "devastation of all the islands of Britain by the gentiles." These were the Vikings, and in the following year they pillaged the Scottish monastery of Iona, and landed in Skye. Even by this early stage it is likely that Viking raiders had established forward bases in the Orkney Islands and the Western Isles. This Viking threat weakened Pictland at a time when it was threatened by invasion from the Scots of Dál Riada; the last phase of a war for supremacy that had lasted for generations. The Scots themselves were forced onto the defensive, and the threat to their seaboard may have helped stimulate them to complete their takeover of the Pictish kingdoms in what would become Scotland.

Apocalyptic invaders

In 798, the Hebridian islands that had not already fallen under Norse sway were ravaged, and the Irish conducted their first raids on the shores of Ulster. By 800, the Vikings were well on their way to controlling the entire north and western seaboards of Scotland, and from their bases in Orkney they were well placed to raid Ireland or the west coast of the British Isles, or Northumbria and the Pictish coastline. Viking-age finds in Orkney and Shetland indicate that settlement and annexation of the islands took

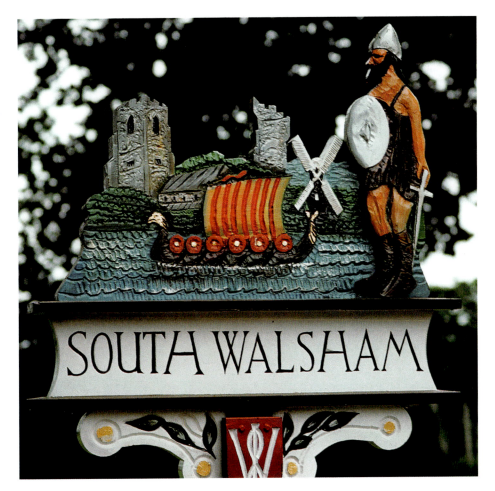

place before the start of the ninth century. This dating is supported by accounts of the first appearance of the Vikings in the Northern Isles as recounted in the later Icelandic Sagas, and obliquely in the *Orkneyinga Saga*.

To the clerics of the Celtic and Anglo-Saxon monasteries in Britain and Ireland, these attacks were simply the fulfilment of the Old Testament prophecy of Jeremiah: "Out of the north an evil shall break forth upon all the inhabitants of the land." Ill omens had been reported for much of the preceding century, so this gloomy mood was commonplace. The venerable Bede himself had expressed concern for the future of Northumbria in his *Historia Ecclesiastica* (731). To British Christians it was the "sixth age of the world," which lasted from "John to the Judgment, in which our Lord Jesus Christ will come to judge the living and the dead and the world through fire." The Vikings were merely another portent of doom and the onset of the end of the world.

This pessimism seemed justified by the Lindisfarne raid, which was seen as "an attack on both the body and soul of Christian England." If these Northumbrian clerics had known that the Vikings had established winter bases only a few hundred miles up the coast, they would have had even more cause for despair.

Above: Memories of the Viking raids still linger on the eastern coast of England. This decorative sign welcoming visitors to the small village of South Walsham, Norfolk depicts a Viking warrior and a longship in front of the church.

Facing: A picture stone from Sweden includes the image of a raiding longship under sail.

Raids on Lindisfarne and Iona

The attacks on the monasteries of Lindisfarne and Iona marked the start of decades of desecration; a series of raids that nearly destroyed the early Christian Church in Britain. Within four years these raiders would return to plunder the most sacred sites in the British Isles.

Below: The Abbey on the island of Iona was built in the early 20th century on the site of the original monastery founded in 563 by St. Columba. The original monastery became a center for Celtic missionary expeditions into Scotland and Anglo-Saxon northern England. The community barely survived the Viking raids of the 8th and 9th centuries.

The *Anglo-Saxon Chronicle* record the first appearance of the Vikings in English waters off the coast of Wessex, ruled at the time by King Beorthic:

"In the year 789, three strange ships arrived at Portland on the southern coast of England and Beaduheard, the reeve of the King of Wessex, rode out to meet them. He took with him only a small band of men under the mistaken impression that the strangers were traders… and they slew him… those were the first ships of Danish men that came to the land of the English."

The same manuscript records that in June of 793 "the ravages of heathen men miserably destroyed God's Church on Lindisfarne with plunder and slaughter." Lindisfarne served as a symbol for the Christian Church in Anglo-Saxon England. Built on the border between the Roman and the Celtic Churches, it drew on influences from both branches of the Christian faith. Anglo-Saxon monarchs and nobles donated money and commissioned works of religious metalwork in order to help secure the favor of both the monks and the Almighty, so the island monastery was a repository for the wealth of the early Church. For the majority of monks, their days were spent in prayer, in the recording and illuminating of manuscripts, and in the preaching of the word of God. They survived by harvesting the island's cultivated slopes and fishing in the surrounding sea.

This peaceful life of self-sufficiency and spirituality came to an abrupt end on that dreadful June morning when Viking raiders swooped in from the North Sea. The monks were slaughtered or driven off, and the monastery itself was plundered and then put to the torch. The Vikings suffered no remorse for their sacrilege because they had no reverence for the Christian God. There was no guilt in destroying one of Christianity's most sacred places. With the plunder loaded aboard the waiting longships, the raiders departed, well before any local nobles were able to gather their retainers and come to the monks' rescue. For the English, this was an unprecedented atrocity even in an age when murder and mayhem were commonplace.

Unholy Barbarism

The monasteries of the period were vulnerable to Viking attack. Not only were they a lure with their caches of costly objects of veneration to loot, but many were built on or close to the coast. In an age when roads were extremely rare, it was easier to spread the word of God by boat than by foot. Within a few years, other monastic sites fell prey to the Norsemen.

To the Celts of Ireland and Scotland, the raiders were unholy pagans, and even the recently converted Anglo-Saxons of England were unable to understand how any people could be so barbarous. In reality, although the devastating raids in the eighth century gave the Vikings a reputation for destructiveness, the culture that had spawned them was just as sophisticated as the cultures on the islands they attacked.

Celtic Scotland experienced its first recorded attack in 795, when the monastic island of Iona was pillaged. The church on the Isle of Iona had been founded in 563 by St. Columba, but it barely survived the Viking raid; the first of three attacks on the settlement in just over a decade (795, 802, and 806). In Wales, small monasteries at Carmarthen, Llancarfan, St. David's, and Llanwit were plundered, as was the English settlement at Jarrow. Celtic Ireland

also experienced its first onslaught in 795, the same year that Iona was attacked.

The massacre of the entire monastic population of Iona in 825 marked the end of this phase of destruction, as the raiders gave way to Norse settlers. Although far from safe from the Vikings, the monasteries were now partially protected by secular Viking overlords, at least for a price. It is a testimony to the faith of these early Christian monks that they kept returning to their sanctuaries and rebuilt them, preserving the faith in what must have seemed a Godless age.

Above: A small boat lies upturned on the shore of Holy Island (Lindisfarne). The monastery founded here by St. Aidan in 635 became the first victim of Viking raiders at the end of the 8th century. Today, only 13th-century ruins of a priory remain.

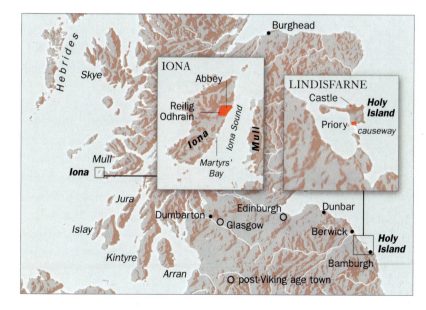

Attacks on Ireland

As a relatively small domain, Ireland was particularly vulnerable to Viking depredations. During the first half of the ninth century the size and destructiveness of the Viking raids increased. After laying waste the countryside, the Norsemen returned to Ireland to conquer and occupy the island.

Facing: Celtic crosses and a round tower are among the ruins of the monastery of Clonmacnoise, which flourished between the 7th and 12th centuries. It was repeatedly plundered and burned by the Vikings, native Irish, and Anglo-Normans, until it was finally destroyed by the English in 1552.

At first, raids on Ireland were sporadic and relatively random; just the odd ship or probe by a few raiders. The first concerted Viking raid came in 795, when Rechru (Rathlin Island, north of where Dublin is today) was assaulted. This level of attack was bad enough for the fragile economy of the disunited island, and it slowly damaged the coastal communities, as people fled inland. What followed was much worse. The *Annals of Ulster* record in 820 that:

"The sea spewed forth floods of foreigners into Erin, so that no haven, no landing-place, no stronghold, no fort, no castle might be found, but it was submerged by waves of Vikings and pirates."

Clearly the pace of raiding had increased and the sea-raiders began to penetrate inland, using rivers such as the Shannon to strike into the very heart of the country. The great Celtic monasteries at Clonfert, Kells, and Armagh were all plundered, and even Clonmacnoise monastery in the very center of Ireland was sacked.

The pace stepped up even more in the 830s. In 831, a Viking raiding party captured the King of Louth, and two years later Derry in Ulster was attacked, a settlement previously thought too big to assault. In the same year the monasteries of Lismore and Clondalkin near Dublin were taken. As was happening in England, the Celtic Church of Ireland was brought to its knees by these raids.

No effective defense

The local kings of Ulster, Connaught, Munster, Meath, and Leinster tried to turn the tide, but their efforts were in vain. Although a string of round fortified towers was built to guard the coasts, without the support of a powerful fleet and army, these fortified positions were bypassed easily. It was impossible to defend the entire coast and the Vikings had the advantage of mobility and surprise. By the time Irish forces arrived to counter a raid, the Vikings had often looted what they wanted, and returned to their ships. For 836, the *Annals of Ulster* record that the first prey of the Vikings was southern Brega where they killed many and took many captives. By now these raids were frequent, and forces were getting large enough to plunder entire regions. In the same year, the *Annals* recall that there was "a most cruel devastation of all the lands of Connaught by the pagans."

In 836, Vikings raided the area around Lough Neagh, plundering the kingdoms and monasteries of the north. The Vikings were not just looting towns and monasteries. This was the period when the Viking leader Turgeis established control over Ulster, and gained a series of coastal footholds. By 840 he had established fortified bases where Norse raiding parties under his overall control could spend the winter without returning home to Scandinavia. They also established slave markets so that Scandinavian traders could buy their captives, and save the raiders the problems inherent in shipping slaves themselves.

These *longphoirts* were really small coastal fortresses, the first being at Dubh-Linn (Black Pool), which soon developed into a thriving Norse town, then a city. The Vikings used these winter bases as trading settlements, and fortresses from which to launch attacks deep into the Irish heartland. They also subdued the local area, as an entry in the *Annals of St-Bertin* for 847 attests:

Ireland, 795–850

ATLANTIC OCEAN

ULSTER
Larne
Bangor
Armagh

CONNAUGHT

IRISH SEA

Kells
MEATH
Clonmacnoise
Clonfert
Dublin
Kildare

Limerick
LEINSTER

MUNSTER
Waterford
Wexford

Cork

☐ area of major Viking settlement

"After they had been under attack from the Vikings for many years, the Irish were made tributaries to them; the Vikings have possessed themselves without opposition of all the islands around about and have settled them."

At this stage, the focus changed from viewing Ireland as a source of plunder to a potential land to colonize. In the second half of the ninth century, a struggle began between the Irish, Danes, and Norse for control of the island. Rather than ravage the land, the Norse sought to protect it as a source of wealth and power in its own right. Ireland had proved an easy island to plunder. As a place to colonize, it was going to be a completely different story.

The Great Danish Raids

For the most part, the Vikings who raided the shores of Celtic Scotland and Ireland were Norse (Norwegians). Those who devastated Anglo-Saxon England were Danes. In 789, three Viking ships were sighted off Dorset. A decade later raids were ten times that size, and by 850 fleets of over 300 longships made their appearance off the Saxon shore.

Below: Helmeted warriors carrying round shields fight with swords in the top panel of this picture stone from Gotland. Below, a longship full of Vikings prepares to land and raid.

Viking raids fell first on the shores of Northumbria, a region of Anglo-Saxon England. These were most probably the work of Norsemen, working their way south from their new winter lairs in the Orkney and Shetland Islands. Although the historical records are vague about the bases used by the raiders, at the same time (c.793) or a little earlier, the first probes by Danes were made against the southeastern corner of England. It would be another three decades before they returned in strength.

Strength is a relative term, and there is no reason to doubt that Danish longship raids struck the English coast in small numbers throughout this period. But the raids remained sporadic until about 835, at which point a concerted campaign began. The *Anglo-Saxon Chronicle* for that year records that; "In this year the heathen devastated Sheppey." The following year the West Saxon (Wessex) King Ecgberht fought off a raid by 35 ships launched against Carhampton in Somerset, and two years later another large-scale raid was driven off in Cornwall.

The busy Wessex port of Southampton was attacked in the 840s, and the *Anglo-Saxon Chronicle* records suggest that each year these raids increased in size and intensity. It seems that the Danes were testing Saxon defenses; probing all along the coast, moving the focus of their attacks from Cornwall (where they encountered some local support from the largely Celtic population), moving east toward Sussex and Kent, then around into East Anglia. In 842 "there was great slaughter in London… and in Rochester."

Although the Danes had established winter bases on the other side of the Channel on the Frankish coast, it wasn't until 850 that they established their first fortified winter camp at Thanet in southeastern England, an event that marked the start of a permanent Danish presence in the country. Within five years Sheppey had also become a Danish stronghold and, as Danish numbers increased, the raids evolved into what amounted to a full-scale assault on the Anglo-Saxon kingdoms of England. In 865 a "heathen host" led by Ivar (Yngvarr) the Boneless and his brothers Ubbi and Halfdan landed in East Anglia. Tradition has it that they were the sons of the Viking chieftain Ragnar, who had been captured by the Anglo-Saxon King of Northumbria, cast into a pit, and was bitten to death by snakes.

Growing menace

At the time, Northumbria was in a state of civil war, but its two claimants set aside their differences and joined forces to repel the Danish invaders. Ivar and his army marched on York, captured the city, and in 867 his Vikings defeated the Saxons, killing both royal claimants in battle. With York in Danish hands and Northumbria laid open to conquest, the Danes rapidly consolidated their gains, and established a Danish state in northeastern England. This was only the beginning of a campaign of conquest that would split England for a century.

The Saxon king of Mercia repulsed a Danish sortie in 869, after which Ubbi and Ivar the Boneless turned back south into East Anglia. There, they defeated the Saxon army of King Edmund and executed him. The death of a Christian monarch at the hands of pagans was seen as a martyrdom, and led to Edmund's canonization. St. Edmund's martyrdom would provide a Christian focus for Anglo-Saxon resistance to the Danish invaders in coming decades, but for the moment, nothing could stop the Danish onslaught.

The momentum continued. In 870, Halfdan led his Vikings into Wessex, where they captured Reading. Using the fortified town as a base, they fought for control of southern England. The *Anglo-Saxon Chronicle* records:

> "…during the year, nine pitched battles were fought against the host in the kingdom to the south of the Thames, besides those frequent forays that Alfred the king's brother, and earl's and king's thanes rode on, which have never been counted."

Under the guidance of King Æthelred and his brother Alfred, Wessex proved to be a tougher proposition. At the Battle of Ashdown (871) the siblings halted the tide of Viking conquest. Following Æthelred's death later that year, Alfred assumed the royal mantle. The Vikings decided that further invasion was impractical, and sued for peace. For the moment the surviving Anglo-Saxon kingdoms were secure. However, so too was the new Danish realm in England.

Below: Despite its small scale, the North Sea can throw up some of the worst weather anywhere in the world. Due to the sea's relatively shallow depth, high winds generate gigantic waves that threaten even modern shipping. This proved no barrier to the Vikings, whose longships rode all kinds of weather to reach the shores of England, Scotland, Ireland, and France.

Extracting Danegeld

By the 870s, the Danish Vikings had managed to carve out a new kingdom for themselves in northern and eastern England. For the next decade, while cities such as York thrived under the control of Scandinavian merchants, the Danes and Saxons were locked in a bitter struggle for control of Anglo-Saxon England.

Above: This gold brachteate (pendant) would have been worn on a warrior's chest, suspended from the neck, to offer the wearer magical protection. It is pictured here slightly larger than lifesize (4 inches diameter).

Following his capture of the territories collectively known as the Danelaw (formerly Northumbria, Anglia, and Mercia), Ivar the Boneless sent King Guthorm (or Guthrum) south to invade Wessex, the largest remaining Anglo-Saxon kingdom in England. During the course of 877, Guthorm and his allied leaders captured Exeter on the western borders of Wessex, and extracted tribute in return for leaving the land in peace. This tribute was known as Danegeld (*lit*. Danish money) and its regular extraction from the Saxon kings was a form of protection racket that continued throughout the ninth and tenth centuries.

Saxon nobles were not the only ones to pay Danegeld, and anyone capable of paying but unwilling laid themselves open to brutal retribution. The Viking habit of slitting the noses of erring taxpayers led to the expression "paying through the nose." The payment was meant to sate the Vikings' appetite for raiding, but for Guthorm, it was only the beginning of his campaign of conquest. He dispatched a raiding fleet to land on the coast of Wessex while marching his army south to link up with it. The Saxons were caught in the pincer movement. Guthorm captured Chippenham in January 878, then wintered inside Wessex, extorting Danegeld and living off the spoils.

The Saxon king Alfred the Great (r.871–99) was caught unawares by the invasion, which had split his lands in two. While the Danes paused to consolidate, the Saxons did manage a victory in Devon during Easter 878, and this gave Alfred renewed hope. He prepared to bring the Vikings to a decisive battle. In May, the two armies met at Ethandun, on Salisbury Plain, and Alfred was victorious. The Viking warlord agreed to Alfred's terms and surrendered. Part of the agreement required Guthorm and 30 of his commanders to be baptized. Guthorm took the Christian name of Athelstan to mark his conversion.

The two leaders entertained each other for several weeks after signing the resulting Treaty of Wedmore before the Vikings withdrew to Chippenham for the winter. Early in the following year, Athelstan led his men back to Danish East Anglia. Here he demobilized his army to occupy and farm the land and so consolidate their hold on that corner of England.

Uneasy co-existence

Under the terms of the Treaty of Wedmore, Athelstan agreed to leave Wessex in peace, and hostages were given to safeguard the commitment. In addition, the conversion of the Viking leader marked a change in relations between Viking and Saxon, since it removed the religious divide between the two peoples, and ensured a modicum of Church control over the affairs of both kingdoms.

Although the treaty failed to halt Viking attacks on Wessex, it did prevent any major campaigns of conquest. Instead, a succession of English kings ensured peaceful relations by

paying Danegeld. This practice continued until, in 1002, Æthelred the Unready inflamed Saxon passions in the Danelaw and encouraged an uprising. It was put down but led to a renewal of full-scale war between Viking and Saxon.

Ultimately, Alfred the Great's principal achievement was the continued survival of the Anglo-Saxon people, but his treaty also ensured that over half of Anglo-Saxon England remained under Viking rule until the 11th century. Both sides fought to preserve their boundaries, and Alfred's last campaigns centered around the defense of London and Essex. Following Alfred's death, Edward the Elder (r.899–925) continued his predecessor's vigorous defense of the English realm. He even managed to roll back the Danish frontiers from the Mercian midlands to the banks of the Humber. The struggle would be renewed, but in the meantime, both sides had to co-exist in order to strengthen their economy and military muscle for the next round of conflict. Paying the shameful Danegeld was preferable to the launch of an unplanned war.

The Danelaw

For two centuries, a major part of England remained a Viking state. Despite Norse enclaves on the west coast, the Danes ruled and the kingdom was known as the Danelaw. Its kings relied on military might, Scandinavian settlement, and subjugation of the indigenous Saxons in order to maintain their control of the realm.

York in 866 was a bustling Anglo-Saxon town that had already established close trading links with the merchants of Frisia (now Holland). Since Frisia had earlier fallen under Viking control, when the Danish Vikings led by Ivar the Boneless captured York, he had both ends of a vital commercial link. Under the

(Derby, Leicester, Lincoln, Nottingham, and Stamford) would inevitably fall with it.

During the ninth century the frontier between Saxon and Viking had been established in a diagonal line across Britain, stretching from the Mersey in the west to Maldon in Essex on the east coast, a line demarcated in part by Watling Street, the old Roman road. The Saxons built a string of fortifications along this line to create a virtually impenetrable barrier.

On the northern side of this line, the Danelaw Vikings lacked the political unity or the strength of military readiness to oppose the spread of the Saxon forts. While attacks against these defenses almost always ended in failure,

Above: The shallow draft of the longship meant that even the smallest of British rivers could act as a highway for Viking predatory "tax" raids.

Danes York became one of the most thriving marketplaces of the Viking world. Viking merchants flocked to the city, so that by 1000 York was "filled with the treasure of merchants, chiefly of the Danish race." It was the economic cornerstone of the Danelaw, and if the city fell, the Five Boroughs of the Viking kingdom

the Saxons used their strong position to launch campaigns of conquest into Danish territory. In settling down and building their mercantile concerns, it seemed that the Vikings were losing their taste for raiding. It was also obvious that with time the Saxons lacked much worth plundering. In 886 the frontier was established by treaty, and both sides were left to continue their own political development.

War spreads across Britain

In the west, Norse inroads into the Danelaw north of the Mersey took the form of a Norse-Irish invasion. Conflicts between the Norse and the Danes continued to weaken the Viking position until the union of Saxon Mercia and Wessex under King Athelstan (r.925-940) posed a threat the Norse could not ignore. A temporary alliance was formed between the Norse, Welsh, Scots, and Irish, and the two groups decided the issue at the Battle of Brunanburgh (937). Athelstan's Saxons were triumphant, and when the Saxon king established his nominal suzerainty over the Northumbrian Saxons, he effectively isolated the Danelaw on two sides. It seemed as if the Saxons were winning their struggle for England, and when York was recaptured in 959, the Danes appeared to be doomed.

However, the tide turned following Athelstan's death. A succession of three Wessex kings failed to maintain a firm grip on the Vikings and the Saxon offensive finally ground to a halt with the accession of Edgar the Peaceable (r.959–75). The conversion of the Danish king Harald Bluetooth in 980 (*see pages 38–39*) robbed the Saxons of a religious rationale for further war on the Danes, and a fresh wave of Vikings helped to bolster the defenses of the Five Boroughs. A Viking foray at Maldon led to a battle between Viking newcomers and Saxons, an English defeat that has been remembered in one of the great epic poems of Anglo-Saxon literature, *The Battle of Maldon*.

With the Danes once again in the ascendancy, the Saxons were forced to bide their time, and pay Danegeld, hoping the Vikings would stay away from their lands. Inevitably, these protection payments only produced a temporary respite, and King Olaf Tryggvasson of Norway appeared in the 990s, an ally of King Sweyn Forkbeard of Denmark. These were no longer mere raiding parties but national armies; well-armed, well-led, and highly trained. Only a political split between the two kings and the conversion of King Olaf saved Wessex and Mercia from destruction.

The Danish attacks continued by both land and sea, and so too did the demands for Danegeld. Following a final, failed military campaign, Anglo-Saxon England accepted that the Danes were there to stay and from this point onward the two peoples began to merge and unite in a way that had not been possible during the centuries since the Vikings first arrived off the Saxon shore.

The density of Viking settlement in England between 875 and 950.

- parish names with Scandinavian origin
- southern limit of the Danelaw

Crisis for the Franks

Viking attacks on the British Isles had only been a prelude. Across the Channel lay a much richer kingdom ripe for plunder. Viking enclaves on the Frankish coast provided bases for a campaign of conquest in 845 that would shake the very foundations of the emergent western European civilization.

Right: Gothic reliquary bust of Emperor Charlemagne the Great, founder of the Frankish Carolingian Empire. Charlemagne styled himself *Carolus Magnus*, hence "Carolingian." Thus the terms Carolinginian or Frankish Empire are interchangeable.

A friar from the monastery of St. Germain-des-Prés near Paris described the crisis that befell the Franks: "In the year of our Lord 845, the vast army of Northmen breached the frontier of the Christians." The appearance of a Viking army at the very gates of Paris was a brutal realization of the prophecy of Jeremiah which claimed that the "chosen people" would suffer divine punishment from the north.

The Carolingian Frankish Empire was already wracked by civil war following the death of King Louis I the Pious (r.814–40). The depredations had started decades before, in 810,

when Danes led by King Godfred invaded Frisia, which was then part of the Carolingian Empire. Although the invasion was little more than a raid, it proved a lucrative venture, and the Danes returned ten years later. In 820, a large-scale Danish raid on the Frisian coast was repulsed and the Vikings were forced to look elsewhere for plunder.

It was probably the same group of Danes who appeared in the Seine estuary later that year, but again, the local Frankish defenses proved too strong, and the attackers withdrew. For a time it seemed that the Danes were content with attacking the softer English coast, but in 834 they returned, sacking the Frisian town of Dorestad, the site of the main Carolingian mint. Louis I, son of the Emperor Charlemagne, had split his lands between his three sons, and from 829 onward, the Frankish kingdoms were weakened by near-constant wars between the siblings. These divisions provided the Vikings with an opportunity to exploit.

Louis built a string of forts to guard the Frisian coastline, and during his final years he maintained a standing army at Nijmegen, in readiness to counter any full-scale Viking invasion. Following his death, his sons were too

Viking incursions into the western part of the Carolingian Frankish Empire in the ninth century.

NORTH SEA

Dorestad
Utrecht · Nijmegen
Walcheren · Duisburg
Antwerp · Asselt · Rhine
· Cologne
· Aachen

EAST FRANKISH KINGDOM

ENGLISH CHANNEL

Rouen
· Bayeux · Seine · Reims
Jeufosse · Paris · Verdun
St-Germain · St-Maur-des-Fossés · Metz
· Melun
· Chatres · Troyes
BRITTANY · Orléans · Sens
· Angers · Tours
Noirmoutier · Nantes
WEST FRANKISH KINGDOM
· Poitiers · Loire
· Limoges · Lyon
· Saintes
· Bordeaux

Carolingian kingdoms in 888

● Viking winter camps

KINGDOM OF ASTURIAS AND LÉON

PROVENCE
Nîmes · Arles
· Toulouse · Camargue (region)

MEDITERRANEAN SEA

involved in their civil war to care about the seaward defenses of the Empire.

An empire overrun

In 841, the Vikings sailed up the Seine for the first time, plundered Rouen and attacked the abbey of Jumièges. The following year they returned to exact Danegeld from the towns along the Seine, and Quentovic was pillaged, probably because its citizens refused to pay the raiders. The establishment of three stable kingdoms from the divided ruins of the Carolingian Empire in 843 failed to stop the increasingly ferocious Viking attacks.

Inevitably the worst affected kingdom was the western Carolingian territory of Charles the Bald (r.843–77), who had already suffered Viking depredations in the Seine valley. In 845 the sack of Paris was only prevented by the payment of 7,000 pounds of silver. Inevitably such concessions just led to further attacks, and larger demands. Over the next two decades, no river valley in the Western Frankish Kingdom was safe from the Vikings. They even sailed up the Rhône in the late 850s, and wintered on the Mediterranean coast. In 851 Vikings wintered in the Seine valley, and within a few years permanent Viking settlements were established on the Loire, as Nantes was attacked, followed by Tours in 853.

Blois was attacked in the following year, but raids on the cities of Orléans and Poitiers were thwarted; at least on a local feudal level resistance to the Vikings was increasing. Charles the Bald still appeared incapable of defending his realm. The western portion continued to be the focus of devastating Viking attacks for a quarter of a century after the death of Louis I, and although some areas resisted the raiders, elsewhere the Vikings had a free rein. By 865 the pace of attack slackened, as the Vikings

Below: A matrix used in the manufacture of helmet plaques. The image depicts two Viking warriors wearing helmets topped by figures of boars, animals associated with Frey.

became increasingly embroiled in affairs in England and Ireland, and in Danish-Norwegian rivalry. When they returned, they came in even greater numbers, and for some, their objective was conquest, not just plunder.

To the Gates of Paris

The Western Frankish Kingdom suffered the brunt of Viking attacks during the mid-ninth century, but raids down the rivers to the east became increasingly popular for the Danish adventurers. The Western Franks enjoyed a brief respite until, in 879, the Vikings returned to the Seine. This time their objective was Paris, the jewel in the Frankish crown.

Facing: From the island of Vernon in the River Seine, the Vikings launched their attack on Paris in 845 that resulted in Charles the Bald, King of the West Franks, paying them 7,000 pounds of silver to go away. The Danegeld payment worked but failed to keep the Norsemen out of Normandy.

The western Frankish kingdom of Charles the Bald was all but destroyed by Viking raiders, but further to the east, the lands of his two brothers were far from unscathed. The central Frankish kingdom of Lothair (r.840–55) was bisected by the Rhine, while to the east, the Elbe flowed through the kingdom of Louis the German (r.843–76). Both rivers became avenues for Viking attack. While the townspeople along the Seine and the Loire enjoyed a brief decade of peace due to Viking involvement elsewhere, the rest of the former Carolingian Frankish Empire continued to suffer.

In 845, a large raid led by King Horik of Denmark led to the destruction of Hamburg. Six years later the Danes returned, raiding down the Elbe. In 858 it was the turn of the Weser, and Bremen was pillaged, then put to the flame. Another major raid took place in 862, but on the whole the Eastern Franks escaped the worst of these attacks due in part to the strong defensive stance of the Duke of Saxony, the most powerful German warlord in the north.

To the west, the middle kingdom inherited by Lothair went relatively unharmed except along the Frisian coast, where Lothair had neglected to maintain the coastal defenses erected by his father. Dorestad and the region of Batavia were both plundered, but the worst came after Lothair's death, when the realm was ruled by his son Lothair II (r.855–69). In 863 a large Viking expedition attacked the old Imperial city of Xanten on the Rhine, and the Vikings reached Neuss, a day's row from Cologne, when they were bribed into turning around.

Viking savagery in the middle kingdom was largely kept at bay by such bribery. The elder Lothair gave the Danish exiled king Harald the island of Walcheren on the Schelde estuary to use as a base. In return Harald discouraged further raids into the lands of his benefactor. A similar deal was struck in 850 with Harald's nephew Roric, whose raids into Frisia were rewarded with the gift of Dorestad and its hinterland. This deal did much to secure the safety of the middle kingdom, but the arrangement did little to benefit the Western Franks.

Repulsing the attackers

After a decade of peace, the Vikings returned in 868. In the intervening period the defenses of several Frankish cities had been improved, and Orléans was able to withstand a determined Viking attack that year. Defenses were also improved along the upper Loire and the upper Seine, so when the Vikings did come back, the Franks were ready for them. However, this policy meant virtually abandoning the coastal regions; Bordeaux and Nantes became ghost towns. In 879 a Viking force of 700 ships and 40,000 raiders rowed up the Somme and the Seine rivers, and occupied Flanders. In 882 a raid reached Cologne and Trier.

Three years later, the Vikings moved on Paris. Here, fortified bridges spanned the river, blocking the Vikings' progress. An initial Viking assault on the city's northern wall was thrown back. The invaders unusually settled for a slower investment and laid siege to the city. In the spring of 883, just as the Vikings were preparing to launch a final assault, Prince Charles the Fat of the Eastern Franks arrived with a relief force, and drove off the Vikings. It was a military stalemate. While the Vikings roved around the city to plunder the area beyond Paris, the Franks improved their defenses. Realizing that they had lost the initiative, the Vikings eventually moved westward into Brittany, where they were defeated and destroyed in 891. Although the raids continued, and Viking enclaves remained in the estuary of the Seine and in Frisia, the Franks had managed to weather the Viking storm.

Plunder of the Western World

When the pagan Vikings set off on their raids across the North Sea, they fell upon some of the richest monasteries of Celtic Scotland and Ireland, and Saxon England. Gold, silver, money, and jewelry were their prizes, and this plunder included some of the richest examples of early-medieval artistry in existence.

Before the Vikings arrived off the shores of the British Isles, churches and other religious centers had become storehouses of wealth. Both the Celtic and Anglo-Saxon cultures produced exquisite examples of craftsmanship in precious metals and other materials, and most of these objects were inspired by the Christian faith. Wood and bronze reliquaries to hold the bones of saints, gilt-bronze statuettes of religious figures, illuminated manuscripts encased in jewel-studded covers, and bishops' croziers were all to be found in these places, and all became plunder for the sea raiders.

The plunder available from Ireland was particularly plentiful. The island had enjoyed over three centuries of peace before the Vikings came, and the Celtic church had thrived on the patronage of Ireland's secular rulers, and on its own growing control of lands, people, and property. With few real towns, the Celtic monasteries formed the cornerstones of Irish culture, and consequently the institutions became repositories for the wealth of the land.

When the Vikings first arrived in Ireland in 795, they discovered that these monasteries were veritable treasure troves of plunder, and set about sacking each community in turn. The loot was often melted down, then shipped back to Scandinavia in longships. It is a staggering testimony to the efficiency of the Viking raiders that today, of all the Celtic Irish art to survive from the late eighth century or early ninth century, roughly half of it can be found in the museums of Scandinavia. The plunder of the Vikings remained in the Viking heartland for over a thousand years, buried as grave goods in places like Oseberg and Birka.

Experts at extortion

The extortion of Danegeld became a lucrative source of revenue in the ninth and tenth centuries. Taking a financial tribute was a practical option—the raiders were pragmatic enough to recognize that a plundered and razed town was eliminated as a source of future revenue. Surprisingly, very little Frankish or Saxon coinage has been found in Scandinavia. The ninth century hoard of plunder found at Hon in Norway contained a cache of Carolingian silver coins and Anglo-Saxon jewelry, but this is a rarity.

By contrast, Celtic, Anglo-Saxon, and Frankish coins hoarded by Vikings are frequently found in Britain or Ireland. For example the Cuerdale treasure chest was stashed by a Viking raiding party in Ireland about 903, and it contained over 7,000 silver coins, including a high proportion of Carolingian ones. Another hoard found on the banks of the Ribble in Lancashire, England also contained many coins. The Ribble silver is of Irish origin and was probably buried on the river bank after the Vikings were expelled from Dublin in 902.

If the coinage managed to reach Scandinavia (gold or silver) it seems it was melted down for use in barter or to form the raw materials from which Viking artisans could create their own works of art. To the Vikings, the exchange of silver was commonplace, but native Danish, Swedish, or Norwegian systems of national coinage were only introduced in the 11th century. This meant that silver was valued only for its purity and weight, not for its conformity to a regulated system of coinage. In these circumstances, the melting down of precious metals was a sensible option for the looters.

Plunder did not only come in the form of gold, silver, or religious artifacts. Entire villages or monastic communities were carried off as captives, either to be used as hostages in return for a ransom, or taken back to Scandinavia and sold into slavery. Slave markets thrived in the trading towns of the Viking world, even in Russia and Germany. In return for an amount of silver, the unfortunate slaves were sold into a life of servitude and hard labor. The Viking raiders almost ruined the economic and social life of the lands they ravaged, and threatened to extinguish Christian faith by the systematic destruction and despoiling of the religious centers in their quest for plunder.

Facing: This hoard of coins found in Sweden illustrates the extent of Viking travels, since these coins are mainly Byzantine and Islamic. Perhaps the farthest afield any object traveled was a miniature figure of Buddha seated on a lotus petal. Having started life at some point in 6th-century India, it must have been handed on from trader to trader across the Silk Road before ending up more than 5,000 miles away on the Swedish island of Helgö.

Left: Another Swedish hoard was found by a farmer in a field near Visby on the island of Gotland.

from Raiders to Rulers

Following the Treaty of Wedmore, the newly baptized Danes consolidated their English possessions. What followed was the creation of an Anglo-Danish state, shaped by the increasingly peaceful co-existence of two former enemies.

Above: Viking burial ground at Lindholm Hills, Denmark. There are 628 graves, 200 of which are marked by the outline of a ship in stones.

Alfred the Great, King of Wessex, reconquered much Danelaw territory during the late ninth century (*see pages 66–69*). The Vikings were slowly forced back toward their capital of York, which fell to the Saxons in 959. While this was happening, the Danes were busy creating a Scandinavian realm, organized and ruled on Danish lines. To all intents it was considered an extension of the Danish homeland. Because it provided a sizeable chunk of revenue for the Danish crown, its kings took an active interest in its defense.

In 878, the Viking's Danelaw England amounted to some 25,000 square miles, and it contained a handful of large settlements such as York and Lincoln, as well as populous and fertile river valleys, such as the Humber and Trent. Just how many Danish migrated to the Danelaw is unknown. Some scholars argue for a relatively low number and that the Danes only created a ruling aristocratic stratum—having ousted any Anglo-Saxon nobles—and left the rest of the English social orders untouched.

Another argument says that there was mass migration from Denmark to the Danelaw during the ninth and tenth centuries, and that these colonists intermingled with the local Saxon populations in all areas, and on all levels. This seems a more realistic approach, since it is supported by the linguistic evidence. The Danes who settled in France soon adopted the Frankish tongue, but those in the Danelaw kept their own language. Hundreds of place names in this part of England end in the suffix –*by* (e.g. Grimsby, Whitby, Kirby, Selby, and Derby), and other Scandinavian place names exist throughout the region. Danish words entered the English language—*happy, wrong, scant, low, anger,* and dozens of others. Supporters of this theory argue that no mere aristocratic elite could have had such an effect on the English tongue, but it took decades of influence from neighbors, farmers, and merchants to alter the Saxon tongue in such a manner.

The Danes and Saxons clearly intermingled, intermarried, and adopted elements of each other's identity until both were largely fused into one. Clearly there would have been friction between the two cultures during this process. In one contemporary text, Saxon chroniclers complained that their Danish neighbors washed and combed their hair "in order to overcome the chastity of the English women"!

Foundations of English law

The Danes also introduced their own legal system into England, with a written law (a development of the unwritten legal codes used in Denmark), a system of courts, and even an appeals procedure. It established the principle of trial by jury, and a legal code from the Danelaw mentions that a court consisted of 12 thanes (local minor nobles), who swore an oath on holy relics to deliberate with impartiality. It also included the instruction:

"Let the judgment stand on which the thanes are agreed. If they differ let that stand which eight of them have pronounced."

This was the first establishment of the jury system, and the provision for a majority verdict. These principles are now enshrined in most legal systems in the modern courts of Europe and America.

The Anglo-Saxon re-conquest of the Danelaw in the mid-tenth century came about because the Danes were too busy squabbling with the Norwegians (and within their own realm in Denmark) to divert military resources to England. This changed in the last decades of the century, when Æthelred the Unready (r.978–1016) succeeded to the English throne. A new breed of Norwegian invader (the most famous of whom was Olaf Tryggvasson) was

matched by a new attitude among the Danes, and the Anglo-Saxons' lack of military preparedness under Æthelred the Unready encouraged the resumption of raids into England. Æthelred's response was not war but appeasement, as he followed the age-old trick of buying off the Viking raiders. As ever, this only encouraged them to come in greater numbers. This time, the new wave of Vikings were not raiders. They were Danish kings, set on the conquest of the whole of England.

Below: The Bound Devil on a cross at Kirkby Stephen, Cumbria, in the northwest of England is actually a depiction of Loki fettered by his son's intestines after contriving Baldur's death. Loki embodied deceit and trickery.

CHAPTER 5

Viking Art & Literature

Left: Detail of carving on one of the sledges found in the Oseberg ship-burial. Scandinavian artifacts produced in the 5th to 7th centuries AD—before the true Viking age—have been found in several burial sites in mainland Sweden and on the island of Gotland. The earliest form of true Viking art recognized by most historians is named after the stunning Oseberg ship-burial find on the Oslofjord, Norway, which has been dated to c.834. Many intricately carved objects were found inside the ship, including this sledge.

The Vikings have long been portrayed as primitive barbarians; pagans from across the sea who had no interest in art, culture, or the written word, but only saw worth in rape and pillage. This does the early medieval Scandinavians a disservice. Although they did not fully adopt the Latin script of Christian Europe until the closing years of the Viking Age, they had their own form of crude but effective written language.

The survival of Viking sagas (or tales) were the written version of traditional spoken tales; recording the Vikings' mythological roots as well as the historical lineage of their ancestors, and the exploits of their contemporaries. These sagas, most of which were finally recorded in writing in the 13th century, provide a priceless window into the cultural, political, and economic development of Scandinavia during the Viking era. They also provide a frame of reference to help us interpret the archaeological remains the Vikings left behind, by allowing us to understand the references to religion, people, or events that have been recorded in the surviving artifacts of the era.

Above all, the sagas provide us with a means to understand what drove the Vikings to ravage the coastline of Europe, embark on trading voyages deep into the Russian wilderness, or set sail across uncharted oceans to discover new lands. The Viking sagas are windows into the past which are virtually unique in early medieval history.

In addition to the written cultural legacy, the Vikings left behind them an artistic heritage in the form of richly-decorated domestic objects, clothing fixtures, and weapons. Trends in the development of Scandinavian art during the Viking age can be identified from the priceless objects the Vikings buried with their dead, or hid in secret caches to prevent their loss. Because of this hoarding, a great deal of material has survived to the modern day.

The Runemasters

For all their endeavors, the Vikings left few written records, apart from the Skaldic legacy of the 13th-century sagas, which post-dates the true Viking age. Instead, they inscribed their weapons, jewelry, and marker stones with their runes, the mysterious stick-like markings that served as their written alphabet.

Below: The Common or Danish runes are known as *futhark* for the first six symbols. Each character had a word associated with it. Variations in the script mean that these associations were not constant throughout the Viking world, and differed with time and place. Other new symbols were added as the Viking language developed. Runic characters were grouped to form words, but each also had a specific meaning (shown below)—an early form of shorthand writing.

According to Viking legend, Odin, the chief of the old gods of Scandinavia, gave the runic alphabet to the Scandinavians as a gift. He was also the god of poetry, knowledge, and mystery, and his personal knowledge of runes was meant to have come from an even higher being. In his own quest for knowledge, Odin hung in Yggdrasil, the windswept tree of life. for nine days and nine nights. In that time he gained his knowledge of the runes, and he subsequently passed this knowledge on to the mortals whom he ruled. So much for the legend. The real origin of the runic alphabet is far less straightforward.

Runes have been ascribed to the Bronze Age Greeks and Etruscans, although there is no indication that any southern European development of an alphabet was shared by the inhabitants of Bronze Age Scandinavia. In the Dolomite Mountains of Italy examples of runic script dating to the first century BC indicate that there may have been some Celtic antecedent to the Viking runic system. It has been suggested that migrating Germanic tribesmen took the alphabet north into Scandinavia at some time during the following four centuries.

There is a strong indication that similar runic scripts were used in other pagan Germanic regions during this period. Certainly by the ninth century, the Viking runic script was well established as a form of communication throughout the Viking world, and was different from any other runic form in Germanic lands, including Anglo-Saxon England or Frisia, where early runic inscriptions are also found.

Rudimentary alphabet

The basic runic alphabet of 16 characters is known as *futhark*, after the first few characters of its script. An individual letter was known as a *rune*, while *runic* refers to the alphabet in its entirety. Each rune combined both an individual meaning as a letter in its own right with another, more specific meaning. These meanings may well have varied with region or time, and there is indeed evidence of a certain degree of variation in the meaning of runic lettering.

In its most common form (known as the Danish *futhark*) the double meaning of symbols seems to have been universally understood. As an example, of the 16 runic letters, the first, representing the letter *F* can be used in combination with other letters to spell a word. But it can also stand alone, for instance when

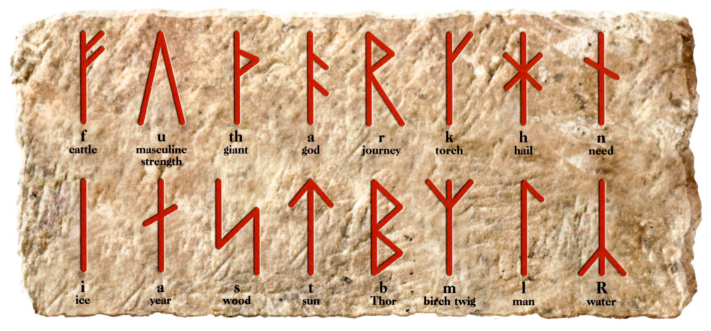

f	u	th	a	r	k	h	n
cattle	masculine strength	giant	god	journey	torch	hail	need

i	a	s	t	b	m	l	R
ice	year	wood	sun	Thor	birch twig	man	water

used to represent the word "cattle."

Of the most common variations, "short-twig" or Norwegian/Swedish *futhark*, differed slightly from the universal form. It appears that as the Viking language developed, new symbols were introduced to represent letters that had been missed from the original alphabet. Previously, rune writers (or runemasters) substituted one of the older standard 16 letters for a completely new one, which consequently means that some runes are difficult to read. Similarly the letter *n* is omitted before a consonant, making it even harder to read the scripts, unless the reader is a trained runemaster. When runes were carved on surfaces other than wood, the limitations of wood grain were no longer a consideration, and curves could be introduced to speed up the writing process. As a result, inscriptions on bone, stone, or metal tend to have more rounded features than is otherwise the case.

It was a simple alphabet, designed more for carving into wood or stone than for writing. Even the slopes of the lines were designed so that they would not be obscured by the wood grain, which would have made them difficult to read. Although the style of writing was cumbersome, particularly when it came to carving long messages, it also meant that the means to write it were everywhere: on stones, trees, or on buildings. Some runic inscriptions also took the form of graffiti, such as at the Maeshowe burial tomb in Orkney, where a Viking adventurer extolled the beauty of a girlfriend called Ingjeborg. Although few wooden objects with runes carved on them have survived, a wealth of runic inscriptions on grave finds and marker stones still exist, and give us an insight into this lost Viking language. As a consequence, scholars have been able to unravel most of the mysteries of the runes.

Above: The "graffiti" at Maeshowe. Not all Viking runic scripts extol warrior-like virtues. This stone inscription on Mainland, Orkney Islands reads more like a love letter.

Left: Central detail from an 11th-century rune stone at Mariefred, Sweden. Inscribed within the outline of a serpent, these runes honor a Swedish Viking who died while seeking glory far from home.

Viking Stone Sculpture

For centuries the Gotlanders had produced carved stone monuments, recording ancestral deeds. Elsewhere in Scandinavia the erection of such stones was virtually unheard of, until the arrival of Christianity. From the 11th century, stone sculpture and runic inscriptions on monuments became the distinctive artistic and written legacy of the late Viking age.

Stone markers on the island of Gotland were decorated with scenes from Scandinavian mythology, the epic legends of gods and mortals which later developed into the pre-Christian religion of the Vikings themselves. That they also recorded the deeds of their ancestors provides a rare reference to Scandinavian life stretching from the fifth century until the end of the Viking age four hundred years later. Over 400 such stones cover the island, and of these 30 are large, elaborate, and highly decorated examples of their kind, containing a wealth of information for scholars.

For example, the Ardre stone dating from the start of the Viking age, combines a knotted ring of "gripping beasts," surrounding scenes depicting the arrival of a Viking hero in Valhalla, riding on Odin's steed. Below it the artist depicted scenes from Scandinavian legend, with Sigurd in the blacksmith's forge along with his patron, Thor, the god of war, who is shown fishing for the Serpent of Life. Inevitably the stone also shows a well-defined early representation of a Viking ship, crewed by the warriors who at the time of carving were just beginning to plunder the vaults of Christendom.

As Christian influence spread through Scandinavia, the Gotland tradition of raising stone memorials spread to the mainland kingdoms. Often these were covered with runic inscriptions that allow modern scholars to determine who raised the markers, and why. In addition, most were decorated in the prevailing artistic styles of their time, usually the late phases of Viking art known as Ringerike and Urnes (*see pages 98–99*). As with much Viking art, certain conventions predominated, such as the inclusion of mythological or fantastic animals and beasts, elongated into ribbons, and intertwined into a decorative pattern of "gripping beasts" that is distinctively Scandinavian.

One of the best known examples of this type of marker is the memorial stone erected in Jelling to commemorate the royal parents of King Harald Bluetooth of Denmark (*see picture, page 39*). Commissioned by their son, the three-sided stone is both a symbol of the new-found Christian faith in Denmark as well as an embodiment of the art of the late Viking age. It contains the representation of a large animal fighting with a snake carved in the contemporary

Urnes style, as well as a depiction of the Crucifixion. A runic inscription around the edges of the monolith records the details of the newly converted Christian monarch's parents.

Beacons of the new religion

Similar stones began to appear elsewhere, and through them the spread of Christianity can be traced across Scandinavia. Particularly fine examples of the genre are found at Skårby in southern Sweden, Ringerike in southern Norway, and Lingsberg in central Sweden. Of these, the Alstad stone from Ringerike was decorated with scenes from the pre-Christian legend of Sigurd, and gave its name to the Ringerike style. Missionaries often sought ways to use existing mythology to further the understanding of their Christian message, and the large stones may have served as a means of interpretation that the local pagans could understand.

Increasingly, Christian symbols became popular on these marker stones, as did runic inscriptions. In some cases, the inscriptions tell of the Vikings themselves, such as the stone at Lingsberg which says that the Viking Ulfrik (whom it commemorates) "took two payments of gold in England." Although thousands of these rune stones exist across Scandinavia from the late Viking period, they are most common in central Sweden. However, they also appeared in the Viking colonies, and some memorials are distinctly pedestrian. An example from Lincoln in England records that "Thorfast made a good comb." The St. Paul's stone in London carries the message that "Ginni and Toki had this stone set up." Others, more useful to modern historians, record the deeds of those Vikings who conquered lands overseas, or traded in Russia or the Frankish Empire.

Facing: The incised stele from Funbo in Sweden dates from the 9th century, and incorporates runic lettering into the body of a serpent-like beast similar to that pictured on page 83.

Below: Detail from the 10th-century Stele of Sanda, from central Sweden. It contains a representation of Vikings, mythical animals including "gripping beasts," and Scandinavian deities, with a runic inscription running around its top.

Viking Skalds

Runic inscriptions tell us that Vikings honored the values of kinship, heroism, honor, honesty, and virtue. Skaldic verse—the form of Viking poetry recorded in runic inscriptions and in the later Icelandic Sagas—also celebrated these same ideals.

Facing: This carved 8th-century funerary stone from Gotland depicts the kind of poetic imagery that inspired the Skaldic verses. Many stones bore similar imagery (*compare to the fragment pictured on page 35*). Odin is shown at the top, riding his eight-legged horse Sleipnir toward welcoming Valkyries in front of Valhalla. The center panel contains a longship and warriors, and the lower panel shows Loki and his wife Sign, and Thor and Hymir fishing for the Midgard snake.

The most basic forms of Skaldic verse found on runestones relied on simple alliteration for poetic structure. The term itself derives from the Icelandic word *skald*, meaning poet. Freed from the constraints of carving on stone, Icelandic verses developed into more complex forms. The collected prose narratives and verses are known as the Sagas.

These elaborate Viking poems written down in the 13th century were versions of the previously unrecorded spoken poetry of the Viking age. Roving bards entertained during wintertime with heroic poems of legend, history, and stirring deeds, of men, virtue, and battle. (In fact, to Anglo-Saxons the term *skald* meant a Scandinavian court bard.) The Skaldic verses provide a rare insight into Viking culture and society, and the code of ethics they lived by.

The Skaldic verses vary in length from a single stanza (small enough to record on a runestone) to longer eulogies, probably designed to please the royal patrons who hired the skald to recite for them. Most skalds were well-educated Icelanders, who traveled the Viking world, educating and entertaining the courts and households of their time. Others were attached to the households of kings, princes, or earls, to record their deeds for posterity and to recount their exploits over the winter hearths.

Some recitals would have been extremely lengthy, such as the *drápa*: poems with a chorus or refrain that were reserved for the most exclusive royal patrons. Shorter Skaldic verses, known as *flokkr*, record the exploits of less exalted clients, or cover the events of a particular campaign or raid. Other verses were used to honor particular patrons, or served as eulogies after their death.

Of course, the skalds had to please their patrons and must therefore be considered less than accurate in their boasts. However, they do serve to provide a basic summary of the events of their age, and of the virtues that the Vikings considered most worthy.

Complex verse forms

Skaldic poetry frequently uses a predetermined form of imagery (called *kennings*) to serve as a form of shorthand. For example the *tree of the Valkyrie* was a warrior who stood his ground in battle—like a tree. The skald's audience, well-versed in the alliteration and *kenneling* heard in the poems, would have had no trouble in unraveling the intricacies of this form of poetry.

Skalds employed other conventions. Every poem followed a set pattern, or *dróttkvæt*. Each verse or stanza consisted of eight lines, and each line of six syllables. Of these, three were stressed, and three not, although the order in which this stressing occurred could vary from line to line. In every even line, two of the stressed syllables had to rhyme, and on every odd line, two needed to partially rhyme, where they ended with the same consonant, but contained different vowels. In the same odd line, two of the three stressed syllables needed to begin with the same sound, and these had to alliterate with the first stressed or unstressed syllable of the following line.

Clearly the composition of such Skaldic verse was a skilled occupation, and gifted poets were highly prized and well rewarded. While this *dróttkvæt* system meant that the task of composition was formidable—particularly when the poem ran for more than a few stanzas—the system also made it easier for skalds to memorize the words of these unwritten masterpieces. As well as the individual verses, the *flokkr* or even longer *drápa* had to conform to a set sequence, involving an introduction, a middle section, and a set ending. The longest also involved the inclusion of a chorus or refrain, used to separate groups of stanzas from each other, like chapters in a book. From these Skaldic poems we can see that the aristocracy of the Viking world enjoyed sophisticated and cultured entertainment, and they reveal a new facet to a complex and vibrant people which would otherwise have gone unrecorded.

The Icelandic Sagas

When Scandinavians first began to record the previously unwritten poetic testimony of their Viking ancestry, they created a vision of a heroic age. If today the Vikings seem somewhat larger than life, this is mostly due to the way they presented themselves, and the style in which their descendants chose to record their exploits.

Facing: Sumburugh Head in Shetland; the southern tip of the archipelago, close to the Viking settlement of Jarlshof. The Icelandic Sagas have given us a better understanding of what historic events took place in key Viking-age locations such as Shetland.

Skaldic verse was almost exclusively an Icelandic phenomenon. When these poems and narratives were finally set down in writing during the 12th and 13th centuries, the Icelandic chroniclers were simply drawing on their own cultural roots, and recording the stories that had been passed down to them over the generations. Consequently the bulk of the epic Scandinavian prose and verse now known as the Sagas came from Iceland, although other Scandinavian examples do exist (from Norway and Denmark).

The perception of the Vikings is based on two sources: the historical views of the people whom the Vikings encountered through raid or conquest, and the Sagas. When the Sagas were written the Vikings had already passed into history. Scandinavia had become little more than a fringe region of Europe, whose real political and cultural center lay to the south. Accordingly, the Vikings were already legendary figures, symbols of a past heroic age of warriors, mighty

Right: Regin the Blacksmith reforges Sigurd's broken sword. Detail from a carving in Hylestad stave church, Norway.

battles, and stirring deeds. Inevitably, medieval chroniclers chose to take the old Skaldic prose at face value, without challenging its historical integrity. This scholastic gullibility means that the impression passed down to us of the Vikings is colored directly by the saga writers and the earlier skalds.

It follows that in any reading of the Icelandic Sagas, it is almost impossible to separate fact from fiction. Any historical view based solely on these chronicles will be distorted. It is also virtually impossible to know where the recorded words of the old skalds ended, and the reconstructed segments designed to fill in gaps by the later Icelandic chroniclers began. In spite of these limitations, the Sagas provide modern scholars with their best view of the Vikings and their times.

The Sagas divide into several forms, while the Skaldic verses are a related yet distinctive grouping in their own right. Many Skaldic poems were probably recorded faithfully by the Saga writers because the stanzas were too difficult for later generations to edit with any understanding. Any distortions, therefore, are those of the skalds in exalting their patrons. Unfortunately the majority of these complex and elegant poems contain little of concrete value for historians. It is necessary to turn to the epic narratives that form the bulk of the Icelandic Sagas for more detailed information.

Windows on Viking society

The *Konungasögur* (Kings' Sagas) were the first to be written down in Iceland, in about the middle of the 12th century. They cover the whole sweep of Scandinavian history, and describe the fate of kingdoms and empires, particularly the fates of the kings of Denmark, Sweden, and Norway. *Heimskringla*; the *Gesta Danorum*, and the *Orkneyinga Saga* are all prime examples of this type. Another example, *King Harald's Saga* written by Snorri Sturluson, was an addendum to the Sagas of the Danish Kings, and provides us with a superb view of Viking politics and warfare during the late 11th century.

The *Islendingasögur* (Family Sagas) were written later, during the 13th century, and deal with the feuds of Icelandic settlers, or the exploits of explorers, adventurers, or brigands. The *Saga of Halldor Sorrason*, and *Njall's Saga* are prime examples of these works. They record

in often extensive detail the lives, loves, and tribulations of Viking society.

The third group are the *Fornaldarsögur* (Heroic or Mythological Sagas), which record Scandinavian mythology, and the heroic Eddic poetry that evolved as a rival to Skaldic verse (*see page 36*). Written in the 14th century or just before, these sagas provide us with our detailed understanding of the Viking gods such as Odin and Thor, Frey, and Freyja. Of all the Sagas, they are the least useful to historians, but probably the most widely known to posterity.

The Royal Sagas

Among all the medieval texts of Scandinavia, two mammoth histories are the source for much of the written evidence we have on the men who ruled Scandinavia and beyond. Together, they trace the histories of kings, princes, and dynasties, and provide an insight into the Viking political and military framework.

Right: The Vikings were great storytellers, and the life history of the authentic personality Olaf Tryggvasson (also Saint Olaf) allowed for vivid embellishments. In the Flateyjarbok, the 14th-century Icelandic collection of sagas, Tryggvasson is depicted in the illuminated capital (left) dying at the Battle of Stklestad, and undertaking two of his legendary feats (right), the killing of a wild boar and a sea-ogress.

The *Heimskringla* (Kings' Chronicle) was written in Old Norse by the Icelandic chronicler Snorri Sturluson in about 1230. *Gesta Danorum* (Feats of the Danes) was written in Latin by the Danish cleric Saxo Grammaticus in about 1300. Both were based on earlier accounts of their subjects in prose and verse that had been written down by a previous generation of chroniclers. Both histories were written in different styles, and for very different reasons.

Snorri Sturluson's masterpiece is in the traditional and concise style of contemporary Icelandic literature. His storytelling abilities are in part a reflection of the older Skaldic and Eddic traditions, in which events were told with realism, but constructed to maintain the suspense of the listener (or reader, later). Of the two authors, the work of the Icelandic writer is the best known because his style is more suited to modern tastes of historical documentary.

By contrast, the Saxo text relies more heavily on contemporary Latin styles, in which rhetoric and Roman moral and martial values have been used to overlay the Scandinavian subject. In other words, *Gesta Danorum* was written for a Latin audience, not a Scandinavian one, and it was largely designed as an exercise in political ambition. In it, ancestors of the contemporary Danish monarchs are portrayed as men of heroic stature in the Roman model in order to enhance their status in the eyes of all Europe. *Gesta Danorum* should be viewed as a history suited to the age in which it was written, although it appears to be an accurate enough reflection of its Viking subject, given the constraints of Saxo's style and his motives in recording it. Unfortunately, because the original material from which Saxo culled his facts has now been lost, we are unable to compare his version to the older Skaldic verses.

Tale of kingship

Olaf Tryggvasson, the late tenth-century Norse king, is a good example of Snorri Sturluson's portrayal of a Viking hero in the *Heimskringla*. His image as "the most feared Viking" of his age is largely the work of the Icelandic writer, and it is difficult to distinguish between colorful episodic padding to his biography and factual incidents. For instance, Olaf's royal father was killed when Olaf was an infant, and the child and his mother fled Norway, only to be captured by pirates. The infant was sold into slavery but managed to kill his pirate captor, before being

adopted by a king of the Rus. On reaching adulthood, the young hero gathered a band of followers around him, allied himself with the Danes, and then led them on a campaign of conquest in England.

While he was campaigning, Olaf encountered a mysterious hermit, who made a prophecy that Olaf's followers would rebel. Forewarned, Olaf was able to quash the rebellion, and in return, he adopted the hermit's Christian beliefs. Olaf then seized the crown of Norway from the dynastic usurpers who had killed his father, and forcibly converted his new subjects. Five years later, treachery by his wife led to the king being attacked by overwhelming numbers of his wife's Swedish allies in a sea battle. Foreseeing the end, he jumped overboard and drowned;

although a legend that he survived as a monk persisted for decades.

This tale contains elements that can be verified from other sources, but clearly the account of his conversion, the exploits of his childhood, and his final climactic battle have been embellished to provide the reader with a more gripping tale. Separating fact from fiction is virtually impossible, and scholars are left with Snorri's account of King Olaf, and nothing more. All we can do is to regard the histories of Saxo and Snorri with some degree of skepticism, while enjoying the mythical, romantic, and heroic strands the sagawriter weaves into the pages of his history. After all, that is the Viking way of storytelling, so what better way to tell the story of the men who ruled the Viking world?

Viking Art and Ornamentation

The vitality that the Vikings displayed in their raiding, conquest, and exploration also spilled over into their art. Viking art is usually characterized by its use of intricately composed ornamentation, which in turn developed from a centuries-old Scandinavian tradition.

Right: This pendant, or amulet, of a man wearing a horned helmet and holding a sword and two spears probably represents a priest of the cult of Odin. Dating from the 9th century, it was found among a female burial site in Uppland, Sweden.

Scandinavian art's complex decoration can be traced back to the fifth century, well before the Vikings. At the same time, the outside influences of those they conquered were also absorbed. Vigorous, confident, Viking art amalgamated the traditional with the new into a fresh, vibrant style all of its own—symbol of a restless age. Artistic development continued until the last century of the Viking age and the coming of Christianity. Then, following its brief flourish of pagan culture, Scandinavian art disappeared as a unique style. Christian artists preferred to copy the new Romanesque style, which had become the unifying cultural symbol of a Christian Europe.

Viking art is not a "fine art" of highly developed visual representation. Like their physical and temporal neigbors the Celts, the Vikings rarely painted. Their art is almost exclusively applied—the ornamentation and carving of everyday objects such as weapons, domestic utensils, or even longships. Within these constraints, metalworkers, jewelers, and carpenters decorated functional objects with a dynamic that is still startling in its functional beauty today. The Vikings clearly had a love of embellishment that brought dignity and color into their lives.

Surviving examples of Viking art are limited. We have to rely on a small number of grave sites and chance finds. Information on textiles and

Below: A pair of gold 10th-century Danish brooches, with elegant filigree work.

clothing is even more scarce since, along with many wooden objects, these have perished over the intervening years. Certain key finds such as the well-preserved and extensive collection of artistic material from the Oseberg ship-burial suggest that the richness of Viking art was much greater than most of the surviving traces hint at. For example, the Oseberg Tapestry find is virtually unique as an example of textile decoration in the Viking world.

"Gripping beast" motif

The arrival of Christianity is another limiting factor. Christian burial practices radically altered the Viking traditions of burying with grave goods, and most ninth- and tenth-century Scandinavian artifacts that have survived come from pre-Christian burial sites. Like the Oseberg ship, many of these were the graves of royalty or important leaders, and their richness indicates that art played a major part in Viking culture. From this patronage, artisans created masterpieces—a magnificent legacy of decorative ships, horse-fittings, weapons, beds, wagons, and jewelry.

After Christianity supplanted older pagan beliefs in the later Viking age, the information from burials ceases. The hoards of buried plunder found throughout Scandinavia offer little evidence, for their contents were generally stolen from the Celts and Franks. Fortunately, there is the artistic output from the burgeoning marketplaces and towns of the Viking world, and Christianity did bring a fresh kind of art in the shape of stone crosses and sculpture. As an art form, sculpture had previously been confined to the Baltic island of Gotland. Ornamental markers celebrated the dead, important events, and battles, but they also displayed the last vestiges of a unique cultural style that was exclusively Viking.

Art historians have divided the Viking age into six distinct styles, but one common factor stands out, and unites all of them. The "gripping beast," a creature whose paws grip itself, other creatures, or the borders surrounding it, was a stylistic constant

throughout the Viking age. It appeared in the Oseberg carvings, and continued in use into the Christian period. This dynamic image clearly appealed to the Vikings, and may be seen as an apt representation of the vibrant people who colonized the continent of Europe.

Below: The simplified drawing based on the stem/stern post of the Oseberg ship, pictured on page 46, makes it easier to see the manner in which the "gripping beasts" motif works. This example is unusual in featuring humans, rather than animals. Even in earlier art (**left**) with a more abstract appearance, the "gripping beasts" motif can be seen in the creature at the brooch's bottom. This 7th-century Vendel-style brooch from Aker, Norway, has cloisonné enamel work with precious stones.

93

Early Viking Art

It is not possible to precisely date the six major styles of Viking art, and two or three styles may have existed concurrently. However, historians have provided a rough timeline based on grave finds such as the sumptuous ones found in the Oseberg ship-burial, which gives its name to the first of these styles.

Below: Detail of a sled post from the Oseberg ship-burial. The rich interlace carving is ornamented with metal studs. In this section, a dragon, jaws agape, can be seen biting another part of itself—typical of the "gripping beast" motif common in all phases of Viking art.

Oseberg (or Broa style) lasted from the late eighth until the mid-ninth century. Borre style overlapped the end of the Oseberg period by a decade, then continued right through the phase of Viking colonization and conquest until the mid- to late 11th century. This made it the longest artistic period of the Viking age. The first style (named after the ship burial at Oseberg near the Oslofjord and the grave site of Broa on Gotland) was essentially one of carving and intricate bronzework, while the Borre style which followed marked the flourishing of Viking metalworking, particularly the working of gold and silver.

The Oseberg burial (dated approximately 834) produced a wealth of wood carving; the decoration of the burial ship itself, plus the wagons, beds, sleds, and domestic items together made up one of the richest pre-Christian burial finds in Scandinavia. The designs were clearly the work of master craftsmen, and most contained the "gripping beast" motif. Most spectacular of these are two dragon-head posts. The first (*see picture, page 116*) is decorated with a three-dimensional carving of "gripping beasts" that swarms with sinuous life. This vigorous and spectacular carving is one of the most widely known pieces of Viking art. It marks the start of a unique period in Scandinavian artistic development, even though by that time the "gripping beast" was a centuries-old Scandinavian motif.

By contrast, the second dragon-head post is altogether more restrained (*see picture, page 6*). The head itself is carved in a relatively realistic manner, with an intricate interlacing of carved animals forming the neck of the animal, while its face, jaws, and eyes are portrayed in a lifelike manner. The skill with which this piece was carved earned its creator the nickname of the "Academician" among Viking historians.

Another spectacular Oseberg carving is the large wagon or cart, which contains intertwined snakes slithering down its legs, as well as heroic humans, gods, and mystical animals. The sumptuous carvings found at Oseberg suggest an artistic period that was experimental, vibrant, and dynamic. Unfortunately, few other wooden artifacts remain with which we can compare the Oseberg decorative style to later pieces, or identify an artistic shift from one style to the next.

A similar decorative style is found in the collection of gilt-bronze bridle-mounts found at Broa. Distorted animals curve and intertwine in the decoration, but the framework is provided by larger animals whose paws grip the frame of the metal— the archetypal "gripping beasts," similar to the two Oseberg headposts.

Art for all

The Borre style that followed is exemplified by fine jewelry, most notable being the exquisite collection of filigree brooches and ornamentation produced in Denmark during this period. The style is named after bronze bridle-mounts that were everyday pieces, most probably copies of richer gold or silver objects. Despite this, the pieces demonstrate a newer, finer artistic style, where delicate interlacing and filigree work and the addition of tiny inlays of precious metals combine to produce some of the most beautiful artifacts of the Viking age.

While the "gripping beast" motif remains popular, another form of interlacing (known as "ringchain") as used on the gold spur find from Værne Kloster, ends in the profiles of animals and introduces a new and possibly extraneous influence into Scandinavian art. The Borre

period lasted for almost 150 years, and continued to be used in parallel with other, later identifiable artistic styles.

What is particularly interesting is that this style lent itself to reproduction in non-precious metals. In objects like the Borre bridle-mounts, the filigree designs used in other gold or silver brooches or decorative items have been reproduced in a simpler style, and would have been sold to a wider range of less exclusive patrons. While some art historians have labeled these less exclusive offerings as second-rate, they indicate a growing spread of wealth in Viking society through the economic windfalls of raiding and commerce, and a widening of the cultural base that supported Viking artisans.

Above: The intricate filigree work on this gold spur is typical of the Borre style.

High Viking Art

The artistic style known as Jelling overlapped the populist art of the Borre phase and lasted for a century. It was a style of metalworking which resulted in an offshoot: the relatively short-lived Mammen style which began in the mid-tenth century.

Below: The incised ornamentation on this silver beaker found in royal burial mound near Jelling in the center of Jutland, Denmark has become the benchmark of the Viking art style named after the town.

The Jelling style took its name from the ornamentation on a silver cup, found during the excavation of the northern royal burial mound at Jelling, Denmark. The mound marks the presumed burial site of King Gorm of Denmark, and dates from about 958. The style itself covers a period from c.880 to c.985, marking the high point of the period of Viking conquest and expansion.

The cup stands on a small pedestal base, and is decorated around the bowl with an S-shaped spiral of creatures. These beasts are distorted so that their bodies become sinuous interlocking ribbons, bisected by ovals making a ribbed pattern along their tails. A characteristic of the style can be seen in the heads of the beast: almost always shown in profile, they have a downward curling (curlicue) lower jaw. Another feature is a forelock or pigtail to the beast's head, which usually forms one of the intertwining bands of the decoration.

All these features are seen in the Jelling cup. The sinuous beasts are similar to those found in the earlier Broa metalwork of the Oseberg period, and therefore demonstrate that this was a traditional Viking motif. What is particularly interesting is the way it takes the earlier ninth-century design exemplified by the Broa bridle-mounts and transforms it into a highly involved decorative feature in its own right. It is also reminiscent of the Celtic scrollwork that the Vikings would have found on the religious objects plundered from Ireland and Scotland.

Although art historians are reluctant to ascertain any specific influence for this consolidation of an older Scandinavian style, the similarity to Celtic applied art of the same period is striking. Viking artists certainly had direct

contact with the producers of Celtic metalwork. A hoard of intricately ornamented silver brooches discovered at Skaill in Orkney has been dated to c.950. The brooches are decorated with a virtually identical decorative animal motif to the Jelling cup, but the Skaill animals are even more intertwined with offshoots and tendrils emanating from the beasts themselves. This has been seen as an early representation of the Mammen style that followed, but it also reflects the Celtic influences of the Pictish artwork produced in Orkney before the coming of the Vikings.

That similar pieces of Jelling style have been found in other British sites suggests that the style was particularly popular in the Vikings' overseas colonies. In addition, spectacular examples of the style have been found in Norway (at Tråen), in Denmark (at Søllested) and in Sweden, so although probably less popular in Scandinavia, Jelling-style artwork was known throughout the Viking world.

A new realism

The Mammen style developed from the Jelling phase, which overlapped and preceded it. Indeed, some art historians are unwilling to differentiate between the two, claiming one is merely a derivation of the other, and not a separate style in its own right. Mammen is characterized by having the animals portrayed with more solidity than previously. They are in less distended shapes and appear more realistic than in the traditional Jelling depictions.

Even more distinctive is the introduction of foliage into Viking designs and scrollwork. While small tendrils could be found in Jelling pieces, these developed into complex swirling and fully-fledged foliate patterns in the Mammen phase. The influence with the acanthus leaf decoration popular in contemporary Carolingian art has been suggested as a likely source of inspiration for these Viking metalworkers. The style was named after the decorated battleax found at Mammen in Denmark's Jutland Peninsula, a find dated to c.970 (*see picture, page 122*). The iron ax is inlaid with silver wire, formed into a foliate pattern, and incorporates a bearded human face and a bird, shown in surprising detail. Indeed this detailing is a third characteristic of the style. It paved the way for the stunningly intricate metalwork and stone carvings which symbolize Scandinavian art of the late Viking age.

Below: This equal-armed brooch with two animals on either side of a "Thunderstone" (Thor figure) typifies the Mammen style. It was found in a grave at Birka, Uppland in Sweden.

Late Viking Art

From the last years of the tenth until the mid-twelfth century, two final phases of Viking art emerged. Ringerike is largely a continuation of the earlier Mammen style, but Urnes is something different. It represents the last fling of independent Scandinavian art and a return to older traditions.

Facing top: The Söderla wind-vane is a quarter circle of open framework filled with an intricate pattern of foliate scrollwork wrapped around a large dragon trapped in the center. A smaller beast has its jaws clamped around the dragon's foot, while a third snake-like beast is wrapped around the dragon's curved tail. A deer on top of the wind-vane is a three-dimensional form covered in swirls that represent the muscles of the legs.

Right: Tombstone from St. Paul's Cathedral, London, England depicting a dragon carved in relief in the Ringerike style. From the reign of King Cnut.

Facing bottom: A silver arm-ring in Urnes style from Hornelund, Denmark, c.10th century.

Ringerike is a region of Norway to the north of Oslo. Several decorated stones were found here, including the well-known Alstad stone. The penultimate Viking art style that the stones represent is nameed after the area. The Ringerike style emerged at a time when Christianity was spreading across Scandinavia, and the erection of carved stone slabs or monuments was becoming common. These are decorated with scenes of birds, dogs, riders, and extensive, chunky foliate spirals. Indeed the foliate designs that developed from Mammen tradition became the main characteristic of the Ringerike period, which lasted about 90 years from the end of the tenth century.

The gilt-bronze ship's wind-vane from Söderla in Sweden (*pictured right*) is an exquisite example of Ringerike applied art. The dragon and other beasts are clearly locked in a struggle, and this theme of combat is reflected in other examples of the Ringerike style. For example, a carved stone monument at St. Paul's Cathedral in London (*pictured below*) dates from the same period, and portrays a different version of a dragon, intertwined with another animal which it is either meant to be fighting, or has just vanquished. Interestingly, when the London find was first discovered in 1852, archaeologists noted traces of the original paint work which covered the stone, indicating that Viking art from this period was almost certainly not monotone. It was clearly placed there during the reign of King Cnut, and suggests that Viking art was widely used throughout the Danish provinces in England as well as in Scandinavia.

Animals entwined

The Urnes style marks the final development of independent Viking art, and represents a development on Ringerike. The two styles

The Maeshowe Dragon carving from Orkney (*see map illustration, page 132*) is a further fine example of Urnes style. A dragon, similar to that on the Ringerike St. Paul's stone, is shown as the centerpiece of an Urnes pattern of interwoven

overlapped for about 50 years during the last half of the 11th century, but Urnes is more sophisticated in its foliate scrollwork. The foliate clusters of Ringerike have been abandoned and instead the beauty of the design relies on the interplay between the interwoven lines and tendrils, many of which emanate not from any foliate pattern but from the beasts or animals portrayed in the artwork.

In some respects, this represents a return to much earlier Viking styles, when distorted beasts intertwined with each other to form simple scrollwork patterns. An early example of Urnes style is the silver bowl found in the Swedish Lilla Valla Hoard, dated to 1050, the start of the Urnes period. The bowl is decorated by a simple lattice of interwoven animal tails incised into its gilded rim. More intricate examples of the style include the small silver brooch found at Lindholm Høje, where a single beast is developed into an elegant and delicate scroll.

The carvings for the wooden Viking church at Urnes in central western Norway (*see picture, page 30*), which are a prime example of the intricacy and delicate workmanship of this phase, provided the style's name. In it, a deer or greyhound-like beast is shown biting the leg of another animal, and the pair are interwoven in a mesh of tendrils of various thickness. Once again, combat between animals is a popular motif, and it marks a return to and a development of the traditional "gripping beast" motif which has therefore survived throughout the Viking age as a popular artistic device.

curves emanating from it. Slowly, these patterns became less common, as religious art in the Romanesque style was adopted and marked the spreading influence of the Church into Scandinavia. The end of the Urnes style also marked the end of a centuries-old tradition of independent Scandinavian art.

CHAPTER 6

Exploring the Northern Seas

Among the Vikings who headed westward across the North Sea during the last decade of the eighth century, a handful came not to plunder but to settle. Others would return to the new-found Viking bases in the islands of Orkney, Shetland, and the Hebrides with their families and livestock, intent on taking advantage of the land and opportunity the Viking migrations had presented them. These first "land seekers" found familiar landscapes but with greater farming potential than they knew in Scandinavia, and they were able to settle into their new island homes with few problems. As Norse rule was gradually extended to the islands, they became fully-fledged outposts of the Viking kingdom of Norway.

Others took a more southerly route in the wake of a new wave of Viking raiders to establish colonies in Ireland, southern Wales, northern England, Frisia, Normandy, and the Loire valley. Already occupied, the arrival of Vikings created tension with the indigenous populations and their neighbors. It also brought the invaders into conflict with other Vikings, as Norwegians and Danes vied for control of parts of England and Ireland. These settlers came as conquerors rather than colonists, and with them they brought the established rule of Viking law, and the authority of the Scandinavian kings.

To succeeding generations of Viking "land seekers," the new territories soon became as restrictive and hidebound as had been the Scandinavian homelands from which they had hoped to escape. Some Norse in Ireland may have learned of earlier voyages made by Irish monks to new lands far away in the north.

A handful of Viking settlers set sail, searching for virgin land in the North Atlantic. In this way the Faroe Islands, Iceland, and Greenland were discovered and settled. From there, Viking explorers continued on into the Labrador Sea, establishing a colony on the remote western shore of Greenland, and probing deep into the Arctic waters of what is now the Davis Strait. Even more spectacularly, Viking explorers used these far-flung colonies as stepping stones on a voyage that would lead them to the continent of North America. Contrary to established belief, America was discovered five centuries before Christopher Columbus set sail, and the remains of the Viking settlement in Newfoundland is a testament to their achievement.

Some historians have believed that the "grapes" which gave Vinland its name must have been discovered much further south than Newfoundland by Leif Eriksson's Vikings, possibly as far south as Florida. This is largely discounted today (*see page 109*).

CANADA

BEAUFORT SEA

Hudson Bay

Foxe Basin

QUEEN ELIZABETH LAND

HELLULAND (Baffin Island)

Baffin Bay

ARCTIC OCEAN

MARKLAND (Labrador)

Leif Eriksson Thorvald Eriksson Thorfinn Karlsefni

Davis Strait

Lake Melville

Western Settlement

LABRADOR SEA

GREENLAND

VINLAND (Newfoundland)

L'Anse aux Meadows

Eastern Settlement

Cape Farewell

GREENLAND SEA

Jan Mayen

Eric the Red

Denmark Strait

ATLANTIC OCEAN

Reykjavik

ICELAND

NORWEGIAN SEA

Faroe Islands

Hebrides

Shetlands

NORWAY

SWEDEN

Orkneys

Bergen

NORTH SEA

BALTIC SEA

DENMARK

Viking vessels in inhospitable Baffin Bay.

The Impetus for Exploration

By the ninth century, the first wave of plundering had passed and there was a settled way of life in the new colonies, which had become absorbed into the kingdoms of Norway and Denmark. But in many Vikings the restless spirit still lived, and these men were driven to sail in search of fresh lands, far from the authority of kings and earls.

Above: The Faroes were already home to a handful of Celtic hermit monks when the first questing Vikings crossed the "frozen sea" from settlements on the Hebrides, Orkney, and Shetland islands.

The reasons behind the burst of migration during the last years of the eighth century are still not fully understood, but limited resources and a growing population in Scandinavia are cited as the main stimuli behind the development of the Vikings as sea raiders. This coincided with an increase in central authority throughout Scandinavia. Areas that had hitherto been self-governing were now swallowed up into the territories of the Scandinavian kings.

It has been argued that as internal order was established both in Scandinavia and in the Viking lands in Britain, the more unruly elements decided to migrate beyond the reach of royal authority. This is a simplified explanation for the impetus that caused the "land seekers" to venture across the uncharted northern seas in the ninth century. The real reasons have still to be

explained, so for now, the resentment of authority has to be accepted as a plausible factor, but by no means the only reason for the phenomenon.

The century of exploration was largely a new manifestation of the restless energy of the Vikings, which had led to the first raids against Britain. This time, though, the objective of these voyages was land, not plunder. The movement that would bring the Vikings to the shores of the Americas had begun, encouraged in part by adventure and in part by an increasing level of hatred of royal authority. Like the American colonists eight centuries later, these Viking settlers resented that their lives were ruled by an overseas king, and that much of their hard-earned revenue was earmarked for the coffers of the kings of Denmark or Norway, or the Earls of Orkney.

By the early ninth century, Norse authority had been firmly established in the new settlements of Orkney, Shetland, the Hebrides, and the Isle of Man. While some Vikings resigned themselves to this semi-feudal overlordship, others decided to move on. In Ireland, Celtic clerics reported rumors of lands beyond the "frozen sea" to the north, and we can be fairly certain that Celtic monks had already discovered the Faroes, even Iceland. In 682, the Irish monk Dicuil wrote that a group of islands (the Faroes) lay two days and nights sailing from the most northerly of the British Islands. He added that Irish hermits had been living there for roughly a century, "but now, because of Norse pirates, they are empty of anchorites [hermits], but full of innumerable sheep and a great many different wildfowl." The Faroes (or *Færeyjar* in Old Norse, meaning the Sheep Islands) would become a first stepping stone on the Viking voyages of exploration around the fringe of the North Atlantic.

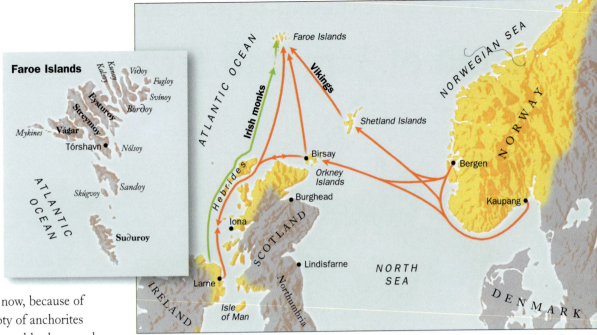

Outlaw refuge

The sources that tell us about these early explorers and settlers are the great medieval Icelandic Sagas, written centuries after the event. The *Orkneyinga [Orkney] Saga*, the *Færeyinga [Faroe] Saga*, *Eiríks Saga Rauða* (Erik the Red's Saga) and the *Grænlendinga [Greenland] Saga* chronicle these events with great detail, but with a level of accuracy that is difficult to quantify. In Iceland itself, the *Æslendinga [Iceland] Sagas* provide a series of accounts of the island's settlement and history, and are probably the most accurate of all these works. They tell how, in about 860, the Viking chieftain Nannod was exiled from Norway and, together with a band of desperadoes, he "went off to make a home for himself in the Faroes for the good reason that he had nowhere else where he would be safe."

The Faroes had already gained a reputation as a refuge for those who were beyond the law. Swept past the islands in a gale, Nannod made landfall on an inhospitable coastline, where ice-laden mountains rose steeply from the shore. Nannod

called the coast "Snowland." Around the same time, the Swedish Viking Gardar Svavarsin was also swept northward in a gale from Orkney, and he too made a landfall on the same coast. Unlike Nannod, he remained to explore the new landfall, and wintered there. He discovered the territory was an island, which he named *Gardarsholm* after himself. The landfall would become better known as Iceland, and what followed would be a virtual stampede of settlers, all wanting to claim a stake in the new land to the north.

Below: The *Gaia* is a working replica of a Viking *knorr* trading vessel, its stern pictured here, docked in Rejkjavík. Ships like this carried thousands of Viking colonists and their possessions across the northern seas to new homes.

Land of Fire and Ice

Above: Loading a *knorr* for a voyage of exploration and settlement.

For some, the Faroes served as a temporary stopping point on a voyage that lay further north over the "frozen sea." Beyond lay Iceland. Over the next century, the first settlers developed Iceland into a thriving Viking colony. The island would also serve as a base for further voyages of exploration to the west.

Floki Vilgerdarson, a Norwegian sea rover, is traditionally credited as being the first Viking settler of Iceland, in c.860. The name Floki was derived from an Old Norse term for pack ice. Intrigued by tales of new lands to the north, he sailed from Norway to Shetland, then on to the Faroes before heading north toward the "land of ice and fire," as its first settlers would soon call Iceland.

The Sagas recall how he carried three ravens with him to act as navigational aids. The first headed south toward the Faroes. The second, launched a few days later, refused to leave the ship. The third flew a few days after that and headed west. Floki followed, making landfall on the western tip of Iceland, after which he was nicknamed "Raven Floki." He landed in a great fjord to the northwest of the island and founded a settlement he called Breiðafjord. But a harsh couple of winters were enough for Raven Floki, and he returned to Norway, dubbing the island

"Iceland" as a gesture of his anger at the failure of his expedition.

Others in Floki's crew were less disheartened. Thorolf Butter (so named because he claimed that butter dripped from the grass in Iceland) spearheaded a new wave of settlers. To land-hungry Norwegians, such tales carried with them the promise of a better life. They also came at a time when King Harald Harfagri was enforcing the central authority of the Norwegian crown in regions that until that point had remained virtually free of outside interference. As the Icelandic Sagas put it: "He made everyone do one thing or the other; become his retainers or quit the country." Vikings were probably not the first Europeans to reach the shores of Iceland. The *Æslendinga Saga Æslendingabók* (Book of the Icelanders) records that—as with the Faroes—Irish monks lived on the island. Apparently, after the Vikings landed: "They went away because they were not prepared to live here in company with heathen men."

Wave of colonization

The *Landnámabók* (Book of Settlers) tells how the first wave consisted of 400 settlers and their cattle, Celtic wives, and Celtic slaves. It appears that they sailed from Ireland or Scotland following the tales spread by the first three

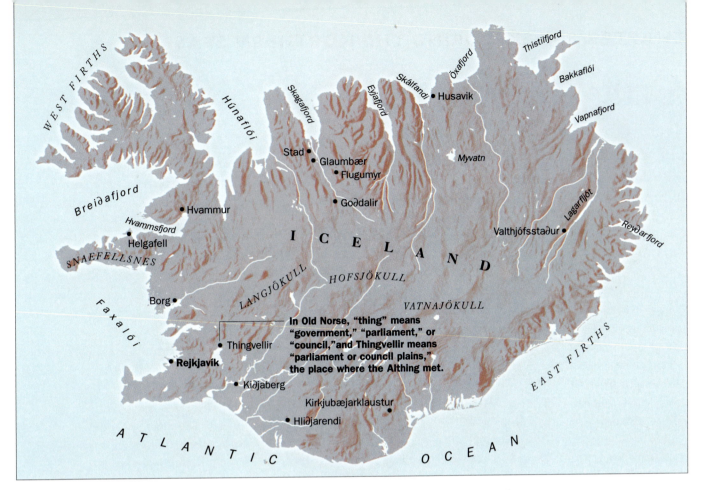

In Old Norse, "thing" means "government," "parliament," or "council," and Thingvellir means "parliament or council plains," the place where the Althing met.

Viking explorers. Over the next 60 years, Iceland was a magnet for Viking settlers, and the population rose exponentially. By 930, when the first Althing (Assembly) was held to forge an island government, there were over 20,000 living there, making it one of the most populous of all the Viking settlements.

The farmsteads established in Iceland were based on those the Vikings had left behind in Scandinavia, Orkney, or Shetland. An example of one at Hofstadir in northern Iceland provides a useful example of these first Icelandic structures: a central hall, with a small family room at one end, plus outhouses. This was the type of settlement built by men like Hjorleif, who harnessed his Irish slaves to pull his plows.

Ingolf Arnasun's first settlement was probably similar, a farm which he established at Rejkjavík (Smoky Bay). This became the site of

the Icelandic capital, and by the late tenth century it was a bustling commercial center. Ingolf was typical of these early settlers. A Norwegian, he had fled from the authority of the Norwegian king and, like many others, his family became native Icelanders, traditionally seen as the offspring of a union between the Viking settlers and their Celtic slave mistresses.

In 930, the settlers gathered at the first Althing at Thingvellir, some 30 miles east of Ingolf's settlement at Rejkjavík. From this point onward Iceland became self-governing by means of this annual national assembly. The once-lawless colony gained a semblance of communal authority. For the more independent-minded, this was yet a further impetus for new exploration to seek a settlement free from the dictat of others. These were the men who traveled to lands even further to the west.

Below: Icelandic wild horses in full gallop. These are descended from stock originally brought to the island by Viking settlers.

Erik the Red

Erik Thornvaldsson Raudi was an outcast. Driven away from Iceland by his neighbors—and rather than return to Scandinavia—he elected to venture further west in search of fresh lands. In so doing, he came across Greenland, a wild and rugged place that would be the next Viking stepping stone across the Atlantic.

Facing: The stone foundations of the Eastern Settlement of Brattahlid still stand. Despite the shift in nearby glaciers, which destroyed some houses, and the astringent climate, by 1090 there were over 3,000 settlers living here.

Below: A view from Brattahlid across Eriksfjord, named by Erik the Red after himself.

Eiríks Saga Rauđa (Erik the Red's Saga), written in Iceland in the 13th century, is probably one of the more reliable surviving accounts of Viking exploration. Its prose is free of the myths, anecdotes, and embellishment that cloud other works. Instead, it provides what appears to be a factual account of a voyage of exploration and settlement, complete with navigational observations, descriptions of landfalls, and details of the men and ships who participated in the expedition.

Erik Thornvaldsson was nicknamed Raudi (the Red) after his red beard, but the Saga adds that it was also a reflection of his argumentative nature. He was born in Jæren in southwestern Norway c.950–60, but an alleged murder led to his father leaving Norway and settling his family in Iceland about 980. The only available land was on the island's barren northwestern coast. Following his father's death, Erik struggled to make ends meet.

He married Thojdhild, the wife of a successful local farmer, and together the couple moved south, establishing a farm at Haukadal, on the Brei afjord. A feud with neighbors led to Erik killing two men, and he was forced to move further west to Oxney. He was soon in trouble again, killing another neighbor's sons during an argument. This led to a three-year banishment from the island by order of the Icelandic Althing.

Gathering together a band of fellow desperadoes, Erik Raudi bought a small *knorr*, and sailed west during the summer of 982. He had already heard Gunnbjorn's tale, a Viking who had been swept west of Iceland by a gale. There, he had spied a group of rocky islands and behind them an uncharted landmass. This was to be Erik's destination. He sailed due west from Snaefellsnes, the westernmost tip of Iceland, Using the stars to hold a westerly course, after four days the explorers sighted land—of sorts. Blocking their path was a vast icecap, and behind it, a range of ice-covered mountains.

Erik skirted the icecap and sailed south until he reached its tip. He then steered north up the western coast, where he found the land more hospitable. The fjords teemed with fish, and were fringed by meadowland. Here, at the head of an inlet he named Eriksfjord, he landed and built his settlement.

Encouraging settlers

Erik spent the three years of exile exploring this vast new land and making allotments to his companions. Then he returned to Iceland to spread news of his discovery. In order to encourage further settlement, he dubbed his new home with the enticing name of Grœnland (the Green Land). On his return to Greenland with his wife, Erik established a bigger, better settlement on Eriksfjord called Brattahlid, in what became known as the Eastern Settlement. Some 400 miles further north, a second group of colonists created a second Western Settlement on the Gothåbfjord, the only other location in Greenland where extensive animal husbandry is feasible all the year around.

Elsewhere, Greenland provided excellent scope for hunting and the waters abounded with fish. The settlers soon began to trade skins, furs, and tusks to Viking merchants from home, for the iron, timber, and corn they needed. Both of Greenland's settlements survived, and even flourished over the next two centuries. But disease, soil erosion, and climatic change eventually conspired to force the Vikings to leave their holdings. The Western Settlement was abandoned by the mid-14th century, and Brattahlid was deserted by 1500.

As for Erik Raudi and Thojdhild, they raised a family, but Erik apparently yearned for his days as a "land seeker." When, in about 986, the settler Bjarni Herjolffson missed Greenland on a voyage from Iceland due to storm and fog, he glimpsed a coastline that was "well-wooded, and with low hills." He had sighted the coast of America, but he turned about and eventually made landfall in Greenland. Although Erik was too old to continue his wanderings, his son Leif Eriksson came of age about the turn of the millennium, and would himself undertake to explore these lands to the west.

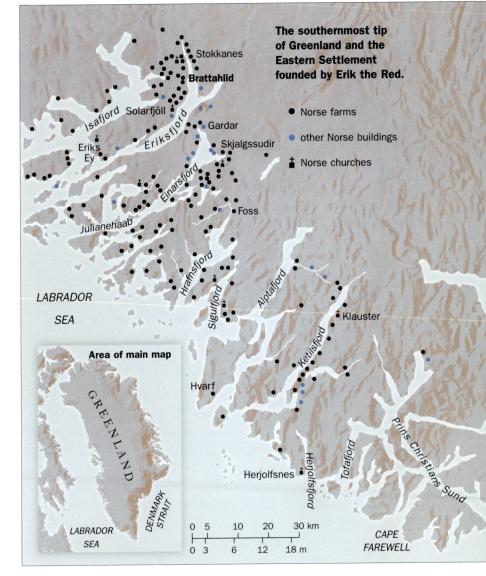

The southernmost tip of Greenland and the Eastern Settlement founded by Erik the Red.

- Norse farms
- other Norse buildings
- Norse churches

Stokkanes
Brattahlid
Isafjord Solarfjöll
Eriks Ey
Eriksfjord
Gardar
Skjalgssudir
Einarsfjord
Foss
Julianehaab
Hrafnsfjord
Sigulfjord
Alptafjord
LABRADOR SEA
Klauster
Ketilsfjord
Hvarf
Herjolfsnes
Herjolfsfjord
Tofafjord
Prins Christians Sund
CAPE FAREWELL

Area of main map
GREENLAND
LABRADOR SEA
DENMARK STRAIT

0 5 10 20 30 km
0 3 6 12 18 m

Leif Eriksson

Leif Eriksson was already an accomplished mariner before he sailed from Greenland in 1001 to search for a rumored land farther to the west that had been glimpsed 15 years earlier by a storm-swept Viking mariner. Eriksson was about to become the first European to set foot on the American continent.

Below: The fall along Newfoundland's Viking Trail. Compared to Greenland's harsh environment, Vinland was a haven of lush grass, plentiful timber, and streams jumping with fish.

Bjarni Herjolfsson, driven off course by a storm in 986, emerged from the Atlantic fog in sight of a landmass that he knew was not Greenland. He continued north and east until he reached his intended destination. In Brattahlid, the stories told of Herjolfsson's accidental discovery aroused the interest of Leif Eriksson, eldest of Erik the Red's three sons and a mariner like his father. The Sagas describe Leif as "a big, strong, strapping fellow, handsome to look at, thoughtful, and temperate in all things." Born in Iceland in about 976, he had moved to Greenland with his parents following Erik's return from exile in about 986. From here, he had pioneered the trading voyage between Brattahlid and the Orkney Islands.

Leif was determined to adventure west in search of the mysterious new land that Bjarni Herjolfsson had spotted 15 years before. Erik planned to sail with Leif, but a fall from a horse forced him to remain in Greenland. "I am not meant to discover more countries than this one we are now in," he told his son. Leif sailed from Brattahlid with a well-provisioned ship and 35 crewmen during the midsummer of 1001. He headed due west until he reached the "black glaciers" which Herjolfsson described sighting on his return voyage. Leif named the inhospitable landmass Helluland (Flatland), and sailed on. This landfall was most probably Baffin Island.

The Vikings continued across what is now the Hudson Strait to reach a coast "level and wooded, with broad white beaches wherever we went, and a gently sloping shoreline." The trees there were tall pines, and to the Greenlanders—who regarded timber as a luxury—the sight was remarkable. Leif named it Markland. The landfall was made somewhere to the west of Cape Harrison, on Canada's Labrador Coast.

Exploring America's coastline

Leif's party sailed on for another four days (two *dægr*, or two-day voyages), and "sighted another shore, and landed on an island to the north of the mainland." This was probably Belle Isle. They pressed on toward the land lying south of the little island and set up a winter camp. Here, the rivers teemed with salmon, good timber was plentiful, and the grass was lush enough to allow winter grazing. This was almost certainly

Newfoundland. Compared to Greenland, it must have seemed idyllic. One of the explorers, Tyrkir Fosterer, discovered grapevines, and so Leif named the place Vinland (Wineland).

This is the story as related in the Sagas, but it has baffled modern scholars. The remains of the outpost uncovered at L'Anse aux Meadows on the tip of the north coast provide excellent evidence that Vikings landed near here (probably in Epaves Bay, off Sacred Bay), but the climate does not permit the growing of grapes. Alternate landfalls have been suggested from the New England coast to as far south as Florida. The answer may lie in the translation of Old Norse, because the words for "vine" and "pasture" are very similar. Still, the Saga specifically mentions "clusters of grapes." Perhaps the Vikings had encountered a form of wild berry that resembled the grapes Tyrkir Fosterer remembered seeing in Germany.

Whatever the explanation, for Leif the name Vinland had a fine ring to it. Very much the son of Erik the Red—the man who had described the inhospitable and icy landmass he discovered as "Greenland" to entice settlers—by referring to Vinland, Leif hoped to encourage fresh waves of explorers to return and develop a settlement.

Leif sailed to Greenland the following summer, but his plans for a second expedition to Vinland were dashed when his father died soon after his arrival. Obliged to remain behind and manage Erik's estates, Leif Eriksson had to leave it to others to take advantage of the new continent that he had discovered.

Above: Viking ships were very seaworthy, but open to all the elements. They were also uncomfortable in the poor weather of the Labrador Sea.

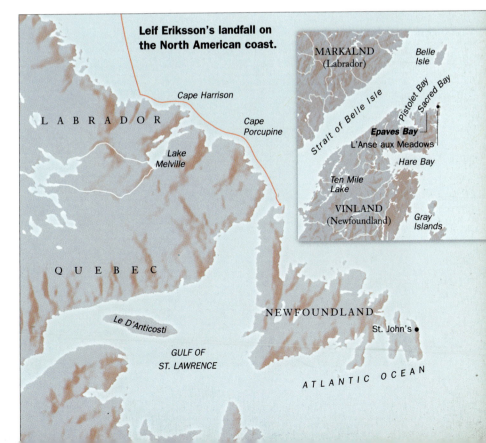

Leif Eriksson's landfall on the North American coast.

Viking Settlement in America

Following the discovery of America in 1001, attempts were made to explore further down the coast of Vinland, and to establish settlements on its shores. Unlike the Vikings who had populated Iceland and Greenland, these settlers had to contend with natives unwilling to concede their land to invaders.

Below:
A reconstruction of the Newfoundland settlement of *Leifsbudir* at L'Anse aux Meadows, founded by Leif Eriksson.

L eif Eriksson was unable to return to Vinland, so his younger brother Thorvald Eriksson made the voyage. He reached the site of Leif's earlier camp (known as *Leifsbudir*— Leif's settlement) and settled there for the winter of 1002–3. The explorers lived on the rich stocks of salmon in the local waters, and spent the following year exploring the local coastline. A second winter was spent in the camp before Thorvald pushed on to the south. His vessel was damaged during the voyage, but the local timber proved adequate to make the repair.

As Thorvald sailed south, he spotted three small craft pulled up on a beach, with men sleeping beneath them. The Vikings waded ashore and killed all of them except one, who escaped into the woods. This was the first contact between Vikings and North American Indians, probably Inuit (Eskimos) or Algonquin Indians. The survivor duly returned with reinforcements, and the Vikings were forced to retreat to their ship. An arrow pierced the *knorr*'s side and struck Thorvald in the armpit. The Vikings retired to the north, but the wound proved fatal, and they buried Erik the Red's son on the shoreline where they had earlier repaired their keel. The expedition then returned to the winter camp. The following summer the party returned to Greenland.

Preparing to return

Next, Erik the Red's youngest son Thorstein attempted to recover the body of his brother, but storms prevented him from reaching Vinland. It was not until 1009 that the Vikings returned, this time under the command of the Icelander,

Thorfinn Karlsefni (meaning "the valiant"). In the intervening years Thorstein died of a fever, and Thorfinn married his widow, so becoming part of the ruling elite of Greenland. Thorfinn's expedition was one of settlement. It comprised 250 men, women, and children, as well as their livestock and possessions. Leif Eriksson's old winter camp was expanded, and during that first winter, early in 1010, Thorfinn's wife Gudrid gave birth to a son, Snorri—the first European to be born in America.

After a harsh winter they ventured south to a landlocked bay they named Hóp, where they traded with the local inhabitants. The Vikings called the native people they encountered Skraelings, a derogatory term for a race they described as "filthy creatures, with ugly hair on their heads, big eyes and broad cheeks." At first, trade between the two peoples went smoothly, but the Indians coveted the Vikings' swords, realizing that they were far superior to their own weapons. When an Indian was killed trying to steal one, a battle broke out, and the Vikings found themselves in a fight for their lives against superior numbers.

They were saved by the antics of Freydis, an illegitimate daughter of Erik the Red, whom the Indians regarded as a warrior-goddess, and the Vikings retired to their settlement. Although the colony remained on American soil for another two winters, the near-constant threat of attack by the Skraelings wore down the settlers' resolve. As the Sagas record:

"It now seems plain that though the quality of the land was admirable, there would always be fear and strife dogging them on account of those who already inhabited the land."

The natives had proved more than a match for the Vikings. The settlers never returned, and Leif Eriksson's land would be all but forgotten until 1497, when John Cabot sailed along the Newfoundland coast.

To this day, scholars and historians are divided over the exact location of the Viking discoveries in America. Some place their colony as far south as New York's upper bay, while others place it on Cape Cod or Narragansett Bay, despite the fact that the remains of the Viking-era buildings discovered and excavated at L'Anse aux Meadows, sit in a location that

The exploration of Markland and Vinland by Leif and Thorvald Eriksson, and Thorfinn Karlsefni, between 1000 and 1009.

main route to Vinland (Leif, Thorvald, Karlsefni)

northwest route of Thorvald and Karlsefni

Thorvald's southerly route

Karlsefni's southerly route

Algonquin Indian settlement

Inuit (Eskimo) settlement

fits almost exactly with Leif Eriksson's description of the place. These buildings appear to have been constructed using two sods of earth, with gravel sandwiched between them. The dwellings would have been uncomfortable yet warm, and easily renovated and expanded on subsequent winters.

To the Middle Sea

Not all Viking exploration was to the north and west. Apart from the traders and explorers who ventured southward along the rivers of Russia, other Vikings sailed south from Britain and Ireland, exploring the Frankish coast as far as Spain, then continued through the Straits of Gibraltar into the Mediterranean Sea to explore the shores of North Africa.

Below: Replica of an original Viking casket. The frame is of gilded bronze and the inset panels are of carved ivory. While Viking jewelsmiths had plenty of local ivory for objects like this, it was the plunder from raids on wealthy cities of the Mediterranean that provided much of the gold used in decoration.

Bjorn Ragnarsson Ironside, son of King Ragnar Lodbrok of Denmark, was one of the principal Viking raiders who terrorized the Western Frankish coastline during the mid-ninth century. His bases on the island of Oisell (probably in the Schelde estuary) were besieged at various times by the Franks under Charles the Bald, then by Viking mercenaries in Frankish pay, led by a chieftain called Weland. Bjorn's base lacked the provisions to withstand a long siege, so he paid Weland Danegeld to leave him alone.

By about 858, Bjorn was free to conduct his own expedition. Spurning the crowded waters of the Seine and the Loire, the Danish prince led his men further south, crossing the Bay of Biscay to reach the northern coast of Spain. Together with his Viking ally Hastein, he had 632 ships at his command, which meant his force may have been as many as 6,500 men.

These Vikings had all heard tales of the Middle Sea (Mediterranean), and the rumored wealth of its shipping and coastal ports was a temptation no Viking could ignore.

The fleet continued around the Atlantic coast of the Iberian peninsula to the mouth of the Guadalquivir, which was in Moorish territory. According to Moorish accounts, the raiders rowed upriver as far as Seville, but found the city too well defended to attack. However, they must have met with some success because two isolated Viking ships were captured off the Spanish coast, laden with gold, silver, and captives, destined for the slave markets of northern Europe. In this case it was the Vikings who were sold, in the markets of Moorish Spain and North Africa. The main Viking fleet under Bjorn's command continued on to the Straits of Gibraltar and, after plundering the Moorish port of Algeciras in the shadow of the great rock, they continued on into the Mediterranean Sea.

The Vikings' passage went uncontested and the fleet sailed south to the North African coast, where at Cabo Tres Forcas (probably Ceuta) they landed and defeated the forces of the local Moorish governor. The Vikings spent a week there, rounding up prisoners, and the Sagas recall the novelty of encountering negroes for the first time, who were duly shipped to Ireland to be sold into slavery.

Bjorn crossed to the north and cruised up the Spanish coast as far as Murcia, looting any settlement or town encountered. The Danish fleet then headed east to the Balearic Islands, which were thoroughly pillaged, before heading northward to the southern Frankish coast. Narbonne was sacked, and the Vikings eventually reached the Rhône, where they established a winter camp in the Camargue region. The camp also provided a haven for raids upriver as far as Arles, and by the spring Viking raiders had penetrated as far as Nîmes before Frankish resistance stiffened, and they were forced to retreat.

Rome saved from pillage

Retiring to their ships and plunder, they sailed east along the Ligurian coast and, probably in the summer of 860, sacked Pisa, before moving on to Luna (Livorno), which Hastein mistook for Rome because of its magnificence. The Vikings gained entry by trickery (*see page 123*), sacked it, then massacred the male population. Laden with plunder, they returned homeward; and a relieved Rome was spared a similar fate.

In 861 Bjorn's fleet returned to Gibraltar but was met by a Moorish fleet. Outnumbered, the Vikings were defeated, and the survivors escaped north along the Spanish coast and hinterland, which they sacked as far as Pamplona. Judging their moment in the spring of 862, the Vikings evaded the Moors, circumnavigated Spain, and returned to their home waters on the Loire. Although only 20 ships survived the expedition, the plunder ensured that Bjorn and Hastein were feted for

Left: A Viking woman's brooch from the 9th century, created from the plunder of Europe.

their achievements as the most successful Vikings of their day.

Although other Vikings would sail into Mediterranean waters, this reconnaissance in force was never repeated. No subsequent Viking expedition was powerful enough to challenge Moorish naval supremacy, so the lands of the Middle Sea were spared further depredation.

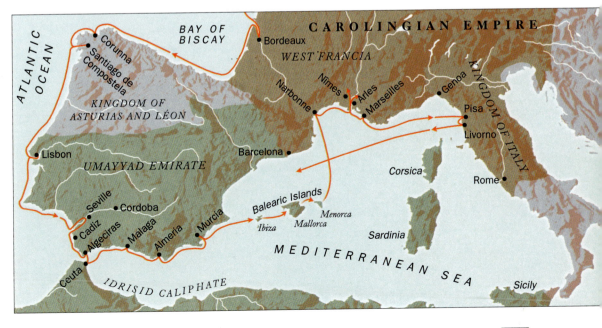

CHAPTER 7

Viking Warriors

The Viking warrior is one of the most instantly recognizable figures of the early medieval period. For over three centuries Vikings inspired fear in the hearts of their opponents, and fought across Europe, Russia, and even in the Mediterranean. They were usually well equipped, at least when fighting away from home, and most were professional soldiers, trained to use their weapons with blood-curdling efficiency.

To Vikings, warfare was a noble pursuit, and success in battle was frequently rewarded with plunder, land, and status. Even if a warrior was killed in battle, had he fought bravely, he was assured a place in Valhalla, feasting in the Hall of the Valkyries until called upon to defend the Gods in a final climactic battle of good and evil. The psychology of the warrior cult, of the *berserkir* blood lust, and of the adulation of warrior heroes in saga and verse, all served to encourage the Viking warrior to feats of valor on the battlefield, regardless of personal risk. The result was a fighter who proved one of the most fearless of his age.

But the usually independent-minded Viking warrior was also a part of a well-rehearsed team that was led by example rather than by decree. The Sagas, however, prefer to dwell on the individual's exploits and are are filled with accounts of the Vikings' skill and ferocity in war, both on land and at sea. Archaeological evidence, certainly, has revealed the brutality with which these battles of old were fought.

On the larger scale, the increasing authority of Scandinavia's monarchs led to the formation of sizeable standing armies and fleets, the organization of troop levies, and the construction of impressive fortifications. These were all signs of significant change. The Vikings had been transformed from the sea rovers of the early eighth century into line soldiers in the powerful national standing armies of the last two centuries of the Viking era. These were the forces that decided the fates of Anglo-Saxon England and Celtic Ireland, and which, in a slightly modified form, swarmed over and colonized Sicily and southern Italy, and, in 1066, returned to Britain to conquer once and for all.

A battle reaches its climax as an earl prepares for the final stand behind what is left of his protective shield wall, which surrounds the rallying point of his banner.

The Viking Way of War

Warfare in the Viking world was brutal and bloody, but it followed certain conventions. Some of theese were shared by warriors in other European cultures, while others were unique to the Vikings. They reflected a code of honor that gave them a respected reputation.

Above: The highly decorated dragon carving recovered from the Oseberg ship shows the way in which the Vikings decorated their longships to strike fear into their opponents.

In full-scale, set-piece land battles of the time, opposing armies drew up in facing lines, usually (but not exclusively) with a main central body and two smaller wings or flanks. Prominent leaders, such as kings or earls, surrounded themselves with a protective bodyguard of veterans who formed a *skjaldborg* (shieldfort) around them. The rest of the army formed a *skjaldborgr* (shieldwall) that presented an unbroken array of interlocking shields to the enemy.

The commander's standard bearer stood close to hand. Banners were the rallying point for the army, and the loss of a standard had a serious effect on the army's morale. Personal standards were also a battle's focal point when warriors of either side were dressed so alike.

Standard bearers, therefore, were hand-picked for strength, experience, and a high degree of honor. Some banners became renowned symbols of Viking prowess. For instance, a black Raven banner was used by the Danes in England in 878; another Raven banner was carried by the standard bearer of Earl of Orkney Sigurd the Stout during the Battle of Clontarf (1014). Captured by the Irish, this banner was said to flap like a raven in flight when the wind caught it. Some banners even had special names, such as Harald Hardrada's *Landeyðan* (Landwaster), or King Sverri's *Sigrflugan* (Victory fly).

Viking commanders were also accompanied by trumpeters, who transmitted signals from one battle of troops to another. Unlike the later Medieval period, Vikings did not wear identifying badges or shields, even when they fought in the personal retinue of a leader. Identification, command, and leadership all revolved around the Viking commander himself, and the visibility of his personal banner.

According to the Icelandic Sagas, before a Viking army went into battle it was customary for the Viking commander to address his men and encourage them to fight well. In the

Brutal combat

As soon as the battle was engaged, both sides attempted to break their opponent's shieldwall. If combat became more fluid, it often degenerated into a series of small mêlées between groups of protagonists, wielding axes, swords, or spears. Swords and spears were easier weapons to wield in confined spaces than a large ax, which needed clear air to be wielded with any effectiveness. This suggests that such weapons were reserved for occasions when the battlefield was less crowded, or when an enemy formation had been broken.

There was little or no finesse involved. The brutal, hacking hand-to-hand fighting continued until one side broke, usually immediately following the death of its commander, and the capture of his standard. Most casualties appear to have been caused in the final stages of a fight, when the losing side attempted escape— with their backs turned to the victors, the losers were quickly cut down.

From the archaeological excavation of battlefields such as Gate Fulford in England or Visby on the Island of Gotland, we can tell that the majority of injuries were caused by swords or ax blows, and that many of the dead were veteran fighters, in that they had received battle wounds in the past. This suggests that where large armies involving levies were concerned, the professional *hird* fought on long after their less-experienced companions had fled the field. After the battle the Vikings buried their dead where they fell, and any plunder was divided among the victors.

pre-Christian period, he would remind them that an honorable death assured them a place in Valhalla. Sometimes, encouragement was given by a skald (*see page 86*), or even by a religious figure, either a Scandinavian bishop or, in pre-Christian times, a religious leader. It was also common practice for the commander to hurl a spear toward the enemy as a symbol that the opponents were destined to die, and that their fate was in Odin's hands.

Left and below right: Typical Viking warriors of the 9th and 10th centuries. Basic clothing was a tunic over trousers, both of wool or linen. The extent of added body armor varied according to the owner's means (*see pages 120–21 for more detail*).

Left: Horns played an important part in Viking warfare, serving to pass on signals and to intimidate the enemy.

117

The Berserkir Phenomenon

In the early years of the Viking age, Scandinavian armies often included berserkir, ferocious and impetuous Viking warriors who were enraged by the heat of battle. The later Icelandic Sagas demonstrate how these men provided a significant boost to the morale of the army, and demonstrated the importance of blood-lust and psychology to the Viking warriors.

Facing: This helmet plaque matrix of the 7th-century depicts two warriors. The one on the right wears the pelt of a bear or a wolf and represents either an *ulfhednar* or a *berserkir*. The piece predates the true Viking age; later *berserkir* did not wear animal pelts. The other figure is probably an *einherjar* (which simply means "belonging to an army"). As a "champion of Odin," his helmet is ceremonial—horned helmets were never worn in the Viking era, except in depictions of gods or pagan priests.

T o the pre-Christian Vikings, their gods were a source of inspiration and solace. It was believed that both Odin and Thor had the ability to alter the course of a battle through divine intervention, and when called upon, Odin could stop an enemy javelin in mid-flight, or take the edge off an enemy sword blade. Even

more visibly, the two deities could incite the *berserkir* (bear shirts) into a psychopathic frenzy. When this happened, their blood-lust became a potent weapon on the battlefield. The appelation *berserkir* is probably derived from their admiration of the bear—an inspirational animal, that worked itself into an aggressive rage if riled. It is also the basis of the modern word "berserk."

By some now unknown means *berserkirs* spent the hours before a battle working themselves up into a frenzy. This gave them increased strength and stamina in combat, and made them shrug off non-fatal blows. According to the Sagas, *berserkir* howled like the savage animals they represented as they closed for battle. The *Haraldskvæði* of c.900 records:

Right: Berserkirs epitomized the fury of Viking warfare.

Full they were of fight, with flashing shields,
Western spearheads, and Frankish wound-blades.

Cried then, the bear pelted, Carnage they had
thoughts of,
Wailed then the wolf coated, And weapons
brandished,

Splendid spectator, Of their bloody sport,
Courage was called forth, And cloaks abandoned.

In this poem, the "bear pelted" and the "wolf coated" charged into battle together, screaming and filled with blood-lust. In the eighth century before the start of the true Viking era, records hint that *berserkir* wore animal skins as part of the ritual, from they which expected to gain some of the former animal's vitality. While most preferred the bear skin that gave the *berserkir* their name, others opted for wolf skins, and were known as *ulfhednar* (wolf coats). According to the evidence of the Sagas, the wearing of animal pelts became less common during the period, but still continued until the Christian era, albeit with individuals wearing a bear symbol rather than an entire pelt—hence the name "bear shirt."

Scholars have tried to explain the phenomenon of the *berserkir* for centuries. Some suggest that they were kept separate from the main army, a collection of the mentally unstable, the outcasts, the lepers, and the plain dangerous. Their blood-rage has been identified as a state of paranoia, a type of lycanthropy, which was either a natural state or, more probably, induced by the ingestion of a now unknown herbal drug or alcohol. In the Sagas, the *berserkir* were treated with a mixture of respect for their

prowess and dislike for their uncontrollable nature. When they are mentioned, they are often portrayed as wild hectoring villains, and shunned by the heroes of Scandinavian literature. In Icelandic law, the peacetime development of a *berserkir* rage was outlawed, and those who gave in to it were classed as petty criminals. This said, *berserkir* were assumed to possess a supernatural ability, inspired in part by Odin. According to the *Ynglinga Saga*, they went into battle:

"like mad dogs or wolves, biting their shields,
strong like bears or bulls, mowing down
everything in their path, impervious to fire and
iron."

In the *Volsunga Saga*, one *ulfhednar* fought and defeated seven opponents at the same time.

This Viking belief in his gods and their support in battle encouraged the *berserkir* phenomenon, and it also led to incredible feats on the battlefield by warriors who were unafraid of death since they were assured a place in Valhalla. Although no pre-Christian version of the Valhalla belief survives, the Sagas do suggest a Viking ethos that encouraged the seeking of death in battle rather than in bed, and the glory of a final fight at the side of companions and a Viking commander. Given these psychological incentives, it is easy to understand why the Vikings were such ferocious adversaries in battle, and why they were so successful.

Above: One of the 12th-century Hebridean Viking chessmen found at Uig, on the Isle of Lewis. Three of the figures are shown biting the top rim of their shields. This peculiarity is described in the *Ynglinga Saga* as one way in which the *berserkir* went screaming into battle.

Viking Arms and Armor

The sword was the Viking raider's principal weapon, but as Viking bands grew into larger warbands and armies, the spear grew in importance. It was a similar story with armor. Usually only professional warriors could afford a full suit of armor, so as Viking armies grew larger, the proportion of armored warriors diminished.

Viking weapons that have been recovered from grave sites are the sword, ax, spear, and bow. The typical Viking long-sword was a straight, double-edged blade made of iron and counterbalanced by a large semi-circular pommel, with the grip protected by a small straight cross-guard. Blades were usually fullered (grooved; a *fuller* is a tool blacksmiths use to make grooves in iron). Fullering increased lightness and strength as well as leaving a channel along which blood could flow (disputed by some historians).

From over 2,000 surviving examples, we can see that while the edges were sharpened, the points of the swords were quite blunt. This means that they were used to hack, not to stab. Sword finds range from the strictly functional to the highly decorative. A Norwegian variant was the long-sax, a former Saxon weapon with a single cutting edge, which was probably a weapon used primarily for hunting. Knives have also been found in Viking grave sites, and were widely used in daily life, but could also serve a purpose on the battlefield.

Spears—cheap and easy to produce— were ideally suited for arming the *leidang* (levy). Viking spears tend to have a broad blade, with cross-guards or lugs extending from the socket. This prevented them from penetrating too far into the victim's body and making it hard to recover the weapon for further use. Smaller spears with narrower blades may have been used as javelins by skirmishers, or as hunting weapons.

Axes and bows were widely used. Ax heads varied with purpose. Two-handed axes were popular among the Danes, and these broad-bladed weapons could cleave through thick armor, shields, or helmets in battle. Smaller axes serves as single-handed weapons, or even as throwing-axes. Bows were commonly formed from single staves, and were similar to those found in other Dark-Age armies.

Most Vikings possessed a helmet and shield, but not all possessed a mail shirt (hauberk). Early helmets were simple conical affairs, save the addition of a spectacle-like fixed visor. Others were formed from four segments, riveted together using bands; some had a flange to protect the wearer's nose. Almost all were made of iron, although decorative helmets in other metals have also been found. Most seem to have been simply constructed and unadorned; just domed conical helmets, without any additional form of protection. It is worth noting that the Vikings never wore the horned helmets so beloved of fiction. The image stems from several illustrations from the early Viking age, where helmets of this kind may have been used for ceremonial or religious functions, but were almost certainly not widely used, and were never worn in battle.

Vikings lose advantage

No complete Viking mail shirt survives, but fragmentary evidence suggests that they were usually thigh length, but became longer during the later Viking era. These hauberks of mail were formed from interlocking rings, in a manner similar to the well-known mail shirts used during the early Medieval period by the Normans. The Viking defeat at the Battle of Stamford Bridge (1066) was partly because Harald Hardrada's army was taken by surprise, and the *hird* were forced to fight without their mail shirts.

Sadly, no reliable archaeological examples of shields have been found. Those from the Gokstad ship-burial may well have been specially commissioned designs for use in the burial mound, but pictorial evidence suggests that round circular shields were the norm. A central metal boss protected the wood and hide shield, and the outer surface frequently appears to have been painted, either with quartered patterns of solid color or, more unusually, simple artistic devices. The long kite-shaped shield which is traditionally associated with the Normans crept into use with the Danes and the Norwegians during the last half of the 11th century.

The typical Viking raider was well armed, and knew how to handle his weapons and equipment. He was usually better trained and equipped than his opponents, but as time went on, the quality and quantity of Saxon and Frankish arms and armor improved. From the tenth century, the Viking warrior could not expect to have any advantages over his opponent other than his ferocity and skill.

Below: Archaeological evidence indicates that Viking chain mail remained unchanged between the 9th and 11th centuries. It was similar to that used all over Europe.

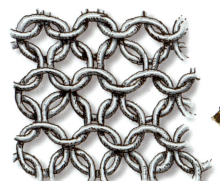

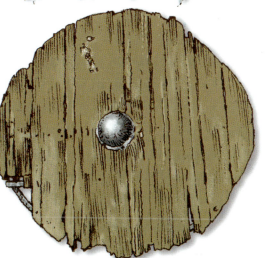

Above: This helmet with its spectacle-like fixed visor and noseguard dates from the 7th century. The elaborate eyebrow ornamentation points to its ceremonial origin, since it was found in the Vendel ship grave in Uppland, Sweden.

Facing left: This 10th-century sword shows its fullered blade (also in cross-section, enlarged). The blunt point indicates that Viking swords were slashing not stabbing weapons.

Facing right: Swedish Vikings favored a straight-bladed spear like this example made from bronze. It has a decorated silver hilt.

Left and above: Front and back views of a shield found in the Gokstad ship-burial. Approximately three feet wide, they are made from wood and bound around the edge in leather, and were originally painted either black or yellow. The metal rim and wooden ribs in the back view are modern.

Viking Battle Tactics

Vikings were typical of warriors of the age, but what set them apart from other Europeans was the dedication of the hird. These professionals developed their own battlefield tactics, which were designed to take full advantage of the ferocious reputation that the Viking soldiers inspired in their enemies.

Right: This splendid iron ax with silver wire ornamentation was found at Mammen, Jutland. Its animal decoration is in the Mammen style, to which it gave its name. The axhead is small at only 6¹/₂ inches in length, and shows slight bearding (a downward extension of the blade), which indicates it was used in close combat to slash at mail shirts. Larger axes were unsuited to close combat because of the space required for warriors to swing them in an arc to strike.

E ssentially sea raiders, the Vikings naturally relied on their ships to provide mobility, and they could attack from any river or coastal water deep enough to accommodate the shallow-draft longship. Initially, Viking raids were small but devastatingly effective. Because their victims had no warning of their coming, they were usually unable to prevent the raiders attacking, then retiring back out to sea. However, as the raids became bigger and warbands, then armies appeared, the Vikings began to display a tactical finesse that belied the notion of them as mere unorganized raiders.

Captured horses were also used to transport troops and materiel from one region to another, but the Vikings preferred to fight on foot. Fortified coastal bases served as secure centers for an army to retreat to, but the Vikings rarely fought defensive battles. Only to offset inferiority in numbers was some use of defensive fortifications made in the Danelaw and in Denmark during the later Viking age.

The Vikings enjoyed a well-deserved reputation for ferocity, and if they failed to break their opponents with a vicious attack, battles became feats of endurance and skill, in which the fittest and best trained and equipped army held the advantage. All too often in the early years, it was the Vikings who were the better warriors. The skill of the professional Viking warrior of the *hird* came through training, both in weapons skills and in battlefield tactics. Tenacious in defense and spirited in attack, Viking tactics reflected these traits of their warrior psyche.

The *skjaldborgr* (shieldwall) was a tightly-grouped array of warriors, whose shields were close enough to overlap and form a protective barrier. Picture stones from the Baltic island of Gotland, and a few depictions from grave sites,

indicate that the degree of shield overlap and the depth of the *skjaldborgr* varied with circumstance. The main feature of the formation was its presentation of a dense, unbroken line of shields, offering mutual protection to the men behind them. These formations could be used defensively, or used as a secure base from which an attack could be launched at the enemy. Clearly, catching the enemy before they formed their own shieldwall, or breaking the enemy's shieldwall, proved a decisive event on the battlefield, and usually resulted in the slaughter of the opponents.

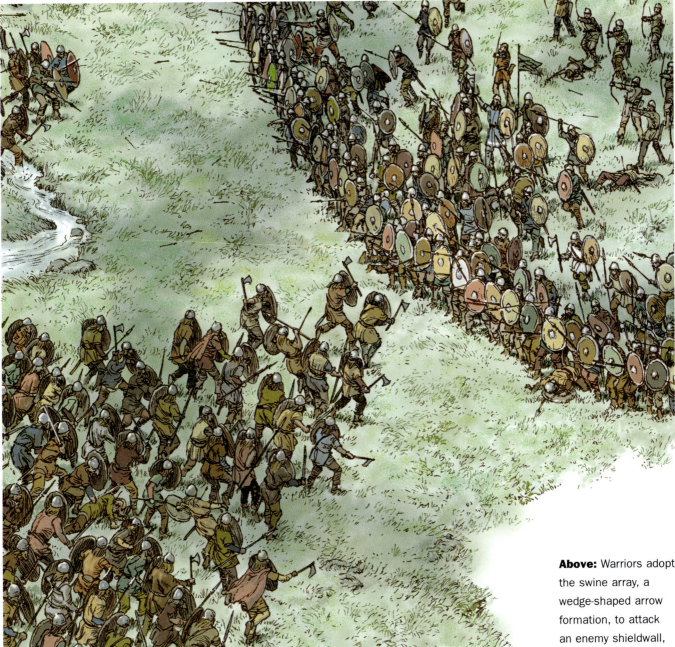

Above: Warriors adopt the swine array, a wedge-shaped arrow formation, to attack an enemy shieldwall, behind which archers aim defensive volleys at them.

Odin's arrow

At the Battle of Stamford Bridge (1066), Harald Hardrada formed a circular defensive shieldwall, supported by small groups of elite troops, whose arrow-like formations darted out from the ring's protection to disrupt the enemy. The invention of this wedge-shaped swine array, as it was known, was traditionally attributed to Odin, the God of War. A front rank of two men was followed by another rank of three, then of four and so on, creating a highly maneuverable unit that could batter its way through an enemy shieldwall using sheer momentum.

The Vikings also made use of archers, either to form skirmish screens, or arrayed behind shield walls, firing over the heads of their colleagues at the enemy formations beyond them. Skirmishing was more often limited to the opening phases of a battle—it was the brutal clash of the *skjaldborgr* that decided victory, not subtle maneuvering. However, Viking leaders were not averse to using deception. In Italy, for instance, Bjorn Ragnarsson feigned his own death to gain access to Luna (Livorno), then he and his "pall bearers" fell on the Italians while others flew false banners to confuse the enemy as to their location.

The Vikings were skilled practitioners of war, and for over two centuries, they proved more than a match for the Saxons, Celts, Franks, or Lombards who opposed them.

The Viking Army

With the popular image of the pillaging Viking raiding band leaping from their longships, it is easy to forget that in the later years large armies mustered to conquer large areas of Europe. These were the forces fielded by the kings of Denmark, Sweden, and Norway that fought for control of the Danelaw in Anglo-Saxon England and the Scandinavian "pale" in Celtic Ireland.

Below: Four swords found in Sweden, typical of the Viking period. All four have large pommels to act as a counterbalance in the tiring act of cutting rather than stabbing. The third from the left is later than the others, identified by its fullered blade.

The nucleus of any large Viking army was the *hird*, a permanent elite force raised and maintained by a king, or at least, by an important jarl, like the Earls of Orkney. The *hirdmen* (or *thingmen*) were warriors who had sworn an oath of allegiance to their master. Although this permanent force was usually composed of his national subjects, it could also include foreign mercenaries. King Olaf II of Norway maintained 60 *hirdmen* at his court in 1020, plus a personal bodyguard of 30 *huscarles* (bodyguards) and 30 *gestrs* (a lesser form of *hird*, they served as revenue collectors, or to maintain the security of the realm).

In 885, King Harald Harfagri (Fairhair) of Norway decreed that each of his subordinate earls should maintain a personal *hird* of 60 men. He should also employ a minimum of four *hersir*, a form of regional military leader, and each of these lesser nobles should maintain their own personal *hird* of at least 20 men. This meant that every earl could draw upon a minimum force of 140 professional soldiers to serve as the core around which a force of *leidang* (the levy) would be mustered. The Viking raiders who ravaged Europe at the end of the ninth century were almost all *hirdmen* in the service of local earls or lesser nobles, but they could also be gathered together for more conventional military service when required.

Farmers as warriors

The *leidang* system evolved in Denmark before the start of the Viking age in the late eighth century, and this became increasingly refined throughout the Viking period. It stipulated the number of ships and men, plus the amount of provisions that a particular region needed to supply to their ruler in time of need. This meant that the main part of any national army was composed of a levy of *bondi* (*see page 19*) or free peasants. The men of the *leidang* could be called on to form armies for invasion, defense, or even a force capable of working on the construction of fortifications. Failure to serve in the levy when called to resulted in the imposition of harsh financial penalties, or worse. On occasion a half or partial *leidang* might be mustered to avoid too much disruption to the fragile agrarian economy of the Viking realms. The full-scale muster was usually reserved for times of major crisis, such as a large-scale foreign invasion. Service lasted from two months to half a year, depending on the nature of the assignment.

This system provided for the creation of large armies or fleets. In 845, King Horik of Denmark mustered a national Viking army of 600 ships, and 50,000 men. The military resources of King Cnut during the early 11th century were even greater and, in theory, he could raise a fleet of 850 ships when he called for a full-scale mobilization. However, trained to farm rather than to fight, many levies would have been unreliable. Their service also curtailed royal revenue from taxation, so when possible, the standing army of the *hird* was relied upon to do whatever military service was called for, and the local levies called only when a battle was imminent.

The typical Viking ship carried between 60–100 men, with the average being about 75. Since vessels were listed by the number of "rooms" or oars they had, a 32-room longship would have 16 oars a side, each pulled by two men, giving a total crew of about 70 men, including the steering oarsmen, officers, and musicians. Some of the armies fielded in the

British Isles may have numbered 20,000 men, and were commanded by a string of royal princes, local rulers (both styled as "kings" in many accounts), and by a host of greater or lesser earls. Far from being a disorganized, anarchic rabble, the Viking army in the field was usually a well-ordered force of professionals and levies, able to count on the support of a ready-made fleet of superb warships.

Above: Manuscript illumination of a peasant with arrows, c.816–35, from the *Gospel of Ebbo*.

Left: During the 10th century, Viking swordsmiths began to copy the outward-curved hilt favored by English warriors. This example from the 9th century was found at Abingdon, near Oxford.

Battles in Poem and Saga

Scandinavian poetry and epic prose was often devoted to accounts of battle, and the part played in them by the heroic patrons of the skalds who recited them. These, and their enemies' poems about them, provide a unique insight into the nature of warfare during the Viking age.

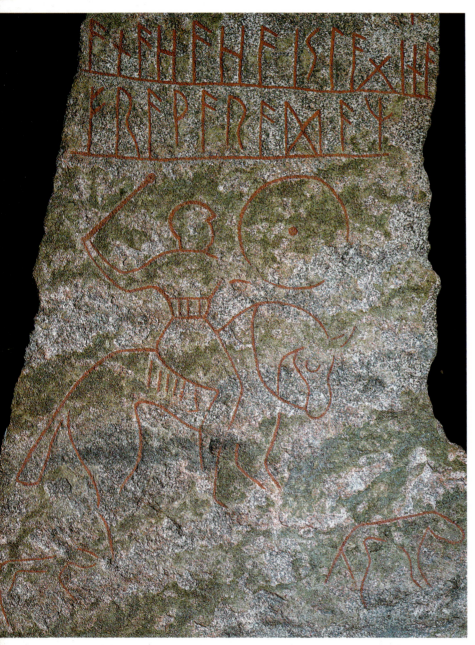

Above: An early Viking rune stone celebrates the valor of a warrior.

Facing: A painted wood carving of a longship on a door at Hedeby, Denmark.

Saxons at one end of a low-water causeway, and the Vikings at the other. The battle began with an exchange of missiles across the tidal creek:

So they stood by Panta's stream in proud array,
the ranks of the East Saxons and the host from
*   the ash-ships,*
nor might any of them harm another;
Save those through arrow-flight fell dead.

The initial Viking attack was thwarted by three Saxon champions (probably a reference to three sub-commanders), so the Vikings requested that the Saxons retire and allow them to deploy on the far side of the causeway, to fight a fair battle. Byhrtnoth assented, and the fight renewed:

Out flashed file-hard point from fist,
Sharp-ground spears rang forth,
Bows were busy, bucklers flinched,
It was a bitter battle-clash. On both halves,
Brave men fell, boys lay still…..

Byhrtnoth war-hard braced shield-board,
Shook out his sword, strode firmly,
Toward his enemy, earl to churl,
In either heart harm to the other.

The sea-man sped his southern spear,
So that it wounded the warriors' lord,
Who with his shield checked, so that the shaft
*   burst,*
Shivered the spear-head; it sprang away,
Stung then to anger he stabbed with ash point."

The poem continues to describe in detail the duel between the Viking and Saxon commanders, whose struggle became the battle's focal point. When Byhrtnoth was killed by a thrown javelin, the Saxons gave up the fight and fled. This example of a heroic duel is a common theme in Germanic and Scandinavian poetry and prose, and can be seen as an idealized version of a battle in which the two commanders inspired their men by example.

In the Viking world it was important to die well in battle, even after the old incentive of a

One of the greatest of Anglo-Saxon poems is an untitled piece dealing with the death of Byhrtnoth, Ealdorman (a Saxon earl) of Essex. It provides us with an account of the Battle of Maldon fought in 991 between Byhrtnoth and a Viking warband. The Vikings demanded Danegeld, and the Saxon leader refused, so both sides prepared for battle, the

place in Valhalla had been replaced by a place in the Christian heaven. For example, in *King Harald's Saga*, the last fight of Harald Hardrada is described by Arnor the Skald:

All King Harald's warriors,
Preferred to die beside him,
Sharing their brave king's fate,
Rather than beg for mercy.

In an age of violence and bloodshed, the Vikings preferred to view their warrior heroes as an elite worthy of emulation. Not all Viking hosts were so selfless in defeat. The account of the retreat of the Danish army following its defeat at the Battle of Ethendun (Edington), on Salisbury Plain in 878, is probably accurate, but runs contrary to the Viking idea of seeking honor in battle. It is a reminder that we should not take everything the Skalds wrote at face value, but rather see it as part of a warrior cult that represented an ideal to be emulated rather than an accurate reflection of Viking warfare.

Upon the Salisbury Plain face to face,
Englishmen eager for home's defense,
Shieldwalls woven in tight protection,
Guthorm's warriors calling to Odin.

The gods of war council the Vikings,
Each man must be valiant,
After death, talk recalls deeds,
And the Valkyries gather valiant men.

Warriors fight fearlessly and strongly,
Before the blade bites his skull,
Little is lost for men who fight well,
And fight again another day.

Guthorm's men fought fiercely, far from their
   home,
But they did not see Odin's favor that day,
Back in Chippenham, weary behind its walls,
But little is the loss, for men who fight well.

They wielded their weapons.
And Guthorm turned his warriors away,
To fight again another day,
Yet Odin gave him fickle fortune.

Guthorm's Army at Ethendun
(Anglo-Saxon poem).

Battles at Sea

With a long tradition of navigation and with a reputation for ferocity, it is no surprise that the Vikings were as happy fighting battles at sea as they were on land. An examination of the accounts of these sea battles reveals a lot about how the Vikings fought, on land or sea.

Viking sea battles are best recounted in the Icelandic Sagas. They indicate that for the Vikings, warfare at sea was fought in a similar way to that on land. Although the tactics were different the objectives were the same— and the consequences of failure usually greater. The Vikings rowed into battle, but unlike the war galleys of the ancient world, the longships themselves were rarely used as weapons, and were not used to ram opponents. Instead, battles at sea involved a long-range exchange of missile fire (usually arrows), followed by brutal hand-to-hand combat, as the two fleets closed and the battle raged over either side's decks.

Sometimes, several ships were lashed together to form a giant (and largely unmaneuverable) fighting platform. When this was done, it was the vulnerable ships on the flanks of the raft that the enemy attacked. The usual Viking tactic appears to have been to send the largest ships into combat first. Then smaller craft came alongside their own longships and fed their crews into the fight. The kings or earls in command of a fleet took a place of prominence in the battle line as a matter of honor, so inevitably, their ships became the focal point in the subsequent fighting.

The *Heimskringla Saga* contains a superb account of a sea battle, fought in 1044 between King Magnus of Norway and Denmark and Jarl Swend, a rival claimant to the throne at Århus off Denmark's Jutland peninsula. Before the fight, Jarl Swend lashed his ships together to form a large fighting platform. King Magnus then readied his men for the attack:

They fought at the bows, so that only the men on the bows could strike; the men on the forecastle thrust with spears and all who were further off shot with light spears or javelins or war arrows. Some fought with stones or short stakes, and those who were abaft the mast shot with the bow. The battle was hot with casting weapons. King Magnus stood at the beginning of the battle within a shield rampart, but as it appeared to him that

Three Viking longships, lashed together to make a fighting platform, are boarded in a two-pronged enemy attack.

matters were going too slowly, he leaped over the shields and rushed forward in the ship, encouraging his men with a loud cheer and springing to the bows where the battle was going on hand to hand. When his men saw this they urged each other on with mutual cheering, and there was one great hurrah through all the ships. Now the battle was exceedingly sharp, and in the assault Swend's ship was cleared of all forecastle men on both sides of the forecastle. Then Magnus boarded Swend's ship followed by his men, and one after the other came up and made so stout an assault that Swend's men gave way, and King Magnus cleared first that ship and then the rest, one after the other. Swend fled with a great part of his people, and many fell, and many got life and peace. There were seven prizes as a result of the battle.

This battle was a brutal slogging match, with Viking warriors fighting from ship to ship, hacking their way from one end of a longship to the other, then moving on to clear the next vessel. This form of combat was similar to the assaults of the swine array formations on land,

but defensive *skjaldborgr* tactics could also be employed. According to *Heimskringla*, at the Battle of Nissa (1062) fought between King Harald Hardrada of Norway and King Sweyn of Denmark, on Harald's flagship:

> The ring of shields seemed to enclose,
> the ship's deck from the boarding foes.
> The Dragonship on the Nissa's flood,
> Beset with men who thickly stood,
> Shield touching shield, was something rare,
> That seemed all force of men to dare.

Harald's men held off the assaults of the Danes, then counterattacked and won the day. The brutality of a Viking sea battle is shown by its aftermath, as Harald searched through heaps of dead Vikings on his enemy's flagship before he found the body of his rival monarch.

Viking fortifications

Early Vikings had little time for fortifications. Instead they relied on maritime mobility to ensure victory. Later, wintering in foreign parts, they started to build temporary defensive camps. Finally, as the rulers of conquered territories or faced with national invasion at home, they built elaborate defenses as symbols of royal power and regional domination.

E arly Viking fortifications were temporary, designed to provide safe winter havens for a Viking warband and its ships. Such camps were preferably located on islands, or in riverine or coastal areas on higher ground surrounded by marsh or mudflats. The natural barriers provided some degree of security, but the camps also needed to be close enough to the water for the Vikings to haul their boats up to protect them from winter storms.

A simple earthen ditch and palisade provided a secure perimeter, while temporary huts made of earth sods, canvas, or timber gave the warriors protection from the elements.

Little trace remains of any winter camps, but the remains of defensive walls can be found on the coastlines and estuaries of Ireland, Scotland, Normandy, and English East Anglia. In both Scandinavia and Britain, the remains of older pre-Viking fortifications, such as hill or promontory forts, were pressed into service, and there is evidence that the Vikings took advantage of sites such as Burghead in Scotland, or Gråborg in Sweden.

Following the initial wave of conquests in England during the ninth century, the Danes found themselves confronted by an increasingly

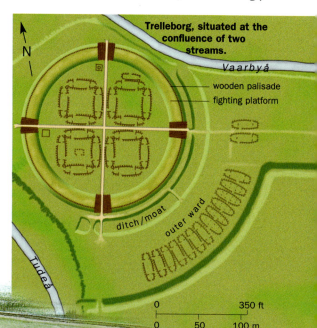

Trelleborg, situated at the confluence of two streams.

Vaarbyå

— wooden palisade
— fighting platform

ditch/moat

outer ward

Tudeå

0		350 ft
0	50	100 m

Above: The stone walls of Scarborough Castle in Yorkshire, northern England. The Vikings used the site as a fortified base long before the 11th century, when it was turned into a more permanent fortification.

militaristic Anglo-Saxon state. A network of Saxon fortifications discouraged further Viking forays into English territory (*see pages 70–71*), and served as bases for attacks into the Viking Danelaw. According to the English contemporary chronicle *Burghal Hideage*, these Anglo-Saxon fortifications were built every 20 miles or so, usually where an existing town or settlement provided some degree of infrastructure for supply, trade and recruitment. Clearly this form of defensive network influenced the Danes, because similar fortifications began to appear in the Danelaw, and even more imposing fortifications were constructed by order of the Danish crown. While the Saxons sometimes constructed fortified lines, such as Offa's Dyke, only one such defensive line exists in Scandinavia, the Danevirke near Hedeby in Denmark, marking the southern boundary of the Danish state.

Danish great camps

In Scandinavia, few settlements were fortified, even the great and burgeoning marketplaces of the middle and late Viking period were poorly defended, usually with the most basic earthen bank, ditch, and palisade. There were a few exceptions, most notably Hedeby and Birka, where a large citadel dominated the town itself, and the surrounding walls were interspersed with watchtowers. In times of crisis, fortified settlements provided a haven for the inhabitants of the surrounding area, replacing the use of old fortified encampments which had provided refuge

for local communities before the Viking age.

The most impressive fortifications in the Viking world are the Danish military camps at Trelleborg, Nonnebakken, Aggersborg, and Fyrkat; circular fortifications laid out with an almost Roman precision during the late ninth century. Simpler and less permanent forts were constructed in the Danelaw, but little or no trace of these survives. The development of these Scandinavian fortifications have been linked to the reigns of King Sweyn Forkbeard and King Cnut, and represent a visible manifestation of royal military power.

They served as training camps for the newly reorganized Danish standing *hird*, and warriors trained in these centers would have seen service in the campaign of conquest and re-conquest in England during the late ninth and early tenth centuries. The Trelleborg forts all conformed to a similar pattern. A circular wooden palisade and wide earthen fighting platform surrounded the fort, sited on the top of a steep bank, while a moat surrounded this perimeter. Inside, buildings were arranged in four groups of four, forming the sides of a small internal courtyard, which probably served as a drill ground. Each square of buildings was sited in one of the four quadrants of the fort, and these were separated by roadways leading to four gates. These forts would have dominated the region in which they were built, and would have played a major part in the imposition of royal power in Denmark at a time when the country was emerging as a nation-state in its own right.

Facing: This reconstruction of Trelleborg military camp shows the four groups of four barracks at the camp's center. Each barracks is about 98 feet long and housed 40–50 men. The 15 houses in the outer ward are slightly shorter. The diameter within the protective ramp is 446 feet. Trelleborg is one of four similar camps, including Fyrkat (*see picture, page 150*).

Northern Europe, c.1000

- Norway and sphere of Norse influence
- Denmark and sphere of Danish influence
- Sweden and sphere of Swedish influence
- sphere of Rus influence
- Frankish kingdoms

A potent symbol of Viking history in Orkney, the Maeshowe Dragon (below) was carved by one of the Norsemen who broke into the prehistoric howe (grave) in the hope of finding valuable grave goods to steal.

Originally under Norwegian control, the Faroes now belong to Denmark.

ICELAND
Rejkjavík

FAROES

ATLANTIC OCEAN

NORWEGIAN SEA

NORWAY

Kaupang

SWEDEN

Sigtu
Birk

Shetland Islands

ORKNEY
Kirkwall

Hebrides

Ullapool

Burghead

SCOTLAND

Scone

Dumbarton

NORTH SEA

DENMARK
Jutland
Skåne

Kalmar

Öland

Jelling
Ribe
Roskilde
Lund

Bornholm

Larne

IRELAND

IRISH SEA

Dublin

Limerick

Jarrow Wearmouth

Whitby

York

DANELAW

Chester

Hedeby

BALTIC SEA

Pavi

Waterford
Cork
Wexford

WESSEX

Winchester London

Canterbury

Wolin

Pomeranians

ENGLISH CHANNEL

Dorestad

Hamburg
Bremen

Weser

Cologne

Poles

BRITTANY

Bayeux

NORMANDY
Rouen

Reims

Paris

WEST FRANKISH KINGDOM

Orléans

Scheide

Rhine

Meuse

Mainz

Frankfurt

Main

EAST FRANKISH KINGDOM

Rhine

Danube

Elbe

Oder

Bohemians

Nantes

132

CHAPTER 8

A Scandinavian Empire

Map labels:
GULF OF BOTHNIA
Staraja Ladoga
GULF OF FINLAND
Novgorod
Izborsk • Pskov
otland
Grobin •
Balts
Neman
Rus
Gnezdovo •
Prus
Elbing
ula
Slovaks

allies of the Orkney Earls. The growing importance of trade, and the economic and cultural influence of the Scandinavian homelands over these overseas provinces influenced this complex political situation.

In Scandinavia, as the Norwegians, Swedes, and Danes struggled with the problems of increasing royal authority and the spread of the Christian religion, the Scandinavian kings found themselves increasingly embroiled in affairs in the British Isles. Although none of these monarchs yet realized it, part of what they were fighting for was the continued dominance of Scandinavia in the economic and cultural development of northern Europe. The ultimate failure of these rulers to impose their military and political will in Anglo-Saxon England paved the way for a change in the cultural axis of the continent, and its new masters would be the 11th-century Norman French—themselves descended from Viking settlers of the previous century.

In the late 11th century, three centuries of Viking involvement in northern European affairs reached a crucial juncture, as three contenders vied for the throne of England. All the rivals had Scandinavian ancestry, but only one of the three was pure Scandinavian. The defeat of Harald Hardrada in 1066 marked the end of the Vikings in England, although Norse enclaves remained in the north of Scotland, where the once-powerful Earls of Orkney retained their lands if not their influence. Almost overnight the political landscape of Europe was changed, and with it came the end of the Viking age, and the emergence of a feudal Europe whose cultural heart was France rather than Denmark, Norway, or Sweden.

C onquests of the ninth century had created a series of Viking kingdoms in Britain, Ireland, and France, which relied on each other for trade and mutual defense, and maintained trade links with Scandinavia. Although rivalry between the Norwegians and the Danes hindered the political unity of the overseas Scandinavian possessions, the political development and ultimate survival of these provinces was intertwined. Norse-Irish from Dublin allied themselves with the Earls of Orkney, the Norse and Anglo-Saxons formed alliances against the Danes in England, and the Anglo-Saxons campaigned against the Scottish

The North Sea Axis

At no other period in history did the North Sea play such an important role in Europe's development. It was the Vikings' highway to the pillage of Britain, then the means of colonization and commerce, and finally the channel for Scandinavian rule—a cultural and economic exchange that transformed northern Europe.

Sailors know the North Sea as one of the most changeable and dangerous bodies of water in the world. It is prone to storms even in mid-summer, and acts as a meteorological funnel for the weather fronts of both the

For the more southerly placed Danes, their natural route lay along the Frisian coast, past the Frisian Islands and the Rhine and Schelde estuaries to the Thames estuary. Throughout the Viking age, these were the two principal routes linking Britain to Scandinavia, routes dictated more by wind, current, and weather than by political or military decision.

Once in Britain, the Viking Danelaw was easier to control from Denmark than the Earldom of Orkney was from Norway due to the problems inherent in organizing large-scale North Sea voyages across the more exposed

Above: These three 9th-century silver coins depicting Viking longships were found in the market-place at Birka, Sweden. However, they were most likely minted in Hedeby, Denmark.

Atlantic and the Arctic. While its predominant currents run north to south, the winds change with an unpredictable randomness, depending on the weather fronts generated in North America and the Atlantic and Arctic Oceans. It is prone to just about every type of weather condition, yet to the Vikings of the late eighth century, the North Sea was a friend; the uncontested route to wealth and land that was unavailable in Scandinavia.

Following the establishment of Viking settlements in the northern isles of Scotland and the first Viking raids into Britain and Ireland, a pattern of North Sea travel emerged. For the Norse the optimum route was to cross from the western coast of Norway between Bergen and Stavanger to the Shetland or Orkney Islands. From here, the route continued on south via the Hebrides to Ireland and ultimately the French Atlantic coast.

northern route. Consequently, the Earldom became a semi-independent fiefdom which controlled Norwegian access to Britain, Ireland, and France. By contrast the Danelaw remained closer ties to its Danish homeland, and the safer coastal voyage encouraged a greater amount of migration than was the case in the north, where Norwegian settlers faced a more grueling crossing.

Medieval colonial powers

The control of these sea routes was vital to the development of the Scandinavian colonies "west over the sea," as they called the islands across the North Sea. When the Anglo-Saxons re-conquered the Thames estuary and much of the East-Anglian coast, they were in a position to threaten the maritime links between Denmark and the Danelaw. York's economic importance declined as a result. Nevertheless,

Viking traders continued to dominate the routes across the North Sea, Irish Sea, and English Channel throughout most of the period, even in the face of an effective Anglo-Saxon navy in the ninth century.

The same ships that transported commodities also transported colonists. As growing numbers of Scandinavians settled in Britain, Ireland, and France, these regions became even more closely linked to the Scandinavian kingdoms. Therefore, for much of this period, the axis of European politics spanned the North Sea from east to west. It was only after the Norman conquest of England in 1066 that this axis shifted across the English Channel, and became a north-south one. The failure of Scandinavian kings and warlords such as Erik Bloodax, Olaf Tryggvasson, King Cnut, King Sweyn, and Harald Hardrada lay in the fact that they failed to consolidate the North Sea axis. As a result they predicated the collapse of Scandinavian political aspirations, and of the empire "west over the sea" in 1066.

Because Viking cultural development was directly linked to the control of all North Sea coasts, this collective failure also brought about the end of the Viking era. Deprived of a North Sea avenue of expansion, the vitality of the Viking age withered within a matter of decades, and the new nation states of Scandinavia became limited to the Baltic arena. It is a matter of speculation how the political landscape of Europe may have looked if the North Sea axis had survived the events of 1066.

Below: The Viking ruins at Jarlshof in the Shetland Islands.

The Earls of Orkney

Vikings first arrived in the Orkney and the Shetland Islands shortly before the end of the eighth century; settlers followed. Within a century the islands were under direct Norse control, governed by the Earls of Orkney on behalf of the Norwegian crown. The earldom extended south and west to encompass much of the fringes of Scotland, and at times its influence would be felt as far south as York and Dublin.

Facing: St. Magnus Cathedral in Kirkwall, Orkney is one of the finest examples of late Viking age architecture. Work started on the structure in 1137. Its combination of Scandinavian and Norman architectural elements reflect the hiring of Anglo-Norman builders during its construction.

When the first Vikings arrived in the Orkney and Shetland Islands, they encountered a peaceable and fertile haven with a well-developed agrarian economy. Archaeological evidence suggests that while some Pictish farms were taken over by Scandinavian settlers during the early ninth century, the bulk of the island population was assimilated into what became a Norse province. The primary source chronicling the development of the islands under Norse rule comes from the *Orkneyinga Saga*, a chronicle of the Orkney Earldom written in Iceland during the 14th century.

In 872, when King Harald Harfagri (Fairhair) became the sole ruler of Norway, refugees fled his rule to Orkney and Shetland, from where they made attacks on the King's realm. The islands had been a haven for Viking sea rovers since the start of the century, but they had avoided the political interest of the Norwegian crown. Now Rögnvald, Earl of Moeri arrived in Orkney on King Harald's behalf, and subjugated the islands, including the Hebrides. Harald granted him Orkney and Shetland, but he chose to return to Norway and instead handed the islands to his brother Sigurd, who became the first Earl of Orkney.

Earl Sigurd promptly expanded his realm by conquering the Pictish territories of northern Scotland and, on his death, his successor Earl Thorstein the Red consolidated these conquests. It is worth noting that when Rögnvald heard of his brother's death, he sent his son to govern Orkney. However, the young Hallad Rögnvaldsson returned home after a year, claiming that the islands were infested with rowdy Vikings, and were ungovernable. The islands were still a lawless place, and as the Saga relates, "In harvest, winter, and spring, the Vikings cruised about the Isles."

Consolidating direct rule

It was only in 895 that Einar, the illegitimate son of Earl Rognvald, pacified the islands and cleared them of the lawless Viking brigands. From that point on, the islands remained firmly in the hands of the Earls of Orkney. The *Heimskringla* claims that Earl Turf Einar "was ugly, and blind of an eye, yet sharp-sighted nonetheless." He defeated an invasion attempt by the Norwegian prince Hálfdan Highleg, who had already killed Earl Rögnvald back in Norway. Hálfdan was duly captured and had his lungs ripped out by way of revenge, as a sacrifice to Odin.

The earldom passed to his sons on Einar's death, most notorious of whom was Thorfinn Skull-splitter. The dynasty ruled until the death of Einar's great grandson, Earl Sigurd the Stout, at the Battle of Clontarf in 1014. The succession was often far from easy, but on the whole the Earldom remained peaceful, and the islands prospered. Sigurd the Stout converted to Christianity in order to marry the daughter of Malcolm II of Scotland. On his death, the earldom was passed around by his children until it devolved into the hands of Thorfinn Sigurdsson, a Norse grandson of the Scottish king. On his death in 1064, Orkney was divided between his sons, Paul and Erlend.

This division resulted in further dramatic rivalry between their offspring, Earl Haakon Paulsson and Earl Magnus Erlendsson. The murder of Magnus by Haakon on the Orkney island of Egilsay in 1115 led to the construction of Kirkwall's St. Magnus Cathedral by a penitent Earl and the canonization of Magnus as a Christian martyr in 1135.

But by this stage, the great age of the Vikings was past, and the Earldom of Orkney was fast becoming a political and military backwater. The might of the earldom had been broken following the defeat of Harald Hardrada by King Harold Godwinsson of England in 1066. Although the islands remained in Norse hands until 1214 (and were ruled by Scottish earls on behalf of the Norwegian crown for another two and a half centuries), the heyday of Orkney as a force on the European stage had passed.

Facing: The Old Man of Hoy, Orkney.

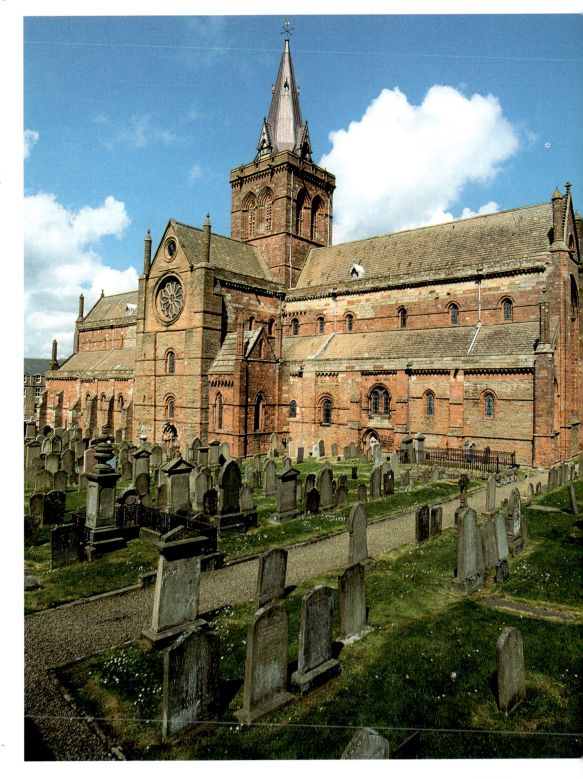

Viking Scotland

Within decades of the first Viking raid of 795 on Iona, Scandinavian settlers had become a major political power in Celtic Scotland. The Vikings were to remain a potent force in the north of Britain long after the abandonment of Scandinavian colonial ambitions elsewhere in the British Isles.

Below: Some of the farmhouses in the Shetland Islands are still based on Viking architecture. In this example, the functional structure of the Viking longhouse is evident.

T he raid on Iona in 795 was followed by others: in the Hebrides in 798; a second raid on Iona seven years after the first; then again in 806, when the population of 68 monks were put to the sword. As late as 825 the monastery was still under attack, and the monk Blathmac was killed for refusing to reveal the hiding place of the reliquary containing the bones of St. Columba. To the east along Scotland's North Sea coast, the Picts were locked in a cultural struggle for survival with the Scots to the west, and the final assimilation of the old Pictish kingdoms into a new Scottish state may well have been encouraged by the Viking depredations. No part of Scotland was more affected by the arrival of the Vikings than the islands lying to the north and west, as the first raiders were followed by Norse settlers. By 800 Orkney and Shetland were firmly under Norse control, and within a decade the suzerainty of the Orkneys extended onto the mainland south into Caithness and Sutherland, and west through the Inner and Outer Hebrides.

Following the union of the Picts and the Scots in 841, the Norse consolidated their hold on their Scottish possessions, although they continued to interfere in Scottish politics. The Norse-Irish King Olaf of Dublin campaigned in central Scotland in the 860s. Viking attacks on the stronghold of Dumbarton Rock in the Firth of Clyde (870) and on the religious community of Dunkeld in central Scotland (903) were only the most prominent of a series of incursions designed to secure plunder and slaves.

This interference continued into the tenth century, with Norse or Norse-Irish contingents supporting Scottish kings or rival claimants, as political necessity dictated.

During the reign of Malcolm I (r.943–54), a Norse-Irish army fought the Saxons on behalf of the Scottish king, and was defeated. In the reign of Kenneth II (r.971–95), a Danish invasion of eastern Scotland was repulsed, and his descendant Malcolm II (r.1005–34) married his daughter to Earl Sigurd the Stout of Orkney to secure his northern borders. Although local Scottish and Norse nobles fought each other for control of the borderlands in the Highlands and Islands, the Scots and the Norse co-existed in relative harmony throughout these centuries.

Waning influence

In 1014, when Sigurd the Stout was killed during the Battle of Clontarf, his lands were divided between his Norse-Scots offspring to ensure the continued alliance between earldom and kingdom. Next, an alliance between the Earl of Orkney and the Mormaer (Earl) Macbeth of Moray led to the seizure of the Scottish throne by the Scottish nobleman, supported by Norse swords. The accession of Malcolm III Canmore (r.1058–93) to the Scottish throne ushered in a period of stability for the kingdom. As the military muscle of the Orkney earls waned in tandem with the islands' economy, the threat of further Viking involvement in Scottish affairs diminished.

Although largely abandoned by Norway, the island fringes of Scotland continued in their largely autonomous way, and it was not until the mid-13th century that Norse influence in Scotland came to a complete end. A largely unsuccessful and costly punitive expedition led by Haakon IV of Norway against the Scots ended in the indecisive Battle of Largs in 1263. The disillusioned king died in Orkney on his return home and, virtually bankrupt, the Norwegian crown decided that the islands were not worth keeping. The Hebrides were duly sold to the Scottish crown in 1266. Although Orkney and Shetland remained Norse until the late 1460s, the islands became little more than economic and political backwaters. The days of Viking Scotland had passed, and the Scots were free to devote their attention to their more dangerous neighbor to the south.

The Norse-Irish

Up until the ninth century, the Norse remained firmly established in Ireland, and it looked as though the complete subjugation of the island was merely a matter of time. Yet within a few years an Irish counter-attack all but evicted the Vikings from Ireland, although an enclave remained in and around Dublin until its gradual assimilation by the Irish during the 11th century.

A Viking cemetery discovered to the west of Dublin and dated to the mid-ninth century provides some indication that by the 840s the Norse were feeling relatively secure in Ireland. This all changed in 848, when (as the Frankish Annals record), "…the Irish attacked the Northmen, won a victory with the aid of our Lord Jesus Christ, and drove them out of their land." The tables had turned, and after a half-century of domination, the Vikings in Ireland were on the defensive.

The following year, the Irish, united under the Uí Néills, attacked Viking Dublin. Two years later, the arrival of a Danish fleet placed the Norse in Ireland in even greater peril. However, the Norse repulsed the threat, and the Danes withdrew in the following year for easier pickings in the Western Frankish Kingdom. Irish and Danes were not the only problem for the small Dublin enclave. A large Norse fleet also appeared in the Irish Sea and tried—unsuccessfully—to force their authority over the existing Norsemen in Ireland.

The brief period of Irish unity under the Uí Néills passed, and from 850 onward, local Irish chieftains forged alliances with the Norse, and the two peoples traded, intermingled, and lived in relative harmony. In 853, Amlaíb arrived from the Hebrides and was acknowledged as overlord of the Norse-Irish, ushering in two decades of lucrative raids into Scotland from Viking bases in and around Dublin. While Viking raids continued elsewhere in Ireland, and Irish resistance duly stiffened, the Norse (or Danish) enclaves around Lough Foyle, Cork, and Limerick were overrun. The Norse-Irish around Dublin became increasingly divided by dynastic squabbles and, in 902, the city was captured by the Irish, and the Vikings expelled.

Centuries-long struggle

The Danes returned in 914. From his base at Waterford, the Danish warlord Ragnall conquered Northumbria (918), while his lieutenant Sitric recaptured Dublin from the Uí Néills. Sitric, followed by his kinsman Godfrid, ruled a mixed Norse-Danish Viking province from 918 until 941, during which period the political development of the Norse-Irish enclave became closely linked to events in England and the Danelaw.

The great Anglo-Saxon victory at Brunanburgh (937) prompted a general Irish rising. Over the next decade, Norse and Irish fortunes swung both ways, and Dublin suffered

Facing: Surrounded by an embankment topped by a timber palisade, 10th-century Viking Dublin was home to a population of about 10,000. Situated at the confluence of the River Poddle and the estuary of the River Liffey, the town was a major trading port.

frequent attacks. Peace slowly returned in the mid-tenth century. For the next three decades the Norse-Irish enclave prospered, until a fresh Uí Néill onslaught in 980 brought defeat at Tara. In the late tenth century, the Irish Uí Briain dynasty rose to prominence. Under Brian Bórama (Bóru) Dublin was captured and turned into a puppet state.

The Dubliners rallied, revolted against the Irish puppet, Sitric Silkenbeard, and called for reinforcements from Orkney and the Hebrides. The climactic battle for control of Ireland was fought on Good Friday, 1014. The Battle of Clontarf was a decisive Viking defeat, and Earl Sigurd the Stout of Orkney was killed. So too was Brian Bórama, which created a power vacuum. Clontarf marked the beginning of the end of the Norse-Irish presence in Ireland, but rivalries between Dublin, Leinster, and the Irish

sub-kings ensured some semblance of Norse-Irish presence would continue in Dublin for a few more years.

In the end it was cultural assimilation that consigned the Vikings in Ireland to history. In recognizing an Irish king, the Dubliners found themselves embroiled in what seemed a never-ending struggle for dominance among the Irish sub-kings. The once exclusively Viking cities of Dublin, Limerick, Waterford, and Cork had become Irish marketplaces, as the Norse settlers, traders, and townspeople gradually became assimilated by their Celtic neighbors. Even a belated and ultimately unsuccessful Norse invasion attempt by King Magnus Barelegs of Norway in 1098 failed to reverse the process. For a few decades Dublin would be an Irish city, until the arrival of the Anglo-Normans in the next century.

The Isle of Man

As the Norse swept south around Scotland in the last years of the eighth century, they came across a small island in the middle of the Irish Sea, located halfway between Celtic Ireland and Anglo-Saxon England. The Isle of Man would serve as the ideal haven for succeeding generations of Viking raiders.

Facing: Carved stone from c.1000, found on the Isle of Man. The relief depicts a scene from the Norse saga of Ragnarök, Doomsday of the Gods, in which Odin is eaten by the wolf Fenrir. In this case the raven associated with the cult of Odin perches on the god's shoulder.

Sodor, or Southern Isles, was how the Norsemen named the Hebrides. With an excellent location for raids south into the Irish Sea, the islands were settled within a few years of the first arrival of Vikings in these waters. Given its even better location and its three or four good harbors, it seems surprising that there seems to be no trace of any permanent Norse settlement on the Isle of Man for a century after the Vikings first sailed past it.

The remains of a Norse ship-burial discovered at Balladoole suggest that the first settlers arrived at the end of the ninth century. A stone cairn set in a corner of an early Christian cemetery marked the site of a boat grave. Of the 40 or more Viking graves so far discovered on the island, only one pre-dates the conversion of the Norwegians to Christianity. At Ballateare, a pagan Viking settler was buried alongside a slave girl, sacrificed so she could serve her master in the afterlife. The mystery of the late settlement of the Isle of Man has perplexed historians, but a relatively simple explanation is that the island was typically too lawless for settlement for almost a century after the Vikings first arrived there.

This had also occurred elsewhere. Before the enforcement of Norse rule in 895, the Orkney Islands were a haven for violent bands of Vikings—pirates happy to prey on each other as much as to raid Saxon or Celtic settlements. Although there is evidence that some former Pictish farms were taken over by Norse settlers, there are few physical indications of permanent Norse settlement until the mid-ninth century. Similarly, the Faroes provided a safe haven for outlaw Vikings. In the Hebrides, the first wave of Vikings came to pillage, and it was only some years later that the first settlers arrived, taking over the farmsteads of the indigenous population. In the main, the real Vikings were raiders, not farmers, and they preferred to live off the local population rather than replace it. In other words, the Isle of Man was a useful pirate haven, but it only became a place suitable for permanent Viking settlement after the first wave of Viking raids had subsided, and the raiders had moved on to France or Ireland.

According to *Heimskringla*, King Harald Harfagri of Norway visited the Isle of Man on his way south on an expedition into the Irish Sea in the last years of the ninth century. This coincides with the start of the era of Norse settlement, and may be regarded as the moment when the island was cleared of desperadoes, and became fit for settlement.

Gradual settlement

The earliest Norse farms on the Isle of Man included small defensive enclosures and strongly-built homesteads. Fortified farms sited on coastal promontories are also peculiar to the island, indicating that even by the start of the tenth century, the island was far from a safe place to settle. Unlike the more established (and law-abiding) Norse colonies to the north, the Isle of Man was virtually unprotected by powerful jarls, or regional warlords such as the rulers of Dublin.

By the mid-tenth century, Viking houses became larger, and the large bow-sided hall at Braaid represents a new confidence and prosperity on the island. It replaced an earlier Norse roundhouse, and was sited amid some of the best farming land on the island. In the tenth century there was a renewal of Norse Viking raids on England, this time against the western coastline of the Danelaw. The Isle of Man became a regular staging post for raids against towns such as Chester and the Wirral (now Liverpool).

The Vikings' legacy is still noticeable today in the Isle of Man. It remains semi-autonomous, and is governed by the Tynwald (from the Old Norse word for Parliament). The Isle of Man remained a Norse possession until 1266, when the sale of the Hebrides by Norway to Scotland forced the last independent King of Man to accept the overlordship of the Scottish crown.

Olaf Tryggvasson

Two great rivals emerge from the pages of the Royal Sagas at the end of the tenth century. The Norse King Olaf Tryggvasson is regarded as a hero for bringing Christianity to Norway. His arch enemy, the Danish King Sweyn Forkbeard, is also idolized in the poems. Whatever the source, both rulers played crucial roles in the development of the Scandinavian Empire.

Below: This Norse Viking tomb from northern England in the unusual hogback form is carved with a relief of the four dwarves who held up the corners of the sky.

O laf Tryggvasson was born c.969, and the details of the death of his father, his exile in Russia, and his subsequent return to Scandinavia as a Viking adventurer have already been recounted (*see page 91*). There is strong evidence to suggest that, after cruising in the Baltic, he joined a Danish expedition to England in 990, and participated in the Battle of Maldon the following year. If this is the case, he was almost certainly in the service of the Danish King, Sweyn Forkbeard. According to the *Heimskringla*, Olaf's raids took him all around the British Isles and beyond during the next few years: to Ireland, Wales, the Isle of Man, the Hebrides, Scotland, Northumbria, and the Western Frankish Kingdom.

By the time he adopted Christianity in 995, he was already regarded as one of the most highly successful Viking raiders of his day, and had amassed a fortune in plunder and Danegeld. According to the *Anglo-Saxon Chronicle*, he and Sweyn led an abortive attack against Anglo-Saxon London in 994:

Olaf and Sweyn came to London, on the nativity

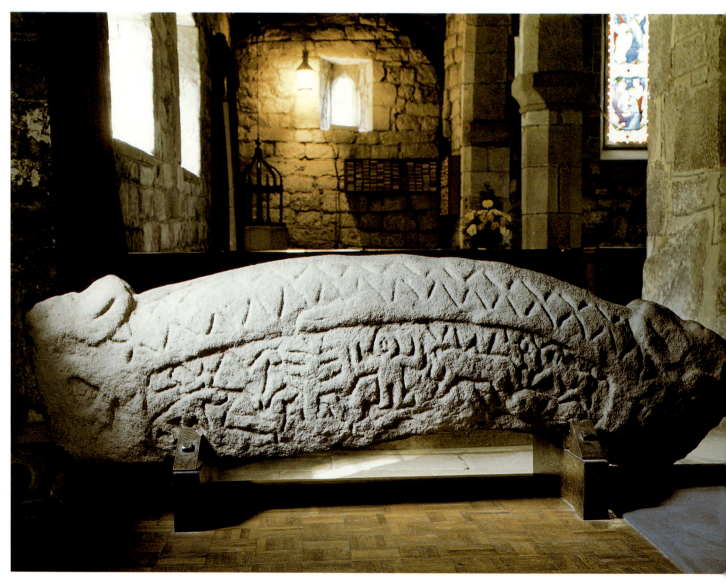

of St. Mary, with 94 ships, fighting constantly the city, and they meant, moreover, to set it on fire. But they suffered more harm and evil than they ever believed any town dwellers could have done them... then they went from there, and wrought the most evil that any force had ever done, in burning, ravaging, and killing, both along the sea-coast, in Essex, and in Kent, Sussex, and Hampshire... they were given sixteen thousand pounds. Then the King sent Bishop Aelfheah and ealdorman Aethelward to King Olaf... Olaf promised them—and also did as he promised— that he would never again come to the English people in enmity.

The timely conversion of Olaf Tryggvasson by Bishop Ælfheah may well have saved the Anglo-Saxon kingdom from destruction.

Norwegian hero

Olaf returned to Norway by way of Orkney in 995, determined to seize the kingdom, and to convert it to Christianity, by any means necessary. King Haakon was taken by surprise and killed by one of his dwindling retinue, and Olaf was duly proclaimed sovereign at Trondheim. He promptly set about enforcing the rule of Christianity on his new subjects. By 1000, his proselytism had created enemies, and his former ally, Sweyn Forkbeard of Denmark, was quick to take advantage of the division within the Norwegian state. Sweyn, who had already subjugated the Danelaw, was clearly one of the greatest commanders of his day. He allied himself with Haakon's son, Jarl Eirik, and the stage was set for a battle between the two former allies.

In 1000, Olaf set sail from Nidaros with 60 ships, including his own dragonship, the *Long Serpent* (see page 44). He was bound for the River Oder on a diplomatic mission, and on his return his small advance party was ambushed by Sweyn and Eirik, probably in the narrow straits between Denmark and Sweden at Helsingør (Elsinore). According to *Heimskringla*, Olaf was heavily outnumbered and, as his force was hacked down, he and his men made a last stand on the deck of his giant flagship. The deck of the *Long Serpent* was covered in the dead, and wet with blood.

As more of Jarl Eirik's men closed in for the kill, Olaf realized that he and his men stood no chance. Rather than surrender, or risk being wounded and captured, he leapt over the side of his flagship. The Danes tried to seize him, but Olaf pulled his shield over his head and sank beneath the waves, meeting "the death his life deserved." In later years, Olaf would be applauded as a Norwegian hero, but in the meantime, he left his kingdom in the hands of its Danish enemies. It would be another 15 years before the Danish overlordship of Norway would be overthrown by Olaf Haraldsson the Stout.

Above: The Norse cross in Halton, Lancashire, England has scenes from the story of Sigurd and how he slew the dragon Fafnir.

York and Dublin

Apart from Anglo-Saxon London, the most prosperous cities in the British Isles in the Viking age were Jorvik (York) and Dublin. The cities were seized from the Saxons and the Irish to become the capital cities of Viking Britain, forming a trading partnership that would dominate northern European trade for a century.

There can be little argument that the Vikings were one of the greatest trading peoples in European history, and at York the Danes expanded the former garrison town and seat of regional government into a bustling port city. As the leading city in the Danelaw, its development was crucial to the commercial expansion of the whole region, and the Vikings brought with them an existing trading network, eager for the produce of Britain.

The Anglo-Saxons of York had already developed tentative trading links with the Frankish Kingdoms and with Frisia. This mercantile trade expanded greatly, and from the mid-ninth century the city began to prosper

through the efforts of its Danish settlers, merchants, and craftsmen. When, in 876, King Halfdan officially turned the Vikings from raiding to settlement and trade, it marked a turning point for the Danelaw. Three years previously, the Viking inhabitants of York had embraced Christianity, and the city joined the community of the rest of Europe, thereby increasing its trading opportunities.

Despite this opening of Saxon and Frankish markets, trade links remained essentially oriented toward the Scandinavian homelands across the North Sea. The city also maintained links with the rest of the Danelaw, Denmark, and Frisia, although increasingly, trade up the English North Sea coast from the Thames to the Humber estuaries was prone to disruption by Anglo-Saxon naval forces based in London or Kent.

There is evidence that the Viking merchants of York traded extensively with the Viking Norman marketplace at Rouen, and cross-country trading connections were maintained with the five boroughs of the Danelaw: Derby, Leicester, Lincoln, Nottingham, and Stamford. In recent years the archaeological excavation of the Coppergate district of York has revealed a significant portion of the old Viking city, and the remains of merchants' warehouses, wharves, stores, and workshops have been discovered. Glassmaking, leatherworking, woodworking, and jewelry production were all practiced in the Viking city. Incidentally, recent glass and jewelry finds from Frankish cities as far away as the Rhine and Weser rivers have produced evidence of trading connections with the Danelaw during the ninth and tenth centuries, so the city's trading links were probably more extensive than had previously been imagined.

Norse-Irish traders

During the ninth century, the small amount of North Sea trade between the British Isles and Scandinavia was the preserve of the Norwegians. By the

Viking Jorvik (York)

▨	Viking streets
▬	main Viking street
▲	Viking finds
▲	main Jorvik site
··········	site of Roman fortress

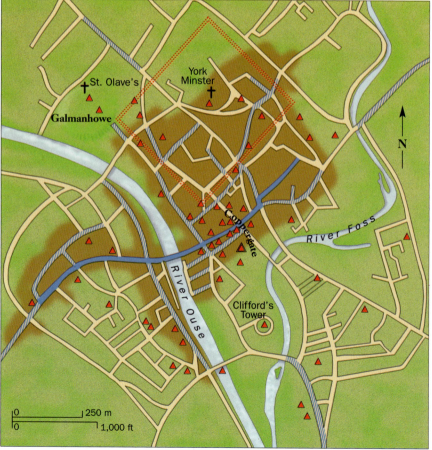

middle of the century, they had developed a thriving trading settlement at Dublin and, by the tenth century, the city had become a bustling commercial center, and would remain so until the end of the next century. All of the great ports of Ireland—Cork, Dublin, Limerick, Waterford, and Wexford—were founded by Norse traders. Originally established as fortified camps, these later developed as marketplaces.

A small Celtic settlement originally existed in Dublin before the Vikings arrived, but the area was occupied in 836, and a new settlement was established. This developed into an administrative center, then into a trading settlement. Its trading routes ran north through the Irish Sea to the Hebrides and Orkney, then on to Iceland by way of Shetland and the Faroes, or west to Norway. The Irish Sea also provided access to the Anglo-Saxon port of Chester, and to Norse and Celtic settlements in Wales,

or Anglo-Saxon ones in Wessex, in the south and west of England.

Further south, Dublin merchants maintained close trading links with the towns on the coasts and rivers of the Western Frankish Kingdom, many of which were already in Viking hands. Coins and trade goods also suggest that the Dubliners traded with the Moors in Spain, since Arabic coins have been recovered from excavations in the Irish capital. Excavations of the waterlogged Viking waterfront area of the city has revealed evidence of metalworking shops, craftsmen's houses, and storehouses.

Dublin, York, and the smaller Viking settlements in Ireland and England flourished under Scandinavian rule, and all seem to have been centers of international trade, linked to the rest of Europe by the North Sea and the Irish Sea, the great highways of commerce in the late Viking period.

Below: Dublin became a thriving Norse trading center. Here, in 1968, archaeologists uncovered a Viking footpath. Although it is rare to find wooden structures of this age, clay mud has preserved examples from as far apart as Novgorod in Russia and Hedeby in Denmark, showing that Vikings employed this technique wherever they went.

Æthelred the Unready

If Alfred the Great and Athelstan represented the high points of Anglo-Saxon resistance to the Danish invaders, Æthelred the Unready was the low ebb. Despite one of the longest reigns in Saxon history, his policy of appeasement left him with one of the poorest reputations of all the Anglo-Saxon kings.

King Æthelred II of Kent (r.979–1016) was nicknamed "Unræd," meaning "the ill-advised," or "evil-counsel." It is a testament to his own failure that it was gradually rewritten as "Unready." Æthelred's problem was Danegeld. He inherited a reasonably prosperous realm but by his death it was virtually destitute, its revenue squandered on paying off the Danes. Even worse, within a year of his death, a Dane sat on the throne of England.

Æthelred (also written Ethelred) has become the historical scapegoat for the decline of Anglo-Saxon England. Undoubtedly, some of this was his fault, but the challenges he faced would have taxed the most gifted of rulers. Only ten years old when he came to the throne, he had to rely on the advice of powerful advisors—men who became the "evil-council" referred to in his epithet. After years of relative peace, the Viking raids on the Anglo-Saxon coast began again within years of his accession. At first they were not particularly dangerous, but this changed in 991. A large Viking warband landed near Maldon in Essex, and defeated the Saxon army sent to meet it.

In the same year, Æthelred had pulled off a diplomatic coup, an alliance with Duke Richard of Normandy. However, the disaster of the Battle of Maldon overshadowed this piece of clever politics. The defeat marked a turning point in relations between the Anglo-Saxons and the Vikings. The *Anglo-Saxon Chronicle* claims that for the first time in a century, the English paid Danegeld to the Vikings in order to discourage their attacks. The first to do so were the Archbishop of Canterbury, whose ecclesiastical seat in Kent was in the front line, and the local Saxon ealdormen (earls) whose lands on the southern coastline of Wessex were vulnerable.

These first payments was made in late 991 or early 992. Further payments of Danegeld were made in ever-increasing amounts three years later in 994, then again in 1002, 1007, and 1012. Tributes continued to be paid for decades after Æthelred 's death and over the half-century following the Battle of Maldon the English paid at least 250,000 pounds' weight in silver to their Viking enemies. Not only did this policy of appeasement fail to work because the Vikings kept returning for more, but the resources available to the Anglo-Saxon state impressed the Danes, and indicated that the kingdom would be a lucrative one to conquer.

A Viking England

The Viking warbands eventually expanded into armies led by senior earls and even kings. In 994, just three years after Maldon, King Sweyn Haraldsson Forkbeard of Denmark arrived in the Danelaw to take personal command of the growing Danish army in England. He possessed the troops and the resources to bring the Saxons to their knees if he wished to launch an all-out invasion. The *Anglo-Saxon Chronicle* describes a succession of devastating raids, from Wales and Cornwall to East Anglia and the center of England. Yet these only brought about a new wave of Danegeld payments, as well as famine and disease in the wake of the destruction.

Below: A ceramic bowl from Denmark.

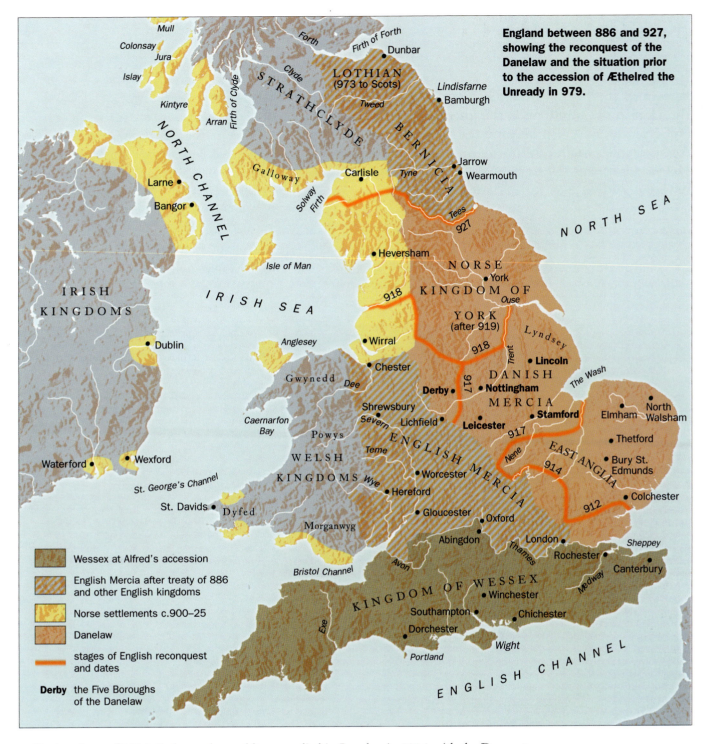

England between 886 and 927, showing the reconquest of the Danelaw and the situation prior to the accession of Æthelred the Unready in 979.

Mull
Colonsay
Jura
Islay
Kintyre
Arran
Firth of Clyde

Forth
Firth of Forth
• Dunbar
LOTHIAN
(973 to Scots)
Clyde
STRATHCLYDE
Tweed
Lindisfarne
• Bamburgh

NORTH SEA

BERNICIA

• Jarrow
• Wearmouth

Tyne

Galloway
• Carlisle
Solway Firth

Tees
927

Larne •
Bangor •

NORTH CHANNEL

• Heversham

N O R S E

918

• York
KINGDOM OF
Ouse

Isle of Man

I R I S H
S E A

I R I S H
K I N G D O M S

YORK
(after 919)

Lyndsey

918

• **Lincoln**

• Dublin

Anglesey
• Wirral

D A N I S H

• Chester

Dee

917

• **Derby** • **Nottingham**

Trent

M E R C I A

The Wash

Gwynedd

Shrewsbury •

• **Stamford**

Elmham •

North
Walsham

Caernarfon
Bay

Lichfield •

Leicester •

917

• Thetford

Powys

Severn

E N G L I S H   M E R C I A

Teme

Waterford •
• Wexford

WELSH

Wye

• Worcester

Nene

914

EAST ANGLIA

• Bury St.
Edmunds

St. George's Channel

K I N G D O M S

• Hereford

912

• Colchester

St. Davids •
• Dyfed

• Gloucester

• Oxford

London •

Morganwyg

Abingdon •

Thames

Rochester •

Sheppey

Canterbury

Avon

Medway

Bristol Channel

K I N G D O M   O F   W E S S E X

• Winchester

Exe

Southampton •

• Chichester

Dorchester •

Wight

• Portland

E N G L I S H   C H A N N E L

Legend:

- Wessex at Alfred's accession
- English Mercia after treaty of 886 and other English kingdoms
- Norse settlements c.900–25
- Danelaw
- stages of English reconquest and dates
- **Derby** the Five Boroughs of the Danelaw

By the winter of 1006–7, those who could flee England did so, and Æthelred's kingdom started to fall apart. Even Æthelred recognized the extent of the catastrophe, and called on the Church for its support in rallying his people. A naval disaster off Sandwich (1006) and the near collapse of royal authority marked the end of any hope. In 1013, Æthelred briefly abandoned his throne and fled to France, as his nobles defected to the Danes.

The death of Sweyn created a brief power vacuum in England, but Æthelred's attempts to recover his power base came to nothing, and he died in London in 1016, with the Danes at the gates. Edmund Ironside, his son, held the throne for a brief spell in 1016, but following his defeat by Sweyn's son Cnut and his death later in the year, the Anglo-Saxons had taken enough. Peace could only be achieved by recognizing a Danish claimant to the throne of England, and so Cnut became King of England, and married Æthelred's Norman widow Emma to give the impression of some continuity. His accession was merely an acceptance of fact. England had been conquered by the Vikings.

King Cnut

Known to the history books as King Canute the Great, the Danish monarch ruled the kingdoms of Denmark and Norway, and also became the king of a new Anglo-Danish realm, following his defeat of the Saxons. His kingdom was the nearest the Vikings ever came to having a unified North Sea Empire.

After Olaf Tryggvasson's drowning in 1000 (*see page 145*), his rival King Sweyn Haraldsson Forkbeard of Denmark annexed Norway and briefly united the Norse and the Danes under one empire. Sweyn's extensive military resources secured the safety of the Danelaw, and brought the Anglo-Saxon kingdom of Æthelred the Unready to its knees. When he died in February 1014, victory in England was within his grasp. His realm was divided between his two sons, Cnut (the elder at 18) and Harald.

While the younger son inherited Denmark and Norway, Cnut became titular master of the Anglo-Danish kingdom of the Danelaw. Aided by Harald, Cnut led a full-scale invasion force

against England in 1015. The Saxons were split in loyalty between the largely discredited Æthelread and his Viking rival. Several Saxon nobles defected to Cnut (who rewarded their fickleness with execution after his enthronement). With half of the Saxon realm already in his hands, Cnut besieged London in 1016. Æthelread had already died by the time the Danes arrived and his son's rule was short. Cnut defeated King Edmund Ironside in the same year at Ashingdon in Essex, and shortly after the two agreed peace terms.

Areas of England outside the Danelaw were divided between them, Edmund keeping Wessex and Cnut gaining Mercia—but within months Edmund was dead. The *Anglo-Saxon Chronicle* records in 1017 that Cnut (r.1016–35) received all the kingdom of England, and divided it into four. These were the Earldoms of Northumbria, East Anglia, Mercia, and Wessex. While he gave two of these provinces to trusted Danish lieutenants (Jarls Thorkell and Erik), Wessex was presented to Godwin, and Mercia to Eadric, both Anglo-Saxon nobles.

Cnut had Eadric executed later in the year for treachery and gave Mercia to another Anglo-Saxon nobleman, Leofric (whose wife was the Lady Godiva of legend). For the next half century until the Norman Conquest, the Anglo-Danish structure was established: a king governed the kingdom, assisted by four powerful and wealthy nobles. These warrior aristocrats maintained their own personal followings of minor nobles, or thanes, who performed the direct administration of the kingdom.

Anglo-Danish integration

Cnut's Danish Settlement was a superb piece of propaganda. It served to bind the two peoples together, and he cemented the relationship in 1017 by his marriage to Emma, Æthelred's widow. Because Emma was the daughter of Duke Robert of Normandy, the foundations had been laid for a future three-way contest for the throne of England. To pay off his forces, Cnut squeezed the last drops of revenue from a depleted Anglo-Saxon treasury.

In 1018, Cnut's brother Harald died, and Cnut became king of both Denmark and England. Although Norway was nominally under Danish rule, it was virtually independent following the death of Cnut's father, Sweyn

Forkbeard. These possessions made Cnut one of the most powerful kings in Europe, ruler of a Viking Empire that stretched around the North Sea and into the Baltic.

Under Cnut's hand, decades of conflict, raiding, and extortion were ended and the war-weary English slowly recovered. In fact, the realm was secure enough for Cnut to make several trips to Denmark to supervise his lands there. He also encouraged integration between Saxons and Danes. When the Earl of Northumbria died, his successor Siward married into the Anglo-Saxon nobility, and it is clear that intermarriage was widespread among all the lower strata of Anglo-Danish society. By the time King Cnut the Great died in Shaftesbury in 1035, his realm was firmly governed, relatively prosperous, and secure from external threat. Three decades later this peace would be shattered.

Above: A figure of Hiberno-Saxon origin on the handle of a bucket, with swastika symbols of Thor.

Facing: The remains of the ramparts of the Viking fort at Fyrkat stand out clearly from the surrounding Danish landscape. This military camp is believed to have housed King Cnut's troops before his invasion of England (*see also Trelleborg military camp, pages 130–31*).

The Normans

At the start of the tenth century, Viking raiders claimed land around the mouth of the Seine. Within years, the region was formally ceded to the Viking settlers. The territory became known as the Land of the Norsemen, or Normandy.

Right: Norman knight and men-at-arms of the 11th century. In the background stands an early example of a wood-constructed motte and bailey castle.

Hrolf Gongu (the Walker) took part in some of the earliest Norse raids on the coast of the Western Frankish Empire. He was almost certainly the third son of Earl Rögnvald of Moeri, and while his illegitimate younger brother Einar claimed the Earldom of Orkney, Hrolf Rögnvaldsson raided the mouth of the Seine. At some stage in the first decade of the tenth century, he seized part of the river mouth permanently.

In 911, Western Frankish King Charles the Simple (r.893–923) realized that he had little chance of evicting the Vikings by force. Instead, he was compelled to reach an agreement with them. Hrolf (or Rollo in his adoptive Frankish language) signed the Treaty of St. Claire-sur-Epte with Charles, who ceded the lands already held by the Viking in what amounted to an admission of defeat. These consisted of the valley of the lower Seine, and the trading town of Rouen. Rollo was named the Count of Rouen, and in return, he was to adopt the feudal system, swear fealty to Charles, and become a Christian.

The treaty worked well for both parties. Count Rollo protected a large part of the Frankish coast from further Viking raids, and the arrangement safeguarded Paris. In return, Rollo achieved a superior position over his fellow Viking warlords. Rollo encouraged the building of churches within his realm, but it seems he still retained at least a partial belief in the older Norse gods. By 923, Rollo had extended his control to include the western part of the province. This incorporated the whole of what is now considered Normandy, including the Cherbourg Peninsula.

About the same time, during the mid-tenth century, French royal accounts first describe this newly extended province as "Normandy—the land of the Normans." Count Rollo of Rouen

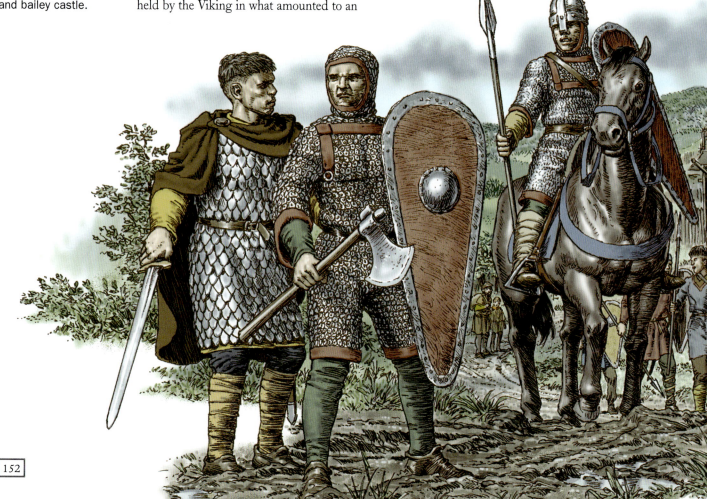

was also styling himself the Count of Normandy, a title that was ratified by the French monarch by 935. Following Rollo's death about 940, his successors (who soon restyled themselves as Dukes) continued his policies of consolidation. The Anglo-Saxon and Scandinavian merchants who traded with Frankish merchants using the Seine as a commercial artery turned Rouen into a thriving trade center from about 1000.

From Viking to Norman

Although Norsemen or their descendants administered Normandy, most of their subjects were Franks. Rather than replace the existing feudal system introduced into what is now western France (Neustria) during the ninth century, the Norman warlords simply adopted feudalism, apparently recognizing its benefits. Parcels of land were handed out to Rollo's followers, and they and their descendants became the future nobles and knights of the Norman state.

He also honored his feudal obligations and

supplied warriors to fight for King Charles when requested. A series of border disputes, revolts by minor nobles, and intrigues honed the military abilities of the Norman Dukes. It has been claimed that all this warfare was a continuation of the earlier Norse warrior tradition, and the nobles and knights in Normandy simply adopted this influence. Whatever the cause, the Norman warrior gained a name for martial ability, and even caused a significant problem for the Norman Dukes themselves. Their answer was to encourage the export of these surplus warriors, which led to the Norman adventurers who carved out their own feudal provinces in southern Italy and Sicily. When Duke William of Normandy invaded and conquered Anglo-Saxon England in 1066, this descendant of a Viking warlord became the ruler of a leading European power. The descendants of the Viking Rollo were now some of the most powerful men in Europe.

Above: The castle of Falaise became the main stronghold of the Dukes of Normandy and was the birthplace of William the Conqueror. As the illegitimate child of a town tanner's daughter and Duke Robert I the Devil, William was known as "the Bastard" before he conquered England and became King William I.

153

Harald Hardrada

The first half of the 11th century had proved a turbulent time for Norway, as a succession of kings, earls, and royal contestants vied for control. From the tumult of battle, Harald Hardrada emerged as the new ruler of the kingdom. The throne of Norway was not enough for the most celebrated warrior of his age, and Harald cast covetous eyes on the English crown.

Below: This length of timber was carved in the first half of the 13th century to illustrate a fleet of Viking longships. An inscription reads: "Here goes the Sea-Darer." Note that three of the ships have wind-vanes on their prows, similar to the one pictured on page 99. ▶

During the reign of Cnut, Denmark and the Anglo-Danish Kingdom of England formed what was virtually a Scandinavian superpower. Through good governorship, a substantial treasury, a formidable military force, and a powerful navy backed Cnut's authority in the North Sea basin. Norway was nominally under Danish control, but in 1015–16, the Norwegian warlord Olaf Haraldsson the Saint emerged as a rival to Danish power, and was crowned. Four years later his authority was recognized by Earl Thorfinn of Orkney. This posed a significant threat to Cnut and, following the death of his brother and his accession to the throne of Denmark in 1018, Cnut planned an expedition to retake Norway.

The campaign was lackluster, because Cnut had to balance his campaigning in Norway (and Sweden) with his commitments in England. Finally, in 1028, Olaf was driven from Norway, and sought refuge in Sweden, where he regrouped his forces. The culmination of the campaign came in July 1030, when an army in the pay of Cnut of Denmark fought against the army of Olaf of Norway at the Battle of Stiklastadir (Stiklestad), near Trondelag in Norway. Saint Olaf was killed, and Norway was once again a Danish province.

When Cnut died in 1035, hope for the independence of Norway was rekindled, and the Norwegians duly crowned Saint Olaf's illegitimate son Magnus Olaffson the Good as King of Norway (r.1035–47). This reclamation of the Norwegian crown by Norwegians was seen as a *fait-accompli* by Cnut's offspring, and King Magnus was left to rule in peace.

Cnut's empire was divided between his sons. Harold Harefoot (r.1035–40) was given England and Hardacnut (or Harthacnut in Saxon) was granted Denmark (r.1035–42). Harold died in 1040, and was succeeded by Hardacnut. When Cnut's second son died two years later, the English crown passed to the Anglo-Saxon, Edward the Confessor (r.1042–66).

Resurgence of Empire

At the Battle of Stiklastadir (1030), the 15-year-old nephew of King Olaf, Harald Sigurdsson Hardrada, fled from the field and went into exile in Russia and Byzantium. He was the son of a minor Norwegian king, and despite his years in exile, and his growing reputation as a military commander in the Byzantine Varangian Guard, he decided to return to Scandinavia. After marrying a Russian princess he arrived in Sweden, where he formed an alliance with Sweyn Ulfsson, a claimant to the Danish throne, which had fallen into the hands of King Magnus in 1042.

Sweyn had already been defeated by Magnus at Heganess, but Harald rejuvenated the rebel force, and the two commanders conquered a significant part of Denmark. Magnus requested a meeting with Harald, and the two concluded a pact. If Harald supported Olaf, he was promised a share of power in Norway. Harald duly switched sides, and campaigned against Sweyn. When Olaf died in 1047, Harald Hardrada became King of Norway (r.1047–66), and Sweyn Ulfsson (r.1047–71) became King of Denmark. The two kings typically spent much of the next two decades fighting each other, until they agreed to sign a treaty in 1064. The feud between the two kingdoms weakened the North Sea axis at a time when it was about to face its most serious test.

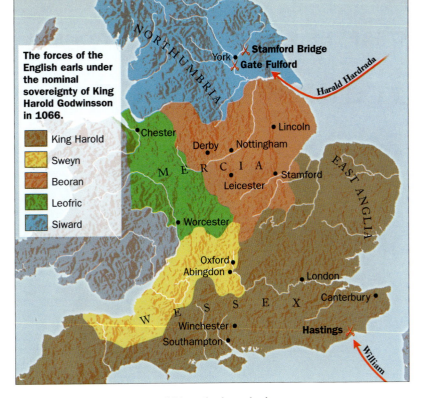

The forces of the English earls under the nominal sovereignty of King Harold Godwinsson in 1066.

- King Harold
- Sweyn
- Beoran
- Leofric
- Siward

Scandinavian overseas ambitions had reached a peak under Cnut, and in the decades since his death, Scandinavian influence in the British Isles and in the rest of Europe had declined. In 1066, Harald Hardrada decided to reverse this situation. The last of the great Viking warrior kings had fought his first battle 36 years before. Since then he had spent most of the time fighting everywhere from Sicily to Norway. His involvement in the succession crisis that gripped England in early 1066 marked the last great involvement of a Viking army in European affairs, and a last attempt to resurrect Cnut's Scandinavian Empire.

▶

When they were not in use, Viking ships were often stored in churches, being the buildings most suited to housing long objects. At the end of the Viking era, many abandoned longships had their wind-vanes removed to be placed on the church's spire.

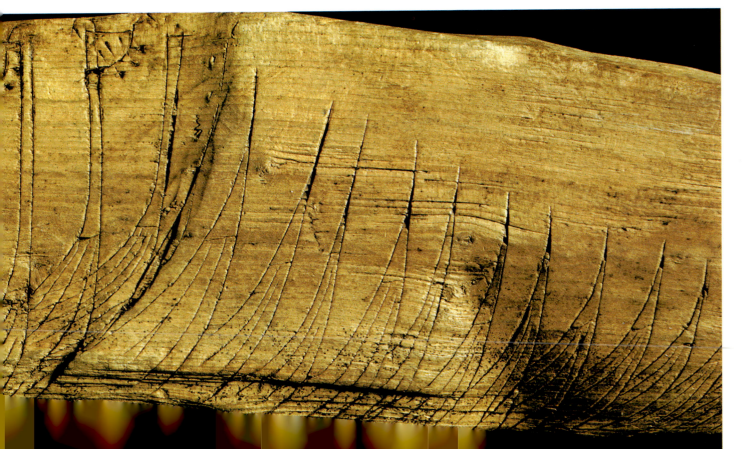

1066: Year of Viking Destiny

The year 1066 was a watershed in European history. In that year three great military leaders fought for control of England: Harald Hardrada of Norway, Harold Godwinsson of England, and William of Normandy. Of these warlords, two were descendants of Vikings, while the third was probably the last of the great Viking heroes, and his death marked the passing of the Viking age.

Above: Both the Normans and the Anglo-Danish used Viking-style *knorr*s for maritime trade during the 11th century. This rendition from the Bayeux Tapestry is actually a Saxon vessel, but the lines on its hull betray its Scandinavian clinker-built method of construction.

On January 5, 1066, King Edward the Confessor of England (r.1042–66) died in his bed. On the following day, his *subregulus*, Harold Godwinsson (r.1066), was crowned in Westminster Abbey. The reason for such unseemly haste was that Harold's claim to the throne was questionable. But he was the strongest Anglo-Danish claimant, and the only man in England capable of uniting the kingdom against rival foreign claimants. To many Saxons Harold was the obvious choice—and he did have a vital political alliance with the Earl of Northumbria to support his claim.

Two foreigners considered themselves to have a better claim to the throne of England. In France, Duke William the Bastard of Normandy had emerged from a blood-soaked minority to establish his authority on the Duchy of Normandy. He was a fifth-generation descendant of Rollo, the Norse nobleman Hrolf Rögnvaldsson, who had created the Norman stronghold. William was also related to King Cnut through his grandfather's sister, Emma, who had married the Danish King of England in 1017. He also claimed the throne of England by moral right (Harold Godwinsson had sworn to support William's claim to the throne).

In Scandinavia, both King Harald Hardrada of Norway and King Sweyn of Denmark maintained claims to the English throne, but while the Danish monarch did nothing about it, Harald and William both decided to invade England and fight for the crown.

King Harold was threatened with an invasion on two fronts: William was expected to invade the south coast from Normandy, and Harald would probably make landfall on the Humber, near the old Scandinavian heartlands of the Danelaw. Soon after his coronation, Harold began mustering an army of Anglo-Danish *huscarles* (or *hirdmen*) to fend off either threat. By the midsummer it looked as if an invasion was becoming unlikely, and most of Harold's army dispersed to their farms. At this point, Harald Hardrada landed at Ricall in the north of England during August, supported by the Earl of Orkney and Tostig Godwinsson, King Harold's disaffected, rebel brother.

The Conqueror

Harald Hardrada immediately marched on York, and destroyed the Northumbrian army sent to block his path at Gate Fulford. The Norwegian king then advanced to the gates of York, and made camp, waiting for hostages and the bloodless surrender of the city. Meanwhile, Harold had learned of the invasion and, having remustered his army, made force-marches north to York. The two armies met at Stamford Bridge on the River Derwent on September 24. The speed of the English advance took Harald by surprise—his men had taken off their armor due to the warm weather.

When Harold appeared, the Vikings raced to form a shieldwall, but part of the army on the west bank of the river were overrun before they could form ranks. A Viking champion held the river crossing until the army formed up, but the English found other crossings. Outnumbered and surrounded, King Harald's men prepared to fight to the death. The battle continued even after Harald Hardrada met his death when an arrow struck him in the throat. Most of the Norsemen were killed, and only a handful escaped to their ships.

Three days later, Duke William crossed the English Channel, and landed near Pevensey. King Harold raced his exhausted men south, and the two armies met at Hastings on October 14. Given the small number of Norman knights who had made the crossing with William, the battle looked like going either way, but late in the afternoon King Harold was reputedly struck in the eye by an arrow and died shortly after. William marched on London and soon had himself crowned King William I the Conqueror of England (r.1066–87). And so the struggle for control of England, which had lasted for centuries, was finally at an end. So too was any remaining dream of a Viking North Sea Empire. The future lay in the axis between France and England, and the Viking world would be relegated to the sidelines of history.

Below: At the Battle of Hastings, William's Norman knights fought on horseback, charging uphill at the better-positioned English *huscarles* and infantry of the levy. The Norman arrows were light and did little damage to the well-armored English, but King Harold was said to have picked an unlucky moment to look up and was struck in the eye. He died shortly after, and the Normans won the day.

CHAPTER 9

Rivers to the East

Viking raiders brought substantial wealth to Scandinavia and eventually carved out new realms in Britain and the Frankish Empire, but it was Viking traders who became the cornerstone of Scandinavian society during the Viking age. In the east, from established trading posts on the Vistula and Oder estuaries, these merchant-venturers sailed far up the rivers of Russia. They even reached the Black and Caspian seas, gaining access to the transcontinental trade routes that stretched from the Orient to the Middle East and the Mediterranean Sea.

To the west, Viking raiders were followed by settlers and traders, who forged commercial links between Scandinavia, Britain, and the Frankish Empire. For the most part western European goods went to marketplaces such as Hedeby, Kaupang, and Birka to be exchanged for goods from central Europe and the East. These Viking ports became thriving commercial centers, attracting traders from as far afield as Moorish Spain and the Byzantine Empire.

Of all the commodities that lubricated Viking Scandinavia's economic development, silver was considered the most desirable. Silver rapidly became the most common medium of exchange. For silver, Viking merchants traded furs, ivory, timber, iron, and slaves. As well as receiving payment for their goods in silver, Scandinavian traders also bought luxury goods to sell to themselves: silks and spices from the Middle East; wax and honey from Russia; glassware and pottery from the Saxons and Franks; and wool and tin from Britain and Ireland. Viking trading ports also became centers of production, as metalworkers, jewelers, and wood carvers took advantage of the economic opportunities this boom in commerce produced.

The greatest beneficiaries of this increase in trade were the Scandinavian kings, who controlled the trading settlements and levied a tax on all exchanges. This provided the means to wage campaigns of conquest in Anglo-Saxon England, and against their fellow Scandinavian kings. If the Viking raider was the symbol of his age, Viking traders and craftsman were at the core of the economic and cultural powerhouse that transformed Scandinavia, and moved it into a new age.

WHITE SEA

Gulf
of Bothnia

Finns

L. Ozero

Lake
Lagoda

Finns

Vaga

SLAVES, FURS,
HONEY, WAX

Gulf of
Finland

Volkhov

Beloozero
(Belozersk)

• Vologda

Aldeigjuborg
(Staraja Lagoda)

Novgorod

Yaroslavl

Murom

Volga

Bulgar

**Volga
Bulgars**

Lake
Peipus

Lovat

Izborsk • Pskov

Volga

SALT
FLAX
HEMP
HIDES
SLAVES

• Grobin

Balts

Dvina

Gnezdovo
(Smolensk)

Ural

bing

Nemunas

Prus

SLAVES

ARAL
SEA

Vistula

Chernigov
(Chernihiv)

Derevlians

Kiev

Dnieper

Don

Volga

Chorzem

Oxus

KHAZARIAN KHANATE

Itil
(Astrakhan)

Dnister

Magyars

Pechenegs

SEA
OF
AZOV

Sarkel
(Volgodonsk)

to Bukhara,
Samarkand,
Tashkent,
China

TEXTILES,
GLASS,
METALS

Goths • Tmutorokan

C
A
S
P
I
A
N

S
E
A

Danube

Baku

**BULGAR
KHANATE**

BLACK   SEA

Kura

SPICES, GEMS,
TEXTILES,
STEEL BLADES

Gorgan

Sinope

Trebizon
(Trabzon)

Tabriz

Constantinople

A n a t o l i a

A r m e n i a

Tigris

ABBASID   CALIPHATE

AEGEAN
SEA

MARITIME STORES,
SPICES, SILK, WINES

Mosul • Arbil

to Baghdad   to Baghdad

HIDES, WOOL,
SPICES

to China

Viking trade and colonization, 800 to 1050

- Kievan Rus, c.1050
- Bulgars
- Kingdom of Hungary, c.1000
- Byzantine Empire c.900
- → Viking trading routes (sea and river)
- ⇢ Viking trading routes overland
- → Arab and international trade routes
- *Finns* Racial/tribal groupings

from Iceland to the Caspian Sea

Before the Viking age, northern Europe was an economic backwater, far from the vibrant markets of the Mediterranean and the Middle East. This changed during the ninth century, as Viking merchants created an intricate network of trade routes by sea, river, and land.

Below: This silver-mounted rock-crystal pendant from a necklace, which originated in Russia at some point between the 10th and 11th centuries, shows Slavic influences in its design. It was part of a Viking hoard found in Gotland and is proof of the extensive trade between the Viking homelands and the new Russian state.

Small trading centers already existed in Scandinavia before the Viking age began at the end of the eighth century. Although these settlements survived and even expanded, the real flourishing of Scandinavian trade came in the middle of the following century, following the opening up of trade routes to the east, through the rivers of Russia. Similarly, other Baltic trading settlements grew up to service

the needs of the Varangian traders who journeyed on the Volga and Dnieper rivers.

The small port of Grobin in Latvia and the nearby settlement at Riga provided ready access to commerce from all around the Baltic, and the river traders to the east snapped up the towns' commodities. Similarly Truso on the Vistula and Wolin on the Oder acted as funnels for trade with the Germanic and Slavic peoples of central Europe. The cleric Adam of Bremen, writing in 1070, described Wolin as the largest city in Europe, after the decline of Hedeby in Denmark. Certainly trade throughout the Baltic and North Sea regions was extensive for much of the Viking period, as traders, trappers, and merchants thrived off each other. They also brought commodities of which there was a surplus in Scandinavia to the marketplaces of the rest of Europe and even Asia.

The chief of these was fur: reindeer, elk, marten, bear, otter, seal, and walrus were all hunted. Fur traders paid Lapp or Viking hunters to bring their hauls south to sell. Eiderdown was also a prized commodity, as was rope made from the skin of sea mammals such as whales, seals, or walruses. Viking whalers hunted in Norwegian waters, reducing whale blubber to produce oil, and collecting whalebone. Narwhal and walrus were hunted for their skin and tusks, and their horns fetched high prices in the markets of southern Scandinavia. Traders ventured north to visit these isolated fur trading outposts and trappers' camps, buying the furs, skins, tusks, and hides in return for silver, trade goods, or luxury items.

Cruel trade

Another staple of the Viking trading economy was slaves. Although slavery had existed in Europe for centuries, the Vikings turned it into a major source of wealth, predating the transatlantic slave trade by some seven centuries. The source of captives varied. The old tenet of "to the victors go the spoils" certainly applied in the ninth century. If the Vikings vanquished a foe such as the Anglo-Saxons in battle, or captured a town or village, the survivors were automatically shipped to Scandinavia, or to a Viking colony, and sold into slavery. The Celts and Anglo-Saxons of the British Isles (including Ireland) were particularly prized for their strength and skills.

In addition, Viking slaving expeditions rights. The marketplaces of Hedeby, Kaupang, and Birka were filled with slaves of all ages. In 870, the sight prompted a Frankish Christian cleric to sell his religious paraphernalia in order to buy the freedom of Christian slaves he found in the marketplace of Hedeby.

Above: A "horn of plenty" containing the belongings of the dead Viking.

ventured deep into central and eastern Europe along the river arteries, while the Scandinavians themselves were not always spared. Several Scandinavian laws condemned the guilty to slavery: for murder, feuding, or simply falling foul of the local authorities or ruling families. The greatest source of all was the Slavic heartland of eastern Europe, and the term "Slav" itself is probably the source of the word "slave" (although Vikings used the term *thrall* instead). In Scandinavian society, slaves were numerous, burdened with heavy agrarian labor, and had no

Amber was a prized commodity, and southern Denmark had rich sources of it. Extensive deposits of iron ore in central Sweden gave Scandinavia another natural resource. Norway, too, had the prized raw materials to produce whetstones and soapstone. If it could be sold or traded, Viking merchants would deal in it—from Icelandic sealskin to Russian children. The trading network created by the Vikings was perhaps their most impressive achievement, although the human exploitation it involved reflected the cruelties of the times.

The Rivers of Russia

In order to reach the wealthy trading markets of the Middle East and Byzantium, Viking adventurers set out from eastern European trade centers to explore Russia's extensive river networks. These rivers became avenues of trade, and Viking merchants provided a trade link between the Caspian and Black Seas and the marketplaces of Viking Scandinavia.

Right: The demand for silver in Scandinavian culture increased during the Viking migratory period. This silver pendant found in Ostergotland, Sweden shows a helmet characteristic of the early Vikings, with the raised eyebrow guards and the beak on the forehead.

irst contacts between Vikings and Russians or Byzantines revealed that the lands further to the east were rich in silver, the most sought-after commodity in Scandinavia. In the late eighth century, the silver deposits of Mesopotamia (mainly from the Kufic region) reached the markets of the Middle East and Central Asia, and were traded for silks, spices, slaves, or other goods.

Although isolated from these Middle Eastern trade routes by an entire continent, the Viking merchants of the Baltic were in fact extremely well placed to exploit this glut of silver. By exploring the rivers that led south and east through Russia, Viking merchants were able to transport surplus commodities of furs, iron, or slaves to trade with Eastern merchants. This economic opportunity created the Viking trade routes along the rivers, and powered the transformation of Viking Scandinavia. Russia's rivers pass through barren, inhospitable, and (in this era) hostile lands. Few merchants, apart from the Vikings themselves, would have considered developing trade routes here. Despite the risks, the Viking marketplaces on the Baltic began to benefit from the newly opened river routes, and a steady flow of eastern silver began to appear in Scandinavia and western Europe.

The two principal river routes across Russia are the Volga and the Dnieper. The Volga is linked to the eastern head of the Baltic Sea by a network of rivers and portages. Traders either ventured south from Novgorod, or east by lake and small river before joining the south-flowing Volga near the modern Russian city of Rostov. At this point, the Volga flows east, then south, passing through the lands of the Bulgars and Khazaks until it finally turns eastward again, emerging in the northwest corner of the Caspian Sea. At its southeastern corner lay the town of Gorgan, which provided access to the silks, spices, and silver the Viking merchants wanted. The Volga also gave access to the Don, which provided a secondary route into the Black Sea. Further to the west, the settlement of Novgorod in northwestern Russia provided a useful trading center, linked by the Volkhov to Lake Ladoga (Nevo) to the north (and its trading settlement of Aldeigjuborg, now Staraja Ladoga). From there, trade continued along the Neva and various portages to the Baltic Sea (sometimes referred to as the "Varangian Sea.")

Network of trade

From Novgorod the Lovat could be followed to its source, then merchants had to cross to the Dvina. Another portage led to the headwaters of the Dnieper near the modern city of Smolensk. From there, the Dnieper takes a southward route to Kiev, then bends to the east and then southward as it flows through the Ukrainian steppes before reaching the Black Sea. This last portion of the Dnieper proved a difficult journey. Not only was it blocked by several rapids and other riverine hazards, it was also subject to attacks from marauding Asiatic horsemen: the Magyars and Pecheneg Turks.

At the Black Sea, Viking merchants followed the western coastline to reach the Byzantine capital at Constantinople. The Varangians—an eastern generic term for the Vikings—gradually assumed political and military control over much of the northern and western portions of these river routes. Throughout the Viking age, the Volga continued to be surrounded by the lands of potentially hostile Bulgars and Khazaks, and Varangian control was never extended further east than the Volga headwaters.

The basis for this security was formed by the fortified Varangian towns of Izborsk, Novgorod, Polotsk, and Smolensk in northwestern Russia, Kiev to the south, and then Beloozero, Rostov, and Murom on the Volga route. The Bulgars

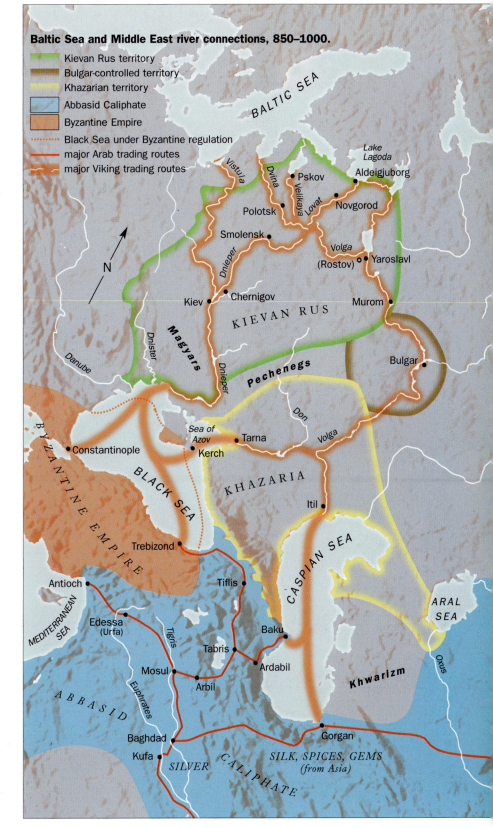

Baltic Sea and Middle East river connections, 850–1000.

- Kievan Rus territory
- Bulgar-controlled territory
- Khazarian territory
- Abbasid Caliphate
- Byzantine Empire
- Black Sea under Byzantine regulation
- major Arab trading routes
- major Viking trading routes

retained control of the river beyond Murom, and tributes and commerce were needed to ensure that the route remained open to traders. As the silver trade died off in the late tenth century, the Volga route was only rarely used, and the Dnieper became the main artery. It remained in use until the end of the Viking age, when the decline of both the Baltic markets and the silver trade finally ended the link between Scandinavia and the Byzantine Empire.

Building a New State: The Rus

As their fellow Scandinavians pillaged and then settled in western Europe, the Swedes looked east across the Baltic Sea for avenues of trade and colonial expansion. During the ninth century, these settlers and traders were given the collective name of the Rus. They went on to help found the Russian state.

Right: Ornate silver-gilt brooches showed off the success and wealth of Swedish Viking traders.

Before 1000, the lands to the east and south of the Baltic were sparsely occupied. The indigenous population clung to the edges of the vast forests that covered the region, and settled on the banks of the great rivers that formed the region's main arteries. This was home to a Slavic people

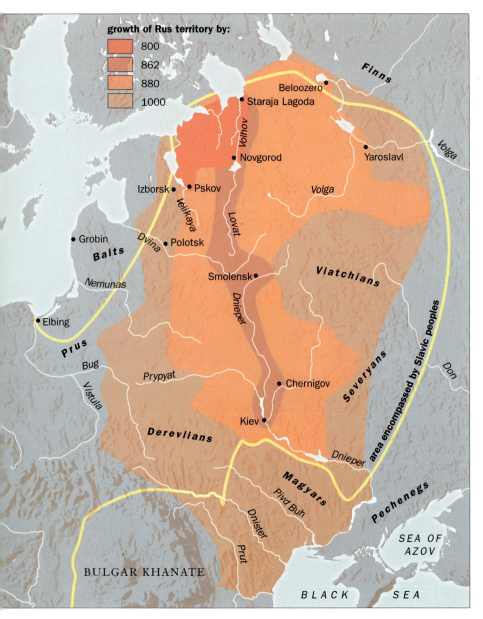

growth of Rus territory by:
- 800
- 862
- 880
- 1000

Finns

Beloozero
Staraja Lagoda
Volhov
Novgorod
Yaroslavl
Volga
Volga

Izborsk • Pskov
Velikaya
Lovat
Dvina • Polotsk
Grobin
Balts
Nemunas
Smolensk
Dnieper
Viatchians
Elbing
Prus
Bug
Prypyat
Severyans
Don
Chernigov
area encompassed by Slavic peoples
Vistula
Kiev
Derevlians
Dnieper
Magyars
Pivd Buh
Pechenegs
Dnister
Prut
SEA OF AZOV
BULGAR KHANATE
BLACK SEA

largely concentrated around the trading centers of Novgorod and Kiev. There was some Persian ancestry here, but the majority shared the same ethnic background as most of eastern Europe.

Beginning in about 850, Swedish Viking traders began to exploit the river route earlier Viking adventurers had recently explored. Before long, they began to found settlements and became more integrated with the indigenous population. These Vikings became known as the Rus from the Slavic derivative of the Finnish name for Swedish Vikings (red-haired).

As numbers increased, they also began to establish a series of protective enclaves along the rivers, encompassing the older Slavic communities in the process. Because the Slavic tribes in the region were less well-armed and organized than the Rus, the Swedish settlements merged together to create a framework of small towns and trading posts.

The *Russian Primary Chronicle*, written in the 12th century by Orthodox priests, provides a useful insight into the early development of the Rus. It gives a date for the creation of a Rus state. According to the manuscript, in 862 the local Slavic tribes collectively declared to the interlopers that: "our land is great and rich, but there is no order in it. Come, rule and reign over us." This unlikely invitation was clearly a vehicle to explain the annexation of these territories by the Vikings, and to lend authority to a later generation of Rus rulers.

According to the *Chronicle*, a Viking leader named Rurik rose to prominence among the Rus and established himself in the formerly Slavic trading town of Novgorod. Using this base, he extended his authority along the river networks, sending his deputies named Askold and Dir down the Dnieper to claim control over the other great Slavic town of Kiev.

Kiev was ideally placed to exploit trade between the Byzantine Empire and the Baltic, and under the rule of Askold it developed into one of Europe's great trading centers, specializing in fur and slaves. In 880, Rurik's successor Oleg led another Viking expedition down the Dnieper to take Kiev, which had traced an independent path since its seizure by Askold. In 911, what is now called the "mother of Russian cities" became the new capital of the Rus. Oleg now controlled a swathe of territory stretching from the Baltic to the northern borders of the kingdom of the Bulgars, far to the south.

Birth of the Russian state

Russia emerged as a political unit during the tenth century. Prince Oleg and his successors forced the other river communities in the region to accept the overlordship of the Princes of Russia. Under Oleg's son, Prince Svyatoslav, the Rus subdued the Bulgars and Khazars,

which extended the southern borders of Kievan Rus along the Volga and Danube. In defending their southern borders, the Rus were almost constantly at war with the Byzantines, Khazars, and Bulgars. Their military prowess so impressed the Byzantine Emperor that he created a Scandinavian bodyguard (the Varangians).

By the start of the 11th century, the lands of the Rus were referred to as Russia, a series of semi-autonomous city-states dominated by Kiev and Novgorod. Around the same time, the Prince of Russia embraced Orthodox Christianity, ensuring a Christian bulwark that spanned eastern Europe. From its early Viking roots, the lands of the Rus had developed into the sprawling Russian state, initiating the dominance of the Russians over eastern Europe for the next millennium.

Above: A statue of Volodymyr overlooks the Dnieper at Kiev. Volodymyr married the sister of Byzantine Emperor Basil II in 988. Part of the marriage settlement was that the Rus ruler should convert to Christianity. Volodymyr was so ardent in his new faith that he made it the Kievan religion and all his subjects had to be baptized in the waters of the Dnieper.

Birka and Kaupang

The first small trading centers in Scandinavia were founded before the ninth century, but the great growth in trade that followed fueled the creation of several significant Viking marketplaces. Of these, Kaupang in Norway and Birka in Sweden emerged as leading Scandinavian centers, second only to the bustling trading town of Hedeby in Denmark.

Facing top: Björko, sitting on Lake Mälar, is the site of the old Viking trading center of Birka, whose remains lie beneath fertile farmland.

Facing bottom: This Viking hoard of coins, jewelry, and a sword was found in th 1960s at the site of Birka.

Birka was founded shortly before 800 on the island of Björko on Lake Mälar, west of the modern Swedish capital of Stockholm. It was probably founded by royal decree, and was governed by a Swedish royal official. As an officially sanctioned trading port, Birka was protected by its location, safeguarded from casual attack by a network of rivers, lakes, and inlets, and guarded by Swedish longships. A rampart surrounded the settlement on the northeastern corner of Björko (which means Birch Island), and the extent of black earth (charcoal deposits from centuries of occupation) inside the semi-circular defensive works indicates that the original town covered some 30 acres.

At its northern end, the natural harbor of Kuggham (the Cargo Boat Harbor and the Korshamn (Cross Harbor) outside the ramparts provided sheltered anchorages and beaches for trading vessels. Additional jetties to the northeast provided ready access to local warehouses and manufacturing workshops.

From the archaeological debris Birka's artisans left behind them, it can be seen that the town was home to metal workers, wood carvers, bronze casters, leather workers, and bone carvers. Unlike Kaupang in Norway, Birka appears to have been a year-around marketplace, offering a place for fur, hide, and ivory hunters to bring their catch during the winter, ready for the coming of the trading ships at the start of summer.

Iron mined in Sweden was traded at Birka, then shipped south to Hedeby in Denmark. Slavers brought their captives across the Baltic to trade on the island. They exchanged them for Arabic silver, Frankish, or Saxon luxury goods (glassware, textiles, jewelry, and ceramics), weapons, or even wine.

Birka appears to have supported a population of around 1,000 at its peak. However, the decline in the silver trade and the rise in land levels (which made the settlement less accessible by portage or waterways) meant that by the mid-tenth century, the settlement was abandoned. From that point on, Paviken on the island of Gotland and the more northerly settlement of Sigtuna in Uppsala became the new centers of Swedish trade.

Norse traders

The Norwegian marketplace of Kaupang (the name itself is old Norse for "marketplace"), located on the western side of the entrance to Norway's Oslofjord, was the principal trading center for the prosperous Vestfold district. Like Birka, it was well-located, on the inner edge of a small bay. Archaeologists have uncovered the remains of a network of houses, storerooms, workshops, wells, and yards immediately adjacent to the shore. Traces of stone jetties running out into the bay show that Kaupang was once a bustling port. The find of a large Viking anchor in the deep harbor certainly points to its having accommodated sizeable trading vessels.

Kaupang was a summer-only market. Norwegian traders came to the port to trade with shipborne or local merchants, who in turn maintained mercantile links extending across the North Sea and the Baltic. Trappers and hunters from northern Norway brought sealskins, fur, walrus ivory (sea-ivory), and walrus-hide ropes, all of which were traded for silver, provisions, and luxury items. At the end of the trading season, the non-resident traders left, and Kaupang reverted to being a regular coastal settlement. The marketplace grew during the late eighth century, and flourished for almost a century and a half. Kaupang, however, never rivaled the Swedish and Danish trading ports

of Birka and Hedeby. In part, this was due to the greater emphasis the Norse placed on North Sea trade, and for that Dublin was by far the most important Norse mercantile port.

Judging from archaeological evidence, ironworking, production of soapstone objects—a major export to Denmark—and, to a lesser extent, the working of precious metals were Kaupang's principal activities. Pottery and glassware from the Rhineland have been discovered at the site, as have coins and jewelry from England, reinforcing the emphasis on North Sea trade.

Hedeby: Viking World Marketplace

The Moorish trader Al-Tartushi described Hedeby in Denmark as "a large town at the very end of the world ocean." When he saw it in about 950, the Danish port was the largest mercantile center in the Viking world. In its heyday, it attracted merchants from as far afield as the Mediterranean and the Middle East.

The Carolingians recorded that in 808 the Danish King Godfred destroyed the Saxon trading port of Reric (probably Rostock), and established a new Viking market at Hedeby, the site of a small Frisian settlement. The Saxons continued to give the place its old name of Slesvig (now Schleswig). This early settlement, which lay to the south of the Hedeby stream, became the center of the new market town.

By 811, the new Viking settlement had been established a short distance to the north of the stream, but by the end of the century this waterway had become the town's focal point. It was widened, dredged, and its banks were lined with wooden wharves, while the beaches on either side served as a landing place for larger ships. Because the city was founded by royal command, its layout was carefully controlled. The streets were laid out running at right angles to the Hedeby Stream, and parallel to the shore of the Haddeby Nor (the enclosed spur of the Schlei Fjord on which the town sat).

A large semicircular earthen rampart, topped by a palisade, enclosed the entire settlement. Further defense was provided by a curving palisade which stretched out into the Haddeby Nor, and which also served to protect the beach and the stream's mouth from the north wind. The entire site encompassed by these fortifications covered some 60 acres, making it the largest trading settlement in Scandinavia. Inside its walls, merchants and craftsmen had their shops, houses, storerooms, and workshops, while additional space was set aside for the tents of traveling merchants or buyers.

Strategic location

By the time Al-Tartushi visited Hedeby, the town was a thriving marketplace. Its success was due largely to its location. At the narrow base of the Jutland peninsula, the Schlei Fjord provided immediate access to the Baltic Sea, while it was only a short land route to the North Sea. Hedeby, therefore, was ideally placed to act as a meeting place for Scandinavian Baltic traders, who in turn provided access to Russia, and the markets of the Middle East, and North Sea merchants. The Danevirke, a series of defensive lines that protected the frontier of the Danish state, safeguarded trade across the peninsula from the Eider or Elbe rivers. Above all, its

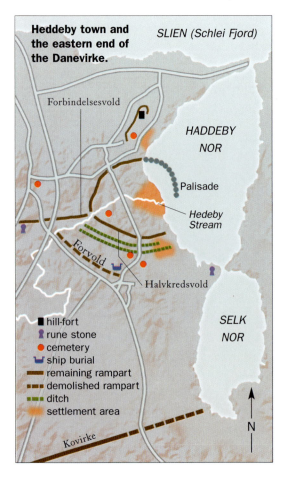

Heddeby town and the eastern end of the Danevirke.

SLIEN (Schlei Fjord)

Forbindelsesvold

HADDEBY NOR

Palisade

Hedeby Stream

Forvold

Halvkredsvold

SELK NOR

- ■ hill-fort
- 🜊 rune stone
- ● cemetery
- 🛏 ship burial
- ▬ remaining rampart
- ▬ demolished rampart
- ▬ ditch
- settlement area

Kovirke

N

links with the Saxon port of Hamburg provided a convenient and popular trading route for merchants from Britain, the Frankish Kingdoms, Spain, or the Mediterranean.

Although the size and vitality of the trading town impressed Al-Tartushi, he was less enthusiastic about other aspects of Hedeby. He called it barbaric, noisy, filthy, and a place where the inhabitants hung animal sacrifices outside their houses. He may have been referring to salted meat or fish, hung out to dry, but the picture of a pagan Viking town was a colorful one nonetheless. What Al-Tartushi would also have noticed were the incredible range of goods on offer: glassware from the Rhine, slaves from Russia, hides from the far north of Scandinavia, and a wealth of jewelry,

textiles, luxury domestic wares, and stunning examples of Viking metalwork.

Hedeby flourished for almost two and a half centuries, producing a substantial revenue for the Danish crown, which in turn provided the wherewithal for the Danish monarchy to indulge in expansionist ventures in the British Isles and the rest of Scandinavia. This also made Hedeby a target for Denmark's enemies, and the end finally came in 1050, when the Norwegian King Harald Hardrada attacked and then burned the town. Hedeby had already passed its peak by the start of the 11th century, and although efforts were made to rebuild the town after its destruction, it was a mere shadow of its former self. A Slavic raid 16 years later finally put paid to the once great marketplace of the Viking world.

Above: At its peak, Hedeby (part of it has been reconstructed) was one of the largest Viking towns.

Facing: Detail of a gold bracteate pendant, usually worn about the neck. Although silver was more important to Vikings, the ease with which gold could be worked allowed Viking metalsmiths to create stunning pieces.

169

Viking Settlements in Russia

The Viking presence in Russia was completely different from that in the rest of Europe. They came as traders, then governed small townships, which in turn developed into city-states. Power was a by-product of trade.

Above: Detail of the dragon-head terminal on a horse-collar found at Sollerstead, Denmark.

Facing top: The Viking influence in Novgorod shows in the style of the wooden church, seen here in a restored village. The original settlement looked more like the reconstruction below.

During the 20th century, political changes altered the perceived view of the Vikings in Russia. In western countries, it was recognized that, as Varangians, they played a vital part in the establishment of Russian townships, and in the subsequent political development of the Rus as a people. However, the communist Soviet view discounted the Viking influence. Today, a more balanced view has evolved through the increased availability of archaeological and documentary evidence.

We know that Vikings from Sweden settled in Russia from the early ninth century, and engaged in trade there. We also know that they founded several of the most important towns in the region, and their descendants developed these centers into fully-fledged political and economic city-states. From the mid-ninth until the early eleventh century, Swedish Vikings and their descendants controlled the towns of Aldeigjuborg (also known as Ladoga, and now Staraja Ladoga), Novgorod, Kiev, and several other smaller settlements, creating a network of Viking towns in the middle of the Russian forests.

Contrary to Viking custom in western settlements, little or no attempt was made to expand control into the surrounding countryside. They remained vibrant, bustling trading centers, rather than bases for military conquest. This did not mean that the Vikings lacked military power in Russia. Punitive expeditions against the Slavs, Bulgars, and Khazaks show that they were more than willing to protect their trade routes with force if required.

Archaeological excavations in Aldeigjuborg indicate that the Viking town had metalworking and blacksmithing workshops from 750 onward. At first, the Vikings were probably seasonal residents, but in time it developed into a permanent trading settlement. During the mid-ninth century, the Rus established outposts deeper into Russia, at Beloozero (The White Lake), then Rostov to the south. From the location of burial sites, it has been deduced that the Vikings living on the headwaters of the Volga integrated more fully with the local population than elsewhere, and traces of their presence can be found throughout the region.

Catalysts for development

By the late tenth century, Novgorod had become the principal Rus settlement in the north, replacing Aldeigjuborg and other small early settlements. It spans the Volkhov, making it well-placed to control trade between the Dnieper and the Baltic Sea. While the main Viking market was established on the eastern bank in about 920, the town grew into a fortified city over the next half century, becoming a regional center of power.

As a Rus capital, Novgorod became the exception to the rule of trade rather than conquest. Its militaristic expansion came at a time when the silver trade between the Orient and the Baltic was ending, and the city thrived on new trade commodities: tin and ore from central Europe, furs from Scandinavia, and grain or slaves from its hinterland. This trading link between Novgorod and Scandinavia reached its peak in the 11th century, and continued after the end of the Viking age.

From the late ninth century, Kiev also became a thriving marketplace and industrial town, and trading agreements between the city and the Khazars ensured access to the East's markets. Despite rivalry with the Byzantines over dominance of the Black Sea basin, Kiev became one of Europe's great trading hubs, supported by secondary Viking settlements in Polotsk and Smolensk.

From left to right:
a Viking merchant-venturer with his wares (9th century); a warrior with baggy pants typical of eastern Vikings; a Kievan Rus.

Viking Industry

Poor overland communications made moving heavy goods difficult. So Viking artisans flocked to the the sea ports, where raw materials arrived and were immediately fashioned into jewelry, weapons, domestic wares, and almost everything the Vikings needed.

Above: Metalworkers made many implements in addition to the all-important military equipment and shipbuilders' nails. This attractively decorated ceremonial fork was made by the lost-wax method of casting, used for large-scale production of metal objects.

Facing: Thor, god of Thunder was commonly portrayed as a blacksmith with his hammer and anvil. This 2½-inch-tall bronze figure was cast in Iceland, c.1000.

Metalworking in both iron or bronze was a skilled and honored occupation, particularly when the object being created was a weapon or armor. Even the god Thor carried a hammer, the tool of a blacksmith, and the legends speak of fabled magical swords produced by master swordsmiths. Located on the outer fringes of the Viking trading towns due to the risk of fire, swordsmiths, blacksmiths, armorers, and workers in brass produced everything from the weapons of war and ships' fittings needed for an expedition to the nails, rivets, and tools needed to build towns. Imported ore was reduced by means of a basic process that used simple bowl furnaces, but it resulted in high-quality iron.

Metalworkers were not limited to the production of domestic and practical items. Bronze casting was carried out in most Viking markets by specialists who created a range of detailed individual objects or even mass-produced runs of cheaper castings. For this, Viking metalworkers used the lost-wax method,

which is still employed today. First, a wax model of the object to be cast is made. Clay is then carefully packed around the wax model to form a mold. When the mold is heated, the liquefied wax is drained off—or "lost." The mold is then ready to accept the molten casting metal.

What the Vikings brought to this technique were mass-production methods to cope with the high demand for repeat items. By their very nature, clay molds are destroyed by the extreme heat of the casting metal each time they are used. In order to permit faster production of simpler items, strips of molds were made, or even hardier stone or bone molds were used.

The Vikings also quarried stone. Soapstone was a major resource in Norway, principally as a substitute for pottery. Soapstone was used to produce domestic vessels, fishing weights or sinkers, spinning whorls, loom weights, and brass-casting molds. Norway was also a source of the schist stone used to produce whetstones, vital for sharpening weapons and tools. The quarry at Eidsborg (Telemark) was an important site, and its products have been found as far afield as Denmark, England, and France. In many cases, raw lumps of soapstone or whetstone schist were exported to the other Viking marketplaces, where local workers fashioned the finished products.

Shipbuilders dominate

Glassmakers used ready-made material imported from western Europe. This included colored tesserae intended for use in mosaics, broken glass tableware, even old Roman windows were used. Hundreds of beads recovered from sites in Denmark, Norway, and Britain indicate the popularity of this usage of glass. Simple beads were made from a single color of glass, but more complex versions incorporated spirals of a differently-colored glass, or even a kaleidoscope of multiple colors, creating objects of incredible complexity and beauty. These were made by the creation of thin glass rods which were then bundled together and fused into larger multi-colored rods. Slicing through the rod thinly produced the finished bead.

According to Viking belief, amber contained magical properties. This made the abundant amber of southern Denmark and northern Germany a popular material for beads, as well as ornaments and gaming pieces. A particularly prized version was jet amber, found only in the vicinity of Whitby, in Viking England. Consequently, nearby York became a leading exporter of amber to the Scandinavian marketplaces. Bone and ivory were other useful materials. The naturally shed antlers of red deer were commonly used in the production of combs, and bone and ivory carvers were also busy in the Viking towns.

For the most part, Viking domestic utensils were made of wood: mugs, platters, buckets, bowls, beds, storage chests, tables, and of course ships. However, pottery manufacture became increasingly important in Scandinavia during the Viking era. Early pots were hand-molded, but by the end of the Viking era, bowls were thrown on potters' wheels. But of all the skilled industries of the Viking age, it was the shipbuilders who transformed a rural agrarian Viking economy into a trading empire that dominated most of Europe.

The Silver Trade

One aspect of the Swedes opening up of the Russian river system was the increase in circulation of much-coveted silver in northern Europe. Viking raids on the British Isles and the Franks provided some silver, but it was trade with the Arabs that began a flood of the precious metal into the Baltic marketplaces.

Swedish enterprise in Russia during the second half of the ninth century resulted in the establishment of several riverside trading settlements in the heart of Russia (*see pages 170–1*). The desire to expand further south toward the Caspian Sea, and its trading potential with even more distant races, eventually brought the Rus into contact with the Khazars of the southern steppes. This nomadic tribe controlled the mouth of the Volga where it emptied into the Caspian Sea. On its far shore lay the largely autonomous Emirates of Azerbaijan and Alid, which, at least in theory, were parts of the Muslim Abbasid Caliphate. These were centers of silver production, and the Rus wanted silver.

While the Rus maintained dominance over the Dnieper—the trading link between the Baltic and Black Seas—Bulgars and Khazars had most of the the Volga to the east under their control. This obliged Scandinavian merchants to pay tribute to the river tribes to allow them to navigate the Volga to the Caspian Sea. The alternative route—taking the Dnieper to the Black Sea, then along its eastern shores past the Bulgar Khanate to the Byzantine Empire—was less attractive. In addition to being a physically more demanding journey, trade in the Empire's capital at Constantinople was regulated, which reduced the Vikings' profit margins.

Arab merchants also journeyed upriver on the Volga. Ibn Fadlan wrote of encounters with Vikings, and the nature of the business they transacted. The main commodities offered were furs, slaves, weapons, European honey, and wax. The Scandinavians traded for silver, although sometimes silks and sugar were purchased.

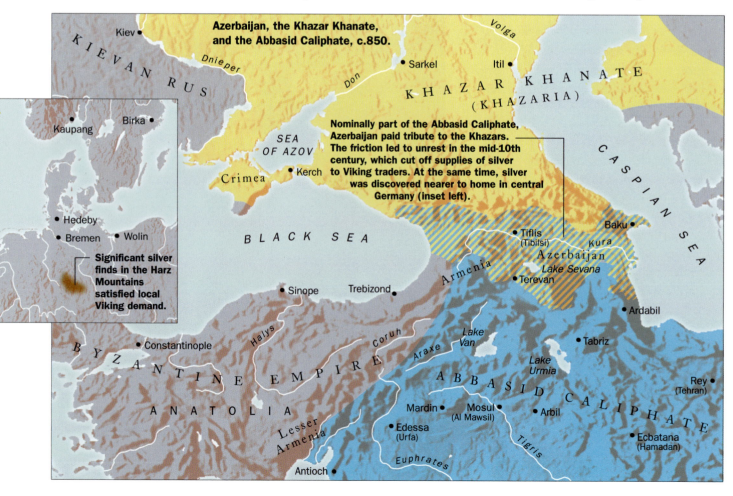

Azerbaijan, the Khazar Khanate, and the Abbasid Caliphate, c.850.

Nominally part of the Abbasid Caliphate, Azerbaijan paid tribute to the Khazars. The friction led to unrest in the mid-10th century, which cut off supplies of silver to Viking traders. At the same time, silver was discovered nearer to home in central Germany (inset left).

Significant silver finds in the Harz Mountains satisfied local Viking demand.

The silver eventually made its way to the Swedish-dominated Baltic Sea markets. Swedish Vikings also traded with the Bulgars themselves, who brought furs and sometimes slaves to the river trading depots, and exchanged them for weapons or western European slaves.

Arabs lose out

Trade on the Volga continued until the end of the tenth century, when it suddenly dried up. The break-up of the Kurdish Emirate of Azerbaijan in the latter part of the century may have destabilized the southern Caspian region and discouraged Arab merchants from using the Kurdish area as a trading base. Similarly, the expeditions of the Russian Prince Sviatoslav against the Khazars (965) and the Volga Bulgars (967) would have damaged relations along the Volga while passions remained inflamed.

A third possibility is a shift in silver-mining operations. New silver veins in the Harz Mountains of the German Empire were discovered at about the same time that the great silver mines of the Eastern Abassid Caliphate were rapidly becoming exhausted. This meant the source of central European silver was more economical and less dangerous to reach.

While it lasted, the volume of the Scandinavian silver trade along the Volga was enormous. Over 90,000 Arabic coins have been found in Scandinavia. These are often referred to as Kufic coins after the mine of Kufa in Mesopotamia, but other mints in Samarkand, Tashkent, and Baghdad are all strongly represented in the hoards. Despite this huge mass, silver was rarely kept in coin form, because melted down into bullion it was easier to store and transport.

Silver was turned into jewelry, most often worn by the merchants and their families to indicate their success and wealth. Much of the silver from Viking grave-find jewelry was of Abbasid origin. Bars, coins, and personal ornaments were also chopped up (creating "hack silver"). For the Vikings, weight of metal was often more important than esthetic appearance. The presence of so many Arabic coins, and over a thousand discovered caches of silver throughout Scandinavia stand as testimony to the importance of the silver trade during the Viking age, and to the enterprise of the Viking traders.

The Byzantine Connection

When the first Viking merchant-venturers reached the Byzantine capital of Constantinople, its size and magnificence must have amazed them. Over the next two centuries, while the Vikings and the Byzantines traded and intermittently fought, a mutual respect developed and matured into an unlikely alliance.

Below: The Vikings who fought in Byzantine service as part of the Varangian Guard, and who then returned home to Scandinavia, sometimes left inscribed stones recounting their deeds.

In the mid-ninth century, Constantinople, capital of the Greek Byzantine Empire, was one of the greatest cities in the world. With a population of around 50,000, it dwarfed anything that existed in Scandinavia, Russia, or even western Europe. It was defended both by virtually impregnable walls and a formidable army. This strength did not deter the Vikings, who raided into the empire c.865 and again in 907. The Varangians, as they were known in eastern and southeastern Europe (a word that could also be translated as "foreigner" or "traveler") impressed the Byzantines with their martial prowess. However, they lacked the numbers to do more than launch hit-and-run raids with small fleets of ships.

Although the Vikings were probably better seamen and warriors than the Byzantines, the latter had one immense advantage over the raiders. Byzantium maintained a well-equipped standing navy, and their ships relied on a secret weapon to ensure victory. When Prince Oleg of Kiev led his Viking fleet against the empire in 907, his ships were attacked by a Byzantine fleet in the Black Sea. The Byzantines used "greek fire"—a jet of combustible liquid similar in effect to napalm—which was fired from hoses mounted on the Greek ships. Faced with such weapons, further attempts to raid the Byzantine coast were abandoned.

While more clashes between the Byzantines and the Rus descendants of these Varangians would follow, a peace treaty between Kiev and Constantinople signed in 912 put an end to further depredations. Following in the wake of the first Viking raiders, Scandinavian traders gained significant concessions from the Byzantine court. This ensured that a flow of furs and slaves arrived in the capital from Russia, and silver, silks, and spices returned to the Baltic.

The Ax Bearers

One other significant commodity appeared in Constantinople from the north. Varangians appeared in Byzantine military service as early as 911, probably recruited from among the defeated raiders of Prince Oleg of Kiev. Military treaties between Kiev and Constantinople during the second half of the tenth century produced a number of contingents of Varangian mercenaries in Byzantine service. The Byzantines were so impressed with the Vikings in their service that they were banded together to form a special elite bodyguard, charged with protecting the emperor.

For a hundred years from the late tenth century onward, the Varangian Guard became a major attraction for young Viking adventurers

prepared to brave the journey from Sweden to Constantinople in return for the prospects of unimagined wealth. In addition to acting as imperial guards, the Varangians grew to become a major core in the Byzantine standing army. In this capacity, they served throughout the Byzantine Empire: in Italy, North Africa, Anatolia, and the Middle East.

The Byzantines knew them both as the Varangian Guard and as the "ax-bearing guard," named after their weapon of choice. Perhaps the most famous Viking to enter Byzantine service was Harald Hardrada (*see pages 154–5*), who became King of Norway, and whose death at

Stamford Bridge in 1066 marked the effective end of the Viking age. The Varangians remained in Byzantine service even after the cataclysmic defeat of the empire's army at the hands of the Seljuk Turks at Manzikert (1071). Although the Guard survived as a unit, they were virtually destroyed as an effective fighting force by the Sicilian Normans at Durazzo ten years later.

By the mid- to late 11th century, Kiev and Novgorod were effectively Russian rather than Viking cities, and while relations between the Rus and the Byzantines continued to oscillate between peace (and trading) and warfare, this development extends beyond the scope of our study. While Swedish Vikings still journeyed to Constantinople in search of trade or military service, their numbers diminished. The newly civilized Russians and the increasingly developed Scandinavian kingdoms had little time for the anachronism that was the Varangian merchant-venturer. By that time, faced with a Muslim onslaught from the east, the Byzantines had greater problems to worry about than the supply of furs and slaves.

Above: Varangian Guardsmen of the 11th century. They were known at the time for two principal attributes—their axes and their drinking. A 12th-century quote labeled them the Emperor's "wine-bags."

CHAPTER 10

Last of the Vikings

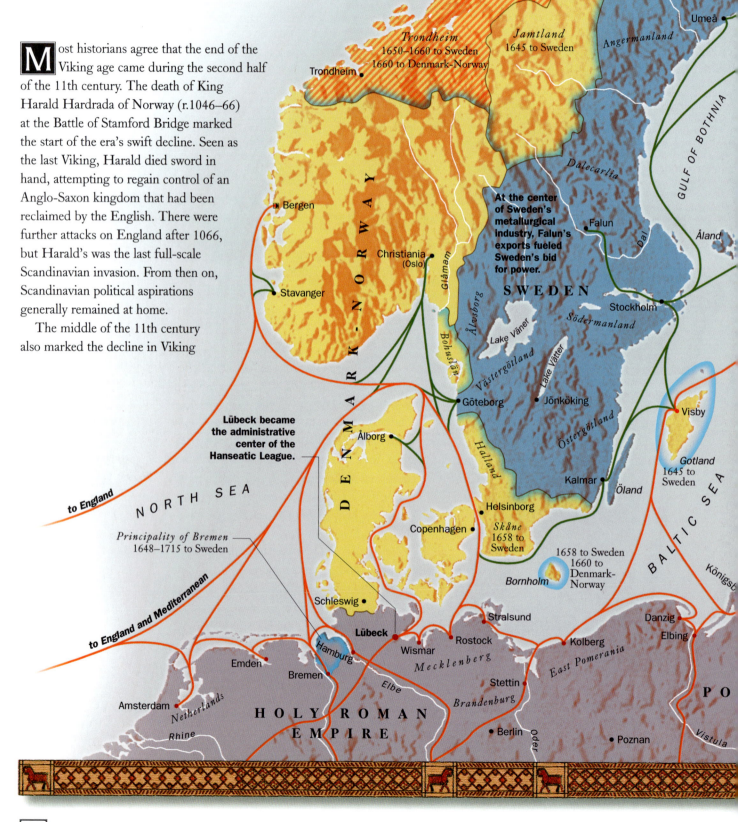

Most historians agree that the end of the Viking age came during the second half of the 11th century. The death of King Harald Hardrada of Norway (r.1046–66) at the Battle of Stamford Bridge marked the start of the era's swift decline. Seen as the last Viking, Harald died sword in hand, attempting to regain control of an Anglo-Saxon kingdom that had been reclaimed by the English. There were further attacks on England after 1066, but Harald's was the last full-scale Scandinavian invasion. From then on, Scandinavian political aspirations generally remained at home.

The middle of the 11th century also marked the decline in Viking

Västerbotten
1560–1660
to Sweden

Trondheim
1650–1660 to Sweden
1660 to Denmark-Norway

Jamtland
1645 to Sweden

Angermanland

Umeå

Trondheim

GULF OF BOTHNIA

Dalecarlia

At the center of Sweden's metallurgical industry, Falun's exports fueled Sweden's bid for power.

Bergen

N O R W A Y

Falun

Åland

Christiania (Oslo)

Glåman

S W E D E N

Stavanger

Ålvsborg

Bohuslän

Lake Väner

Södermanland

Stockholm

Lake Vätter

Västergötland

Jönköking

Östergötland

Visby

Lübeck became the administrative center of the Hanseatic League.

Ålborg

Göteborg

D E N M A R K

Halland

Kalmar

Öland

Gotland
1645 to Sweden

to England

NORTH SEA

Helsinborg

Principality of Bremen
1648–1715 to Sweden

1658 to Sweden
1660 to Denmark-Norway

BALTIC SEA

Copenhagen

Skåne
1658 to Sweden

Bornholm

Königsb

to England and Mediterranean

Schleswig

Stralsund

Danzig

Lübeck

Rostock

Kolberg

Elbing

Hamburg

Wismar

Mecklenberg

East Pomerania

P O

Emden

Bremen

Elbe

Stettin

Amsterdam

Netherlands

Brandenburg

Oder

Vistula

Rhine

H O L Y R O M A N
E M P I R E

Berlin

Poznan

Scandinavia between 1200 and the end of the 17th century. During the 13th to 15th centuries, the Hanseatic League became the leading trading power in the Baltic, but by the 17th century, Sweden had developed into the dominant force in Scandinavian and Baltic politics.

Luleå

1560–95
to Sweden

Österbotten

asa

FINLAND

Karelia
1617 to Sweden

Lake Onega

Lake Ladoga

TIMBER

Nyland

Vyborg

Åbo
(Turku)

Helsingfors
(Helsinki)

St. Petersburg

GULF OF FINLAND

1610 to Sweden

Narva

R U S S I A

Estonia
1561 to Sweden

FLAX, HEMP, HIDES

Reval
(Tallinn)

Novgorod

Dagö (Hiiumaa)
1582 to Sweden

Lake Peipus

Ösel (Saarenaa)
1645 to Sweden

Pskov

FLAX, FURS, GRAIN, HEMP, TIMBER

Livonia
1629 to Sweden

Windau

Riga

FLAX, GRAIN, HEMP, TIMBER

bau

Memel

Polotsk

Western Dvina

Vitebsk

Smolensk

to Moscow

Kovno

to Kiev and Black Sea

Dnieper

■ (blue)	Swedish Empire, mid-16th century
■ (yellow)	Swedish gains to mid-17th century
■ (yellow)	unified Denmark-Norway, mid-17th century
▨	Denmark-Norway gain
●	Hanseatic port/trading center, mid-15th century
■	Hanseatic Kontore, mid-15th century
→	Hanseatic trading routes
→	Scandinavian trading routes.

ND

Warsaw

trade with the Middle East. The once-Viking cities of Russia, such as Novgorod, began to look away from the Scandinavian homeland, which further increased the decay of Viking Baltic commerce. The great cities of Hedeby, Birka, and Kaupang were gradually abandoned. Although new trading ports sprang up, the goods were simply not there to exchange or sell. To compensate for the loss of income from the taxation of trade, the royal treasuries of Denmark and Sweden imposed increasingly heavy customs duties on trade within their borders. The result was that merchants were driven elsewhere. As the sea raiders had become ostracized by a new Christian morality, the Viking merchants vanished through economic pressure, only to re-emerge in part as a new dynamic mercantile community in Germany.

The Viking age was ushered in by the dramatic onslaught of sea raiders on an unsuspecting world. It passed, not with a similar fury but with a meek evaporation, making way for a less colorful world of commerce and national ambition. The Vikings left behind an image that has been passed down through every generation, and still influences our perspective today. While much of the Vikings' world seems alien, the continued fascination with the achievements and horrors of the Viking age shows that the era is one that has captured the imagination of succeeding generations.

This is partly due to the cultural and political legacy the Vikings left behind them, not just in Europe but also in America. In a time when business travelers fly across the Atlantic Ocean in a matter of hours, the efforts of Viking explorers and merchants who sailed the same waters in open wooden boats can only be marveled at. Modern businessmen would also be impressed by the drive and vitality of their Viking counterparts. Indeed, the modern mercantile system owes its origins in large part to these Scandinavian traders. The world of the Viking raider and trader has long gone, but their legacy lives on in our frenetic modern world.

Twilight of the Sea Raider

Harald Hardrada was arguably the "last of the Vikings," but the Norse king was not the last Scandinavian with eyes on England. Danish aspirations to reconquer England were still fresh, but their cousins the Normans had the realm in an iron grip. Within two decades the threat of a Viking invasion passed, and Norman England was left in peace.

With hindsight, Harald Hardrada's invasion of England was doomed to failure. The Anglo-Danes at Stamford Bridge vanquished his Viking army, and in turn, Duke William of Normandy, descendant of a Viking, defeated the same army at Hastings and conquered the kingdom. While it is customary to see Harald's death as the milestone marking the passing of the Viking age, the Danes still harbored ambitions to reclaim the Danelaw.

In 1069, when Saxon rebels in northern England rose in revolt against Norman rule, they appealed to the Danish crown for assistance. King Sweyn III Estridsson of Denmark (r.1043–74) sent his brother Oseborn at the head of a large Danish fleet. He joined forces with the English rebels and seized York, but the Vikings withdrew in the face of William the Conqueror's army.

The Danes remained off the River Humber until William paid them tribute. This throwback to the days of Danegeld seems incredible, given the perceived power of the Norman reign as portrayed in most history books. In fact William's grip on England in the first years was far from firm. He had ventured across the Channel with only a handful of Norman knights to complete the huge task being undertaken. The Normans were ruthless, but they could not be everywhere. It is not surprising, therefore, that the English should have considered the chances of either a Danish invasion or an English rebellion being fair for success.

The last raids

A second opportunity arose in 1075. Two of William the Conqueror's Norman nobles rebelled against their king. King Sweyn of Denmark again dispatched an invasion force to take advantage of the Normans' confusion and support Saxon rebellion. Unfortunately, William

was quicker and the Danish force arrived after he had ruthlessly crushed the revolt. All the Vikings managed was a second pillaging of York—once their own vital city.

A decade later, a political shift in Norman power gave the Danes a third opportunity under another king, Sweyn's son. Cnut II Sweynsson (r.1074–86) had married the daughter of Count Robert of Flanders. Both Robert and the German Emperor Henry IV supported Cnut's continued claim to the English throne. During the summer of 1085, as a Danish fleet gathered in western Jutland, rumors of a Danish invasion forced William I to station troops on England's North Sea coast to repel any attack. The king hired mercenaries to supplement his scant resource of trustworthy Normans. He even destroyed coastal villages and towns to deny the enemy bases should a landing be successful. There is evidence at Colchester of the hasty refortification of the castle there that bears testimony to the seriousness of the threat.

The attack never came, and although Cnut had contemplated it, his gathering of men and ships was probably more posturing than a genuine attempt to reconquer the Danelaw. The Danish king was killed in the following year during a popular uprising against his authority. Only then did William the Conqueror disband his troops, confident that the Danish threat had finally passed. The raids on England immediately after 1066 were the last Viking forays across the North Sea. Baltic traders continued to ply their wares in western European waters, and Danish and Swedish campaigns of conquest continued in the Baltic and eastern Europe for another 50 years. But times had changed and, as a new-found stability in northern European waters encouraged trade, the few remaining Baltic sea raiders were regarded merely as pirates.

Facing: A replica Viking longship sailing at sunset.

Post-Viking Scandinavia

By the last decades of the 11th century, Scandinavia had evolved into a collection of emergent nation-states, controlled by increasingly powerful rulers. When Harald Hardrada's death ended the warfare that had characterized the Viking world in the West, a new era of relative peace and mercantile prosperity was ushered in.

Below: Relief from the side of a baptismal font at Bolum's church in Västergotland. The independence of the Viking spirit was untamed by either the ambitions of kings or the influence of the Church. Even as late as the 13th century, a pagan-animistic image like this creature could adorn a font.

When Christianity came to Scandinavia at the end of the tenth century, the main beneficiaries were its rulers, who used the spread of the new religion and its attendant clerical structure to increase their own royal authority. For the next century the Church became a vital tool of the State, and while clerics in royal service increased the efficiency of record keeping and administration, monarchs courted the support of the Holy See in their affairs. King Cnut I the Great of Denmark (r.1014-35) went so far as to visit Pope John IX (p.1024-32) in Rome. By the end of the century, the Church's authority allied to power of the crown had altered the face of Scandinavian society.

Latin replaced the older runic alphabet, which was marginalized as being a pagan form of writing. Through the clergy, close links were forged with the Germanic and Frankish kingdoms to the south, and the first written laws codified the way in which Scandinavian society was governed. While ecclesiastic historians such as Adam of Bremen recount lurid tales of pagan life in Scandinavia, it was clear that the old ways were dying out. The rapid spread of churches ensured that in order to prosper and trade, the Vikings had to embrace both the new faith and the authority of the State.

For over a century after the conversion of King Harald Bluetooth of Denmark in 960, the Archbishop of Bremen remained the controlling religious figure of all three Scandinavian kingdoms. In 1104, the Archbishopric of Lund was founded in Denmark, followed by the archbishoprics of Nidaros in Norway (1152) and Uppsala in Sweden (1164). The ecclesiastical hierarchy of the area was now truly Scandinavian, and although in Denmark, Norway, and Sweden

the Church and the State continued to squabble and even fight, the two elements of national authority supported each other. Kings and Archbishops needed each other to stay in power, and to continue to control their secular and spiritual subjects.

Adoption of Norman ways

Throughout the 11th and 12th centuries, the three kingdoms continued to war with each other, usually due to some form of argument over succession, or claim to the throne. While this warfare tended to reduce the monarchs' authority from the pre-eminent position reached at the end of the 11th century, it also led to the emergence of a new breed of Scandinavian land-owning nobility. These men were the descendants of the Viking warlords of an earlier age.

For centuries in Scandinavia, where arable land was at a premium, freehold landowners exercised the same rights in Viking society regardless of how much or little land they held. By the end of the 12th century this had evolved into a system that was more akin to the feudal structure found elsewhere in western Europe. In return for protection from roving bands of soldiers, the smaller landowners became the tenants of their larger neighbors. Although the monarchy tried

to prevent this drift toward the creation of a land-owning nobility (and therefore the potential of rival dynasties), the trend continued.

By the end of the century, the Danish kings bowed to the inevitable. They began to grant fiefdoms in return for military service, and soon the habit spread to Norway and Sweden. There was an important difference between the feudal system of Scandinavia and that of the rest of Europe. The Norman and Frankish monarchies were hereditary, but power governed succession in Scandinavia. In this, it was akin to the later German system, where the best man got the job (elected by a college of nobles, however).

Nevertheless, this increased feudalization of Scandinavian society remained largely confined to Denmark and central Sweden. Eleswhere, the traditional independent Viking spirit limited the effectiveness of these non-democratic forms of government. In Iceland, the entire population remained free from the rule of kings or the overburden of a feudal elite. Real power in Scandinavia was economic rather than ecclesiastic or political, and while the kings, nobles, and clerics may have tried to model their society on the rest of Europe, northern European merchants were creating a better world of their own.

Above: Away from metropolitan centers of the late Viking age, traditional values were retained. This church at Hveravellir, Iceland, is built in the same manner as a Viking longhouse, with a turf roof for protection and insulation.

The Vikings Mercantile Successors

Harald Hardrada's burning of Hedeby in 1050 marked a turning point in the economic and mercantile fortunes of the Baltic region. The subsequent decline in Viking trade during the 11th century paved the way for the development of a new Baltic economic system.

Right: Ax in hand, a statue of a Viking woodcutter adorns the front of a building on the Hanseatic Wharf in Bergen, Norway.

Although new mercantile communities emerged to replace the older Viking ones, increased royal authority and administration of Scandinavian trade did much to drive merchants south to Germany. However, the decline of trading settlements such as Hedeby, Kaupang, and Birka were in part compensated for by the growth of a new generation of Scandinavian

townships. On Gotland, Paviken and Visby developed during the tenth century, capitalizing on their central position between Denmark, Sweden, and the sea-river routes to Novgorod. In Sweden, Birka was replaced by nearby Sigtuna, which became a leading market for fur trading by the early 11th century. In Norway, while Kaupang declined, the new township of Christiania (Oslo) grew under royal supervision, exploiting the growth of North Sea trade in the tenth-century .

Further south, the ecclesiastical seat of Lund in Skåne, southern Sweden (but Danish-ruled at the time), encouraged the growth of a new port that also benefited from religious traffic. Århus in Jutland grew into one of the leading ports for Danish-Norwegian trade. Similarly, Bergen, founded by King Olaf III the Quiet of Norway (r.1066–93) around 1070, became one of the most important Scandinavian mercantile ports of the late Viking age. Excavations have revealed that, by 1170, it was a thriving center,

and its extensive wharves and warehouses stored many commodities, including English wool and German wine.

Scandinavian records of the 12th century document the methods used by the kings to impose customs duty—most unpopular. In 1125 Icelanders, who had been forced to pay a *landaurar* (toll) to Norway to offset shipping costs, rebelled against nominal Norwegian authority. Royal officials administered towns on behalf of the king, and imposed customs duties on all trade. In response, Scandinavian merchants formed national guilds for mutual physical and economic protection. Most of these late Viking merchants had extensive overseas interests, and it was little surprise that when royal authority became too oppressive, they simply moved their businesses elsewhere.

The Hanseatic League

The German port of Lübeck, founded in 1143, lies some miles south of the abandoned Viking settlement of Hedeby. From this point on, Germany rather than Scandinavia would dominate trade in northern European waters. The extent to which Scandinavian merchants were responsible for this shift by moving their trade beyond royal authority has never been determined. Certainly, Lübeck had become the

central port of the Hanseatic League by the 13th century. The name is derived from *hanse*, old High German term for troops or company, now associated with "fellowship" or "guild."

Trade disputes involving Visby were settled according to Hanseatic (or Lübeck) law from the mid-13th century onward. As the extension of Hanseatic authority spread to the other major German ports of Hamburg, Bremen, Rostock, Stettin, and Danzig, the power of Scandinavian kings to impose tariffs diminished. Malmö in Skåne became an established Hanseatic depot, while Bergen became a Hanseatic *kontore* (counter, or marketplace). The Hanseatic League had become the new middlemen, safe from Scandinavian regulations and browbeating.

Danish kings opposed the League, resorting to military and naval force in an effort to maintain Denmark's economic and political position in the region. This campaign continued well into the 14th century, by which stage the Hanseatic League was in decline, largely due to the emergence of the Dutch as a maritime economic power. The dealings of the Hanseatic League ushered in a new era for Scandinavia, as part of a structured international maritime economy. Without the pioneering enterprise of the Viking merchants, such mercantile developments would have been impossible.

Above: Waterfront houses in Bergen at sunset. Contrary to Norse kings' wishes, the Norwegian port became a Hanseatic marketplace— recognition that trading power in northern Europe had passed from Viking to German hands. Within a short time, Bergen's waterfront was lined with these Hanseatic warehouses.

Facing: The might and power of the Baltic— the Rathaus (Council house) of Lübeck, the center of Hanseatic League administration.

Vikings in Popular Culture

Following the passing of the Viking age, the perception of these Scandinavian people has altered with time and the political environment. Even the views of contemporary commentators were colored by their own culture or by their reaction to Viking depredations. Today, unraveling the real Viking from the imagined one is an almost impossible exercise.

Above: A postcard of about 1916 shows Leif Eriksson as the archetypical Viking adventurer of popular imagination—complete with fanciful winged helmet.

During the medieval period, Scandinavian writers referred to a "Heroic Age," and Icelandic chroniclers described the actions of their forebears in a far more flattering manner than had the clerics who witnessed the raids for themselves. Both sides had their own tales to tell, and colored their accounts accordingly. Centuries later, we are still trying to unravel the history from the fiction in either kind of source.

Late medieval Swedish and Danish historians vied with each other to portray their own nation as pre-eminent in Scandinavia, while at the same time attempting to make the Vikings themselves appear more civilized in a classical sense than they really were. In other words, the Vikings were already being used for political ends.

Denmark declined as a significant European power after the Thirty Years War (1618–48), and, after Sweden's disastrous war with Russia (1700–21), Viking history entered a new period of realism. In the Age of Enlightenment, the Vikings were portrayed as barbarians resistant to cultural advancement. It was only the emergence of Rousseau's notion of the "noble savage" that saved them from cultural ignominy.

A renaissance followed, driven by a new-found fascination for Norse poetry and sagas. By the end of the 18th century, the Vikings had become the epitome of a golden Nordic age.

This view flourished in the early 19th century, encouraged by a new wave of Scandinavian romantic writers who drew on Viking myths. In 1811, the Gothic Society was formed in Sweden, whose aims included the encouragement of the Viking identity as a nationalist tool. Identifying with both the *bondi* (yeoman farmer) and the Viking sea raider, 19th-century Scandinavians sought political identity from the past, while their writers raced to invoke the ideals of the Viking era in their best-selling literature or poetry. By the later 19th century, this had led to the notion of a common folk history. When schoolteachers began portraying their own view of the past, Vikings and national identity became inextricably mixed.

Toward superman

Fresh archaeological discoveries only fueled this fascination for the Vikings. Composer Edvard Grieg (1843–1907) built a house in what was considered a romantic Viking style, and soon the middle classes of Scandinavia and even Germany followed suit. This new German identity with the Viking age was enhanced by the compositions of Richard Wagner (1813–83), whose *Ring* cycle of operas combined Scandinavian and Teutonic legends. Combined with the *übermensch* (superman) philosophy of Nietzsche, this German fascination for the mystical heroes of the past became explosive.

In the early 20th century, notions of family, homeland, heroism, and racial superiority combined to produce a new semi-religious interpretation of the Viking past, devolved of its native Scandinavian roots. After Adolf Hitler came to power in 1933, the Nazis raised these ideals to passionate heights. Conversely, in occupied Norway, resistance fighters also drew inspiration from their Viking past, referring to the German invaders as "the world serpent."

After World War II, somewhat tarnished by association with the Nazi regime, Vikings were culturally abandoned. Subsequent generations of historians portrayed them as sea raiders, traders, and farmers and not great heroes of a bygone age. Today, the popular image of the Viking is one that has been influenced by this political legacy. Shorn of all political or cultural overtones, the Vikings of film, literature, or even cartoon are no longer icons of an age. Instead they are portrayed as free spirits battling

authority, fighting, raping, and pillaging their way across Europe. In its way, this vision is as inaccurate as any that preceded it. The Vikings continue to be subject to the cultural and political whims of succeeding generations. In recent decades, at least, the growing archaeological heritage has given us a better insight into the Viking age.

Above: In Germany of the 1930s and 40s, Thor's swastika would (in reverse form) find a menacing new meaning for millions. Decoration on a Viking bowl from Norway.

The Viking Legacy

Culture is not a term usually associated with the Vikings, but their cultural significance in the development of European trade, law, language, customs, and political organization was profound. The Vikings helped shape European and global society, and the legacy of their age is still visible today.

After studying the events of the Viking age, a quick glance at the map of Europe will show the extent to which these achievements can be traced today. On the western Atlantic fringes of the continent, Celtic Ireland was dragged reluctantly into the political sphere of the rest of the British Isles, as the Viking raiders, then settlers, established bases and towns around its coast and then in the interior. Wickford, Wexford, Limerick, and Dublin all began as Viking trading outposts. From this point onward, the island was bound to the political and commercial development of the rest of Europe.

To a lesser extent, the same applied to Iceland and the Faroes, or even Orkney and Shetland. In a recent television documentary, a DNA sample of an identifiable Viking warrior was examined and compared to the DNA of the population of various parts of Britain. In Orkney, over half of the population had similar DNA strands, indicating a continuous link with their Viking past.

In England, York developed as a major Viking marketplace, and even today Scandinavian place-names can be traced all over the counties of Yorkshire, while Norse and Danish words abound in the local dialects of northeastern England. Today, most people regard England as a nation of Anglo-Saxons, diluted with a little Norman ancestry. Few realise that for centuries, over half of the country was under Danish control, or that the Normans themselves were descendants of Viking adventurers.

In France, only the name Normandie (Land of the Normans) betrays the region's heritage.

Below: An echo of a Scandinavian past, this monument to the Viking longship stands at the edge of the harbor in Rejkjavík, Iceland.

To the east of Europe, it was the Vikings who built the great Russian cities of Novgorod, Kiev, Rostov, and Vladimir. The descendants of Swedish Vikings created the Russian state, and it was these people who expanded Russia to encompass the rivers linking the Baltic and Black Seas. In Scandinavia itself, although the principal trading centers of the Viking age have gone, the modern cities of Copenhagen, Oslo, Bergen, and Stockholm were all founded by Vikings, or built close to the marketplaces of the Viking realm.

Justice for all

One of the greatest legacies of the Viking age is its contribution to the political landscape of the democratic world. Although the Ancient Greeks considered themselves to be the inventors of democracy, the institutions that governed or adjudicated over the people of Europe were not solely developed from the Greek model but also from centuries of Viking political administration. The Vikings were an inherently democratic people, and their *thing* (parliament) guaranteed that representation was available at a local as well as at a higher level.

The modern democratic system of local, regional, and national assemblies can be traced to the Scandinavian models adopted by later generations of English, French, and German parliaments. When it came to justice, Roman Law contained no mechanism for trial by peers. Instead, it was the Vikings who devised trial by jury, and who first advocated that cases be heard in front of twelve jurors. Even the ritual of swearing an oath in court was derived from a Viking judicial ritual, and can be traced back to the Viking tradition of oath-giving.

Across Europe, traces of Viking culture can still be found in everyday life. The English

language was enriched by its contact with Scandinavia. As one Danish scholar put it: "an Englishman cannot 'thrive,' or be 'ill,' or 'die' without Scandinavian words." The cultural cross-over between the Vikings and the rest of Europe means that today, words, place-names, or even whole dialects have been absorbed into the greater tapestry of European and Anglo-American culture. While identification with the Vikings in popular culture extends from Minneapolis to Moscow, the adoption of English as the world language, and of democracy as the world's most successful form of government, means that the cultural legacy of the Viking Age is now universal.

Above: Actors pose behind their shields before re-enacting a battle during the Viking Festival, held at Århus, Denmark.

Viking and Anglo-Saxon Kings

The spelling of Scandinavian place-names and persons varies considerably depending on different conventions. For instance, this book refers to King Cnut, who may be better known to some as Canute. Similarly Æthelred may be spelled "Aethelred" or even "Ethelred." Caution should also be exercised with nicknames. For instance, Harald Harfagri is translated as both Harald *Fairhair* and Harald *Finehair*.

The earliest Earls of Orkney are known to us mostly through the *Orkneyinga Saga*. It was written about 1200, and while some experts have questioned its historical accuracy, most historians agree that it is based on true events. However, it makes many of the dates hard to pin down accurately, and there may well have been many overlapping earls contesting power at the same time.

Scandinavian Kings, 9th–11th centuries

NORWAY
Harald *Harfagri* (Fairhair) c.872–c.930
Olaf Tryggvasson 995–1000
St. Olaf 1014–30
Magnus 1035–47
Harald Sigurdsson (Hardrada) 1047–66
Magnus 1066–69
Olaf 1067–93

DENMARK
Harald *Bluetooth* c.988
Sweyn Forkbeard c.988–1014
   (King of England 1013–14)
Harald 1014–c.1018
Cnut 1018–35
   (King of England 1016–35)
Sweyn 1047–74

SWEDEN
Eric *the Victorious* c.980–95
Olaf Svenski *Sköttkonung* 995–1022
Anund (James) 1022–56
Edmund Gamul 1056–60

Kings of Wessex and England, 6th–11th centuries

Cynric 534–60
Ceawlin 560–92
Ceola 592–97
Ceolwulf 597–611
Cynegils 611–42
Cenwalh 642–72
Æscwine 673–76
Centwine 676–86
Ceadwalla 686–88
Ine 688–726
Æthelheard 726–40
Cuthred 740–56
Sigebryht 756–57
Cynewulf 757–86
Brihtric 786–802
Ecgbryht (Egbert) 802–39
Æthelwulf 839–58
Æthelbald 858–60
Æthelberht 860–66

Æthelred 866–71
Alfred *the Great* 871–99
Edward *the Elder* 899–924
Athelstan 924–39
Edmund *the Magnificent* 939–46
Eadred 946–55
Eadwig *the All-Fair* 955–59
Edgar *the Peacable* 959–75
Edward *the Martyr* 975–78
Æthelred *the Unready* 978–1014
Sweyn *Forkbeard* 1014
   (King of Denmark c.988–1014)
Edmund *Ironside* 1016
Cnut *the Great* 1016–35
   (King of Denmark 1018–35)
Harold I *Harefoot* 1035–40
Harthacnut (Hardacnut) 1040–42
Edward *the Confessor* 1042–66
Harold Godwinsson 1066
William I *the Conqueror* 1066–87

Norse Earls of Orkney

Sigurd Eysteinsson *the Mighty* 872–874
Guttorm 874–75
Hallad Rögnvaldsson 875
Einar Rögnvaldsson *Turf Einar* 895–910
Arnkell ?–950
Erlend 950
Thorfinn Hausakliuf (*Skull-splitter*) 950–c.963
Arnfinn c.963–?
Havard ?
Liot ?
Hlodver (*Sigurd the Stout*) c.980–1014
Sumarlidid c.980–c.1015
Einar Sigurdsson (*Wry-mouth*) c.1015–26
Brusí 1026–31
Rögnvald 1031–46
Thorfinn Sigurdsson (*the Mighty*) 1046–64
Haakon Paulsson 1064–98
Magnus Erlendsson 1098–1115
   (canonized 1135)
Hakon 1115–22
Paul 1122–39
Harald Maddason 1139–? (*d.*1206)
Rögnvald ?–1158 (canonized 1192)
Harald Ungi 1158–1198
David 1198–1214
John 1214–32 (*died leaving no male issue*)

Index

INDEX